In association with MasterCard

CONTENTS

S0-CYG-441

Cover Picture: The Falcon Hotel, Castle Ashby, Northamptonshire (see page 36)

FOREWORD BY THE EDITOR

*P**eople who use Johansens guides often ask why we never say anything critical about a hotel, an inn, a country house or a business meetings venue which we recommend. The answer is easy. If we knew anything bad to say about one of our selections we would not recommend it*

We visit all establishments regularly and irregularly, overtly and covertly – our professional inspectors non-stop, the rest of us ad hoc; but the many thousands of you who use our guides are really the best guardians of quality. Our recommendations must be reliable, so keep sending us those freepost Guest Surveys which you find among the back-pages of our guides. They provide our inspectors with the first hint of any fall in standards, though, as you will be glad to read, the majority of Guest Surveys are entirely complimentary. In 'The Caterer & Hotelkeeper' a regular columnist recently wrote that a characteristic of Johansens guests is that "they come to enjoy themselves". Keep helping us to help you do just that – to have a good time!

Rodney Exton, Editor

1

KEY TO SYMBOLS

 Total number of rooms

 MasterCard accepted

 Visa accepted

American Express accepted

Diners Club accepted

 Quiet location

 Access for wheelchairs to at least one bedroom and public rooms

 Nombre de chambres

 MasterCard accepté

 Visa accepté

 American Express accepté

Diners Club accepté

 Un lieu tranquille

 Accès handicapé

 Anzahl der Zimmer

MasterCard akzeptiert

Visa akzeptiert

American Express akzeptiert

Diners Club akzeptiert

Ruhige Lage

Zugang für Behinderte

(The 'Access for wheelchairs' symbol (⌖) does not necessarily indicate that the property fulfils National Accessible Scheme grading)

 Chef-patron

 Meeting/conference facilities with maximum number of delegates

 Children welcome, with minimum age where applicable

 Dogs accommodated in rooms or kennels

 At least one room has a four-poster bed

 Cable/satellite TV in all bedrooms

 Direct-dial telephone in all bedrooms

 No-smoking rooms (at least one no-smoking bedroom)

 Lift available for guests' use

 Indoor swimming pool

 Outdoor swimming pool

 Tennis court at hotel

 Croquet lawn at hotel

 Fishing can be arranged

 Golf course on site or nearby, which has an arrangement with the hotel allowing guests to play

 Shooting can be arranged

 Riding can be arranged

Hotel has a helicopter landing pad

Licensed for wedding ceremonies

 Chef-patron

 Salle de conférences – capacité maximale

 Enfants bienvenus

 Chiens autorisés

 Lit à baldaquin

 TV câblée/satellite dans les chambres

 Téléphone dans les chambres

 Chambres non-fumeurs

 Ascenseur

 Piscine couverte

 Piscine de plein air

 Tennis à l'hôtel

 Croquet à l'hôtel

 Pêche

Golf

 Chasse

Équitation

 Piste pour hélicoptère

 Cérémonies de noces

 Chef-patron

 Konferenzraum-Höchstkapazität

 Kinder willkommen

 Hunde erlaubt

 Himmelbett

 Satellit-und Kabelfernsehen in allen Zimmern

 Telefon in allen Zimmern

 Zimmer für Nichtraucher

 Fahrstuhl

 Hallenbad

 Freibad

 Hoteleigener Tennisplatz

 Krocketrasen

 Angeln

Golfplatz

 Jagd

Reitpferd

 Hubschrauberlandplatz

Konzession für Eheschliessungen

Published by
Johansens, 175-179 St John Street, London EC1V 4RP
Tel: 0171-490 3090 Fax: 0171-490 2538
Find Johansens on the Internet at: http://www.johansen.com
E-Mail: admin@johansen.u–net.com

Editor:	Rodney Exton
Group Publisher:	Peter Hancock
P.A. to Group Publisher:	Carol Sweeney
Regional Inspectors:	Christopher Bond
	Geraldine Bromley
	Robert Bromley
	Julie Dunkley
	Susan Harangozo
	Joan Henderson
	Marie Iversen
	Pauline Mason
	John O'Neill
	Mary O'Neill
	Fiona Patrick
	Brian Sandell
Production Manager:	Daniel Barnett
Production Controller:	Kevin Bradbrook
Designer:	Michael Tompsett
Copywriters:	Sally Sutton,
	Jill Wyatt
	Norman Flack
Sales and Marketing Manager:	Laurent Martinez
Marketing Executive:	Samantha Lhoas
Sales Executive:	Babita Sareen
P.A. to Managing Director & regional editorial research:	Angela Franks
Managing Director:	Andrew Warren

Copyright © 1997 Johansens

Johansens is a member company of Harmsworth Publishing Ltd, a subsidiary of the Daily Mail & General Trust plc

ISBN 1 86017 5031

Printed in England by St Ives plc
Colour origination by East Anglian Engraving

Distributed in the UK and Europe by Johnsons International Media Services Ltd, London (direct sales) & Biblios PDS Ltd, West Sussex (bookstores). In North America by general sales agent: ETL Group, New York, NY (direct sales) and The Cimino Publishing Group, INC. New York (bookstores). In Australia and New Zealand by Bookwise International, Findon, South Australia.

HOW TO USE THIS GUIDE

If you want to identify an Inn or Restaurant whose name you already know, look for it in the Regional Indexes on pages 194–197.

If you want to find an Inn or Restaurant in a particular area you can

- Turn to the Maps on pages 183–189

- Search the Indexes on pages 194–197

- Look for the Town or Village where you wish to stay in the main body of the Guide. This is divided into Countries. Place names in each Country appear at the head of the pages in alphabetical order.

The Indexes list the Inns and Restaurants by Countries and by Counties, they also show those with amenities such as fishing, conference facilities, swimming, golf, etc. (Please note some recent Local Government Boundary changes).

The Maps cover all regions. Each Inn and Restaurant symbol (a red triangle) relates to an Inn or Restaurant in this guide situated in or near the location shown.

Green Squares show the location of Johansens Recommended Country Houses & Small Hotels. If you cannot find a suitable Inn or Restaurant near where you wish to stay, you may decide to choose one of these establishments as an alternative. They are all listed by place names on pages 191–193.

The prices, in most cases, refer to the cost of one night's accommodation, with breakfast, for two people. Prices are also shown for single occupancy. These rates are correct at the time of going to press but always should be checked with the hotel before you make your reservation.

All guides are obtainable from bookshops or by Johansens Freephone 0800 269397 or by using the order coupons on pages 199–200.

JOHANSENS AWARDS FOR EXCELLENCE

The names of the winners of the 1998 Awards will be published in the 1999 editions of Johansens guides. The winners of the 1997 Awards are listed below. They were presented with their certificates at the Johansens Annual Awards dinner, held at The Dorchester on 4th November 1996, by Jean Rozwadowski, Senior Vice-President and General Manager Europe, of MasterCard International.

Johansens Country Hotel Award for Excellence
Marlfield House, Co. Wicklow, Ireland

Johansens City Hotel Award for Excellence
The Castle at Taunton, Somerset

Johansens Country House Award for Excellence
Balgonie Country House, Royal Deeside, Scotland

Johansens Inn Award for Excellence
The Manor Hotel, West Bexington, Dorset

Johansens London Hotel Award for Excellence
The Leonard, London W1

Johansens Most Excellent Value for Money Award
Appleton Hall, Appleton le Moors, N. Yorkshire

Johansens Most Excellent Service Award
Alexander House, Turner's Hill, W. Sussex

Johansens Most Excellent Restaurant Award
Freshmans Restaurant, Belbroughton, Worcestershire

Candidates for awards derive from two main sources: from the thousands of Johansens guide users who send us Guest Survey Reports commending hotels, inns and country houses in which they have stayed and from our team of twelve regional inspectors who regularly visit all properties in our guides. Guest Survey Report forms can be found on pages 199–200. They are a vital part of our continuous process of assessment and they are the decisive factor in choosing the Value for Money and the Most Excellent Service Awards.

NESTLING IN 14 ACRES OF LANDSCAPED GARDENS.

WEDGWOOD IN EVERY ROOM.

12TH CENTURY OAK PANELLING IN THE DINING ROOM.

MASTERCARD IN YOUR CORNER.

INTRODUCTION

From The Manor Hotel, West Bexington, Dorset
Winner of the 1997 Johansens Most Excellent Inn Award

I n 1983, my husband Richard and I found ourselves, thanks to a chance dinner invitation, at the Manor Hotel. We were so enthralled by the building, its situation and atmosphere that our friends jokingly suggested we buy it. We did. Fourteen years on from our most expensive dinner date ever, we have yet to feel anything but thankful that we made that fateful decision.

We have spent much of that time raising the standards of the hotel to match the perfection of its surroundings, overlooking Lyme Bay and within hearing of the splendid pebble rush and roar of Chesil Bank. To date we have removed the exterior rendering, exposing the beauty of the original stone building, mentioned in the Domesday Book. We have redecorated extensively, removing all traces of battleship grey, formerly the Manor's main colour theme! We have built a new kitchen, a new skittle room/function room and a new conservatory. We have endowed our existing twelve bedrooms with en suite bathrooms and plan, in the near future, to build new bedrooms, each with a magnificent sea view. Our restaurant is presided over by the brilliant Clive Jobson and features a menu that is fully representative of the cornucopia of our encircling countryside and seascape: from venison, pigeon and fresh local vegetables to lobster, scallops, oysters, crab and haddock.

It is impossible to overestimate the contribution our staff make to the success of the hotel. Many have been with us since the beginning, not just of our ownership of the Manor, but in our previous eight years as tenant landlords of a pub restaurant. They, as much as Richard and I, have worked long and hard to make the Manor what it is today. It is this combination of attentive service, decor, ambience and culinary excellence that guests tell us add up to the perfect recipe, as much for a quick bar snack as for a week-long retreat from the world.

It is with great pride and pleasure that we accept the prestigious accolade of Johansens Most Excellent Inn Award. In just seventeen years, Johansens has grown to become one of the most respected and trusted names in accommodation guides. Their recognition of what we have achieved in the last fourteen means a very great deal to us indeed

Jayne Childs

Arlington Court* –
overall winner of the NPI National Heritage Awards in 1996

Guess who will help you find the perfect place for your pension?

At NPI, we've been helping people find the right place for their pensions for over 160 years now. Helping them find the right balance between growth and security to give them peace of mind about their financial future.

And we've been rather good at it. We are now looking after over £10 billion in assets on behalf of our 500,000 plus policyholders.

Being a retirement specialist, we're confident that we can tailor the right retirement scheme for your individual needs. And the same goes for group schemes.

For more information about retirement planning advice from NPI, contact your Financial Adviser or NPI Membership Services on 0800 174192. Any advice given, or recommendations made by NPI Membership Services relates only to the products sold by the NPI Marketing Group.

NPI
PROVIDING PENSIONS SINCE 1835
Regulated by the Personal Investment Authority.

AS TIME GOES BY YOU'LL BE GLAD YOU CHOSE NPI
National Provident House, 55 Calverley Road, Tunbridge Wells, Kent TN1 2UE. Telephone: 01892 515151, Facsimile: 01892 705611

*Arlington Court photograph supplied by the National Trust Photographic Library/Nadia MacKenzie.

HILDON LTD.
Hildon House, Broughton, Hampshire SO20 8DG
☎ 01794-301 747, Fax 01794-301 718

The White Horse of Kilburn, Yorkshire

Johansens Recommended Inns with Restaurants in England

Castles, cathedrals, museums, great country houses and the opportunity to stay in areas of historical importance, England has much to offer. Whatever your leisure interests, there's a network of more than 560 Tourist Information Centres throughout England offering friendly, free advice on places to visit, entertainment, local facilities and travel information.

ENGLISH HERITAGE
Keysign House
429 Oxford Street
London W1R 2HD
Tel: 0171 973 3396
Offers an unrivalled choice of properties to visit.

HISTORIC HOUSES ASSOCIATION
2 Chester Street
London SW1X 7BB
Tel: 0171 259 5688
Ensures the survival of historic houses and gardens in private ownership in Great Britain.

THE NATIONAL TRUST
36 Queen Anne's Gate
London SW1H 9AS
Tel: 0171 222 9251
Cares for more than 590,000 acres of countryside and over 400 historic buildings.

REGIONAL TOURIST BOARDS

CUMBRIA TOURIST BOARD
Ashleigh
Holly Road
Windermere
Cumbria LA23 2AQ
Tel: 015394 44444
England's most beautiful lakes and tallest mountains reach out from the Lake District National Park to a landscape of spectacular coasts, hills and dales.

EAST OF ENGLAND TOURIST BOARD
Toppesfield Hall
Hadleigh
Suffolk IP7 5DN
Tel: 01473 822922

Cambridgeshire, Essex, Hertfordshire, Bedfordshire, Norfolk, Suffolk and Lincolnshire.

HEART OF ENGLAND TOURIST BOARD
Woodside
Larkhill Road
Worcester
Worcestershire WR5 2EZ
Tel: 01905 763436
Gloucestershire, Hereford & Worcester, Shropshire, Staffordshire, Warwickshire and West Midlands. Represents the districts of Cherwell and West Oxfordshire in the county of Oxfordshire.

Premier House
15 Wheeler Gate
Nottingham NG1 2NA
Tel: 0115 988 1778
Derbyshire, Leicestershire, Northamptonshire, Nottinghamshire and Rutland

LONDON TOURIST BOARD
26 Grosvenor Gardens
London SW1W ODU
Tel: 0171 730 3450
The Greater London area
(see page 15)

NORTHUMBRIA TOURIST BOARD
Aykley Heads
Durham DH1 5UX
Tel: 0191 375 3000
The Tees Valley, Durham, Northumberland and Tyne & Wear

NORTH WEST TOURIST BOARD
Swan House
Swan Meadow Road
Wigan Pier, Wigan
Lancashire WN3 5BB
Tel: 01942 821222
Cheshire, Greater Manchester, Lancashire, Merseyside and the High Peak District of Derbyshire

SOUTH EAST ENGLAND TOURIST BOARD
The Old Brew House
Warwick Park
Tunbridge Wells
Kent TN2 5TU
Tel: 01892 540766
East and West Sussex, Kent and Surrey

SOUTHERN TOURIST BOARD
40 Chamberlayne Road
Eastleigh
Hampshire SO5 5JH
Tel: 01703 620006
Eastern and Northern Dorset, Hampshire, Isle of Wight, Berkshire, Buckinghamshire and Oxfordshire

WEST COUNTRY TOURIST BOARD
60, St David's Hill
Exeter
Devon EX4 4SY
Tel: 01392 425426
Bath, Bristol, Cornwall and the Isles of Scilly, Devon, Dorset, Somerset and Wiltshire

YORKSHIRE TOURIST BOARD
312 Tadcaster Road
York YO2 2HF
Tel: 01904 707961
Yorkshire and Northern Lincolnshire

THE BOATHOUSE BRASSERIE

HOUGHTON BRIDGE, AMBERLEY, NR ARUNDEL, WEST SUSSEX BN18 9LR
TEL: 01798 831059 FAX: 01798 831063

OWNERS: Howard and Susie Macnamara
CHEFS: Danny Clark and Mark Blower

Restaurant: This delightful informal restaurant is on the River Arun at the site of the ancient Houghton Wharf. It is under the same private ownership as the White Horse Inn at Sutton. The inn is full of character, strewn with charts and maritime bric-a-brac, and is Edwardian in style. Weather permitting, you may prefer to enjoy your meal out on the open wooden deck or under the verandah. The attractive staff are friendly and attentive. The Carvery, is without doubt, the speciality here – succulent roast meats are on display, carved for you by the chefs. There is a small but impressive à la carte menu and the fresh fish is a tempting alternative. Extra seasonal dishes are shown on the blackboard in the bar. There is a fine selection of sweets, a good cheeseboard and coffee of the highest class. The set price lunch (two-courses and coffee) is good value and very popular. On Sunday it is advisable to book well ahead. The wine list is well chosen and reasonably priced. **Nearby:** Arundel Castle, Petworth House, Parham House, Chichester (Festival Theatre), and Goodwood Racecourse. Being on the Southdowns Way there are some good walks to be had. The Amberley Chalkpits Industrial Museum is nearby. **Directions: The Boathouse is on the B2139 (Arundel to Storrington Road) where it crosses the River Arun.**

THE NEW DUNGEON GHYLL HOTEL

GREAT LANGDALE, AMBLESIDE, CUMBRIA LA22 9JY
TEL: 015394 37213 FAX: 015394 37666

OWNER: John Winter Smith
MANAGERS: Ian and Rebecca Manley

S: £40–£46
D: £65–£72

Inn: The splendour of Lakeland's most majestic fells is the setting for The New Dungeon Ghyll Hotel. It is built on the site of an ancient Norse settlement, but was rebuilt as a Victorian Hotel in the 1830s. Bought by John Smith in 1991 and completely refurbished, the hotel stands in its own lawned gardens in a spectacular position beneath the Langdale Pikes and Pavey Ark. The comfortable bedrooms are all en suite and offer colour TV, tea and coffee making facilities and direct dial telephones. There are two bars with open fires and the Residents' Bar has an original slate floor. **Restaurant:** The dining room enjoys panoramic views of the Valley and the Fells beyond. A table d'hôte menu is offered and includes a varied choice of both English and continental dishes. Generous portions are served to satisfy the hearty appetite of a keen walker. A good selection of wines is available to complement the cuisine. **Nearby:** The Langdale Valley offers wonderful walking and climbing opportunities in England's most beautiful corner, with abundant wildlife and many places of historical and literary importance. From the hotel guests can walk up Stickle Ghyll to Stickle Tarn and onwards to Pavey Ark, Harrison Stickle and numerous other pikes. **Directions: M6 junction 36 A591. Through Windermere to Ambleside. Follow A593 towards Coniston, turn right onto B5343 to Langdale. The hotel is two miles past Chapelstyle on the right.**

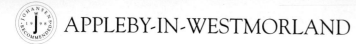 
THE ROYAL OAK INN

BONGATE, APPLEBY-IN-WESTMORLAND, CUMBRIA CA16 6UN
TEL: 017683 51463 FAX: 017683 52300

OWNERS: Colin and Hilary Cheyne
CHEFS: Hilary Cheyne and Stuart Good

9 rms   7 ens

S: £42–£55
D: £62–£84

Inn: The Royal Oak has been a coaching inn since the 1600s and parts of the building are 750 years old. It is a well cared for, traditional hostelry, situated in the oldest part of the north Pennine town of Appleby-in-Westmorland. The oak panelling, beams, stone walls and open fires combine to give the inn its warm, inviting atmosphere. The bedrooms are all individually furnished and all have a private bathroom. Facilities for ironing and clothes-drying are available. Guests will find the owners hospitable and their staff attentive, providing an efficient service. **Restaurant:** An extensive selection of fresh fish, local meat and vegetarian dishes, together with some unusual specialities, are offered to suit all tastes. There are two dining rooms, one of which is non-smoking, and an extensive wine list of over 70 bins. A full Westmorland breakfast is served to set visitors up for a day of sightseeing. The Royal Oak was awarded an AA rosette for its restaurant in 1996. Hand-pumped ales plus malt whiskies are offered in the Snug and Taproom bars. **Nearby:** The inn is well placed for visitors wishing to explore the celebrated scenery of the high moorlands, as well as the numerous castles and historic houses in the area. Running through Appleby is the Settle to Carlisle railway which traverses spectacular remote countryside. **Directions: The inn can easily be located on the south-east approach to Appleby from the A66 Penrith–Scotch Corner road.**

In association with MasterCard

RED LION INN

MAIN STREET, HOGNASTON, ASHBOURNE, DERBYSHIRE DE6 1PR
TEL: 01335 370396 FAX: 01335 370961

OWNERS: Philip Price and Hilary Heskin
CHEF: Hilary Heskin

3 rms | 3 ens

S: £40
D: £65

Inn: The Red Lion is a typical country inn which offers a traditional welcoming atmosphere of good hospitality and homely service. It is situated on the fringe of The Peak District in the main street of the tiny village of Hognaston, just a short drive from the attractive old market town of Ashbourne. With a log fire in the bar, cosy corners, good ales and rustic character this is a welcome retreat for those wanting a relaxing break, or for visitors seeking the opportunity to walk through beautiful countryside. Three individually styled and traditionally furnished bedrooms offer comfortable accommodation. Each bedroom has en suite facilities with a shower. Guests dine in a delightful, sunny conservatory or in the L-shaped bar where the menu is entirely "chalkboard". The choice is extensive and the food is good. Chef Hilary Heskin and her team show considerable expertise in the interesting and imaginative choice of ingredient combinations and sauces that they create and in the way they present them. **Nearby:** Wonderful walking country and some of England's finest stately homes and National Trust properties, among them Sudbury Hall and Kedleston Hall. Boating and fishing at Carsington Water, the famous Crich Tramway Museum and the attractions of Alton Towers. **Directions: From the M1, exit at junction 25 and take the A52 towards Derby and Ashbourne. Hognaston is situated on the B5035 Ashbourne-Wirksworth road.**

ASKRIGG (Wensleydale)

THE KINGS ARMS HOTEL AND RESTAURANT

In association with MasterCard

MARKET PLACE, ASKRIGG-IN-WENSLEYDALE, NORTH YORKSHIRE DL8 3HQ
TEL: 01969 650258 FAX: 01969 650635 E-MAIL: rayliz@kahaskrigg.prestel.co.uk.

OWNERS: Ray and Liz Hopwood
CHEF: John Barber

10 rms   10 ens

S: £50–£75
D: £79–£120

Inn: Ray and Liz Hopwood will welcome you to their country Georgian manor house set amid some of Britain's most emotive scenery, as captured on canvas by Turner during his stay in the early 1800s. Originally built in 1760 the building became an inn in 1810 and it established a tradition of warm hospitality and good food. Yorkshire Life Hotel of the Year award for "outstanding culinary credentials and highly individual period ambience". There are three distinctive bars: one is better known as The Drover's Arms from the BBC TV series *All Creatures Great and Small*. In each of the comfortable bars guests can enjoy an award-winning meal with ales from the cask. Beautifully styled bedrooms include richly draped four-poster, half-tester and brass beds; all thoughtfully appointed to ensure the utmost comfort. **Restaurant:** The panelled Clubroom Restaurant epitomises elegance and sophistication. Only the finest fresh produce, fish and game in season are used for the dishes that comprise the fixed price à la carte menu. Special dinners are held regularly to celebrate events in the calendar. An award-winning wine list complements the menu. The Silks Grill offers steaks, games and fresh fish. It is also available for private functions. **Nearby:** The Yorkshire Dales, Settle–Carlisle Railway, Aysgarth Falls and Brontë country. **Directions: In the centre of Askrigg, ¹/₂ mile from A684 near Bainbridge. This road links A1 at Leeming Bar with M6 at Sedbergh (junction 37).**

THE WINDMILL AT BADBY

MAIN STREET, BADBY, NR DAVENTRY, NORTHAMPTONSHIRE NN11 6AN
TEL: 01327 702363 FAX: 01327 311521

OWNERS: John Freestone and Carol Sutton
CHEF: Gavin Baxter

S: £42–£45
D: £55–£65

8 rms | 8 ens

Inn: The Windmill Inn Hotel was first established as an inn in the 17th century and is situated in the heart of the pretty village of Badby. A traditional thatched country pub, complete with log fires, The Windmill offers good food and a range of cask-conditioned ales. The owners, with their extensive experience of hotel and pub management, have plenty of ideas for regular activities. Winter Sportsmen's Dinners and theme nights with entertainment are popular events. The en suite bedrooms provide comfortable accommodation and the whole hotel is ideally suitable for house party weekends from 12-14 guests. **Restaurant:** Under the skilled eye of Gavin Baxter the kitchen prepares a varied range of freshly cooked dishes.

Many specialities are made and these include Stilton mushrooms, char-grilled Cajun chicken, steak and kidney pie, fresh moussaka and poached salmon with new potatoes. Weddings, functions and business conferences are catered for with ease. **Nearby:** The surrounding woods and meadows provide excellent walking (Badby is the start of both the Knightley and Nene Ways). Cycles may be hired. Places to visit include Althorpe, Canons Ashby, Sulgrave Manor (home of the Washingtons), Blenheim Palace, Silverstone Circuit, Warwick and Stratford-upon-Avon. **Directions: The Windmill is in the centre of Badby, a village located off the A361, three miles south of Daventry on the Banbury road.**

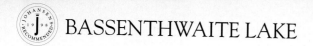

In association with MasterCard

THE PHEASANT

BASSENTHWAITE LAKE, NEAR COCKERMOUTH, CUMBRIA CA13 9YE
TEL: 017687 76234 FAX: 017687 76002

MANAGER: Roger Vorbeck
CHEF: Malcolm Innes

S: £50–£66
D: £86–£112

Inn: This famous 17th century coaching inn is set in lovely gardens and woodlands just 100 yards from the shores of Bassenthwaite Lake. Renowned for its friendly hospitality, The Pheasant has 20 light and airy bedrooms, each comfortably furnished and with private facilities. Three are located in the bungalow next to the hotel. Guests have three lounges to choose from when they want to enjoy a quiet morning coffee or a real Cumbrian afternoon tea with homemade specialities. The bar, with its polished walls and oak settles, is said to be one of the best known in the Lake District. With its traditional setting and convivial atmosphere, this is the perfect place to enjoy a drink before moving on dinner.

Restaurant: The cuisine served in the lovely beamed dining room includes many local Cumbrian specialities, in addition to traditional English food and a wide selection of fine wines. A daily changing menu includes culinary delights to cater for both the meat-eater and vegetarian and there is also a cold buffet available.
Nearby: The Pheasant is within easy reach of the whole Lake District. Usually chosen for its idyllic and peaceful location, the hotel makes a convenient base for guests on fishing, bird-watching or sporting expeditions.
Directions: Signposted off the A66, The Pheasant is 6 miles east of Cockermouth and 8 miles north-west of Keswick.

THE WOOLPACK INN

BECKINGTON, NR BATH, B&NE SOMERSET BA3 6SP
TEL: 01373 831244 FAX: 01373 831223

OWNER: The Old English Pub Co.
GENERAL MANAGER: Andrew Morgan
CHEF: Mark Nacchia

12 rms	12 ens

S: £59
D: £69–£89

Inn: Situated in the centre of the village of Beckington, on the borders of Somerset, Avon and Wiltshire, The Woolpack is a small coaching inn dating from the 16th century. Legend has it that condemned criminals were allowed a final drink here before being led away to the local gallows. The inn has been thoughtfully decorated and furnished to recapture the original character of the building. On the ground floor is the bar area, with its stone floor and open log fire, where fine traditional ale is served. There is also a small lounge. Each of the 12 bedrooms has been individually renovated, each having an en suite bathroom and all modern comforts. **Restaurant:** Guests may enjoy either a quick snack or a more substantial meal in either the Oak Room, Dining or Garden Rooms, where the menus offer freshly prepared dishes, including locally caught game and fish, skillfully cooked by the kitchen team. **Nearby:** There are places to visit nearby in abundance: the Georgian city of Bath, the cathedral cities of Salisbury and Wells, Longleat House and Safari Park, Lacock, Glastonbury, Stourhead, Cheddar Gorge and Wookey Hole, the stone circles at Stonehenge and Avebury, and the tropical bird gardens at Rode. **Directions: Beckington, recently by-passed, is on the A36 Bath–Southampton road on the borders of Somerset and Wiltshire.**

In association with MasterCard

THE BLUE BELL HOTEL

MARKET PLACE, BELFORD, NORTHUMBERLAND NE70 7NE
TEL: 01668 213543 FAX: 01668 213787

OWNER: Jean Shirley
CHEF: Stephen Owens

S: £38–£60
D: £76–£98

Inn: This beautifully restored old coaching inn stands in the centre of the village of Belford, near the old Market Cross. The sophisticated Georgian-style interiors are decorated to complement the original features. Luxurious bedrooms provide every modern comfort and are all unique. There is an elegant residents' lounge and two bars, well stocked with fine malts, rare brandies and vintage ports. The hotel also has three acres of walled terraced grounds, with a putting lawn and organic vegetable and herb garden. Dogs by arrangement. **Restaurant:** The emphasis here is on freshness. Fruit and vegetables from the hotel gardens are combined with an excellent supply of fresh local produce such as Cheviot lamb, Tweed salmon and Craster kippers, to create a range of delicious seasonal dishes. Frequently changing à la carte and table d'hôte menus are served in the garden restaurant, which is furnished with locally crafted tables. For a more simple but substantial menu, try the Buttery. **Nearby:** There is much to discover along Northumberland's scenic coastline – the Farne Islands, Lindsifarne and Berwick-upon-Tweed are among the many interesting attractions. Sporting activities which can be enjoyed locally include shooting, fishing, riding and golf. **Directions: Midway between Berwick and Alnwick, about 14 miles south of Berwick and two minutes from the A1. From A1 turn off at Belford/Wooler junction to join the B6349. The hotel is situated in the centre of the village.**

In association with MasterCard

WHITE HORSE HOTEL

4 HIGH STREET, BLAKENEY, HOLT, NORFOLK NR25 7AL
TEL: 01263 740574 FAX: 01263 741303

OWNERS: Daniel Rees and Susan Catt
CHEF: Christopher Hyde

S: £30
D: £60–£70
Suite: £70

Inn: The White Horse was formerly a 17th century coaching inn and in the early 1900s became the first hotel in Blakeney, a popular boating centre with a main street of brick and flint buildings and a waterfront crowded with sailing craft and cruisers. Set around a shady courtyard, the hotel has six simple and comfortably uncluttered bedrooms, some with good views across the harbour, the National Trust reserve and marshes. All are en suite and have colour television and tea and coffee making facilities. The area is much favoured by artists and the hotel has its own gallery with regularly changing exhibitions. No dogs allowed. **Restaurant:** Situated in the former stables which overlook the walled garden and courtyard, the restaurant is light and airy and has an attractive relaxed style. Chef Christopher Hyde offers a seasonal à la carte menu using local fare as much as possible. Whitebait, herring roe, fish pie, crab and lobster are favourites. Special dishes are introduced daily on the restaurant blackboard. All meals are well presented and complemented by a good choice of wines and ales. **Nearby:** The sandy holiday resorts of Sheringham and Cromer, boat trips to Blakeney Point Nature Reserve where seals may occasionally be seen, the Norfolk Coast Path, Blickling Hall and Holkham Hall. Sailing, fishing, shooting, riding and golf at Cromer and Sheringham. **Directions: From Norwich, take the A140 to Cromer and then the A149 coastal road west for approximately 12 miles.**

In association
with MasterCard

THE CROWN HOTEL

HORSEFAIR, BOROUGHBRIDGE, NORTH YORKSHIRE YO5 9LB
TEL: 01423 322328 FAX: 01423 324512

OWNER: Richard Stables
CHEF: Neil Hanks

S: £50–£70
D: £65–£95

Inn: Few hotels can boast a history as remarkable as The Crown. Centrally situated in the bustling town of Boroughbridge, it stands on the site of a 13th century manor house which was a rendezvous for the 1569 rebellion to place Mary Queen of Scots on the throne. In 1672 it was converted into one of the largest coaching inns on the Great North Road with stabling for over 100 horses. The stables have gone but The Crown retains its historic ambience and many reminders of its past, all combined with the best in modern style and comfort. Each of the 42 bedrooms is furnished to a high standard with en suite bath and shower.

Restaurant: The attractive Tancred Restaurant offers interesting and varied table d'hôte and à la carte menus. Lighter meals are available in the comfortable lounge and bar. Conferences, weddings and private functions can be catered for in the air-conditioned St Helena Suite.
Nearby: Boroughbridge is an ideal centre for visiting the North Yorks Moors, Yorkshire Dales, Rievaulx Abbey, Castle Howard and Knaresborough Castle. Ripon, Harrogate and York are within easy reach. Famous local racecourses include Wetherby, Catterick, York, Ripon and Thirsk. **Directions: Boroughbridge is just off the A1, 11 miles north of Wetherby.**

THE OLD MANSE

VICTORIA STREET, BOURTON-ON-THE-WATER, GLOUCESTERSHIRE GL54 2BX
TEL: 01451 820082 FAX: 01451 810381

OWNERS: Oswald and Audrey Dockery

15 rms 15 ens

S: £39.50–£62.50
D: £59–£119

Inn: The Old Manse was built in 1748 during a period of wealth for all the settlements of the Cotswold hills. Its first owner was Reverend Benjamin Beddome, the village baptist pastor. In recent years, traditional Cotswold stone has been used to add a modern wing to the inn, whilst just a few feet from the porch the wide and shallow River Windrush flows on its way to the Thames. Fully centrally heated, this lovely inn has 12 en suite bedrooms in the main hotel and 3 additional annexe rooms, all with remote control colour TV, radio alarm and tea and coffee making facilities. For added luxury, the Beddome Room boasts a King-size four-poster bed with matching furniture and a double whirlpool spa. **Restaurant:** An elegantly decorated and furnished restaurant offers excellent table d'hôte, à la carte and vegetarian menus and the chef will gladly prepare any special dish on request. Fresh local produce is used wherever possible and there is an extensive wine list to complement the cuisine. **Nearby:** Bourton-on-the-Water has its own motor museum (with one of the country's largest collections of vintage advertising signs), model village (a one-ninth replica of the original), a model railway exhibition and Birdland (with the largest collection of penguins outside America). Also within easy reach is the well-marked footpath route across the wolds of the Oxfordshire Way. **Directions: Bourton-on-the-Water is off the A429 running between Stow-on-the-Wold and Cirencester.**

For hotel location, see maps on pages 183-189

21

THE MANOR HOTEL

WEST BEXINGTON, DORCHESTER, DORSET DT2 9DF
TEL: 01308 897616 FAX: 01308 897035

OWNERS: Richard and Jayne Childs
CHEFS: Richard Childs and Clive Jobson

In association
with MasterCard

S: from £43
D: from £76

Inn: The Manor Hotel, winner of the 1997 Johansens Most Excellent Inns Award and also mentioned in the Domesday Book, is in a wonderful setting, overlooking the beautiful Dorset countryside and spectacular Lyme Bay. The friendly atmosphere is apparent immediately on entering the inn, while the oak-panelling, stone walls and original fireplaces remind guests they are in the midst of history. **Restaurant:** The restaurant is brilliant, with two or three course menus that include wonderful choices – smoked duck breast and mango salad, lobster and scallop ragout, roast salmon and prawns with a lime and avocado salsa or roast pork with sage crust and apple sauce. Vegetarian dishes also feature, and there is a children's menu. The wine list is exciting. Buffet meals, also including seafood, are served in the cosy cellar bar. There is an attractive conservatory for relaxing while children have their own play area outside. There are twelve charming en suite bedrooms and those at the top of the house have splendid views over the sea. **Nearby:** This is Thomas Hardy country and there are famous gardens and historic houses to visit. Chesil Beach and Abbotsbury Swannery are nearby and water sports and country pursuits can be enjoyed. **Directions: West Bexington is on the B3157, 5 miles east of Bridport, 11 miles from Dorchester and Weymouth.**

In association with MasterCard

YE OLDE CHURSTON COURT INN

CHURSTON FERRERS, NR BRIXHAM, DEVON TQ5 OJE
TEL: 01803 842186 FAX: 01803 842473

OWNER: Peter Malkin
CHEF: Mark Hooper

S: £45
D: £65–85

Inn: Step back in time in this ancient manor inn, spend the night, stay for a week, drink with the locals or taste the homemade delights. It's where Agatha Christie stayed and wrote. She donated a stained glass window to the Saxon Church, in whose vaults are buried the ancestors of the Lords of Churston. Churston Court was of such importance historically that its symbol is on the Mayor of Torbay's Chain of Office. In 1016 the Saxon Earls Ulf and his son Ludhael owned Churston Court and ruled this part of Devon as Lords of Totnes. It became a monastery and the ghost of a monk appears in the kitchen. There is a mediaeval passage that runs from Churston Cove to the Inn which was used by Sea Captains after anchoring their ships at the Cove in Tudor times. A welcoming place to stay, great winter fires, comfy old oak furniture, old pictures and friendly staff. The owner Peter Malkin is helped by his girlfriend Kate, his son Oliver, three large and cuddly English Mastiff dogs, Ethelred, Athelstan and Baby Britannia and Blackmalkin the cat. The inn lies in a beautiful setting 5 minutes walk to the sea, golf and tennis next door. All types of boats for hire at Brixham harbour where allegedly Napoleon set foot on his way to St. Helena. **Directions: From Exeter, take A380 to Paignton and then join A3022 towards Brixham. Pass golf course, take 3rd left through Churston Village. Churston Court Inn is beside the church.**

THE BROADWAY HOTEL

THE GREEN, BROADWAY, WORCESTERSHIRE WR12 7AA
TEL: 01386 852401 FAX: 01386 853879 E-MAIL: andrew@thebroadway.u-net.com

OWNER: Andrew and Gaynor Riley
CHEF: Vernon Crowther

S: £47.50–£51.50
D: £80–£95

Inn: The delightful Broadway Hotel stands proudly in the centre of the picturesque Cotswold village of Broadway where every stone evokes memories of Elizabethan England. Once used by the Abbots of Pershore, the hotel was formerly a 16th century house, as can be seen by its architecture which combines the half timbers of the Vale of Evesham with the distinctive honey-coloured and grey stone of the Cotswolds. It epitomises a true combination of old world charm and modern day amenities with friendly efficient service. All of the bedrooms provide a television, telephone and tea and coffee making facilities. **Restaurant:** Traditional English dishes and a peaceful ambience are offered in the beamed Courtyard Restaurant.

There is an impressive variety of à la carte dishes complemented by a good wine list. The cosy and congenial Jockey Club bar is a pleasant place to relax and enjoy a drink. **Nearby:** The inn overlooks the village green at the bottom of the main street where guests can browse through shops offering an array of fine antiques. On a clear day, 13 counties of England and Wales can be viewed from Broadway Tower. Snowhill, Burford, Chipping Camden, Bourton-on-the Water, Stow-on-the-Wold and Winchcombe as well as larger Cheltenham, Worcester and Stratford are within easy reach. **Directions: From London M40 to Oxford, A40 to Burford, A424 through Stow-on-the-Wold, then A44 to Broadway.**

COTSWOLD GATEWAY HOTEL

CHELTENHAM ROAD, BURFORD, OXON OX18 4HX
TEL: 01993 822695 FAX: 01993 823600

OWNERS: Dennis and Ann Evans

20 rms | 20 ens

S: £53
D: £68

Inn: In the days of horse drawn coaches Cotswold Gateway Hotel was a welcome stop over for travellers visiting Burford. Today, this 18th century inn which has recently been lavishly renovated offers its guests every modern comfort and amenity. A friendly and intimate service is offered by the highly trained staff, equal to any found in a family run hotel. All of the bedrooms have been individually designed and furnished and provide a trouser press, alarm clock, television, telephone and tea and coffee making facilities. **Restaurant:** Deservedly awarded its first AA rosette, the spacious and pleasantly furnished restaurant has a daily changing menu of traditional English dishes supported by a good wine list.

The bar, where an exciting range of English and continental fayre is served, has undergone a complete refurbishment. It is a pleasant place to relax and enjoy a drink, while the coffee shop serves informal meals, tea and refreshments. **Nearby:** Adjacent to the hotel is a mews of specialist antique shops offering an array of fine antique pieces. Burford itself has changed little since the end of the 17th century and its streets are lined with exquisite buildings in the honeyed, locally quarried limestone. There are many other pretty Cotswold villages to explore. **Directions:** Burford is on A40 where it crosses A361, halfway between Oxford and Cheltenham.

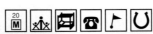

THE LAMB INN

SHEEP STREET, BURFORD, OXFORDSHIRE OX18 4LR
TEL: 01993 823155 FAX: 01993 822228

OWNERS: Richard and Caroline De Wolf
MANAGER: Paul Swain
CHEF: Pascal Clavaud

S: £57.50–£75
D: £90–£100

Inn: The Lamb Inn, in the small Cotswold town of Burford, is everyone's idea of the archetypal English inn, where it is easy to imagine that time has slipped back to some gentler age. The inn is set in a quiet location with a pretty walled garden. To step inside is to recapture something of the spirit of the 14th century: flagged floors, gleaming copper, brass and silver reflect the flicker of log fires and the well-chosen antiques all enhance the sense of history here. The bedrooms, which have recently been refurbished, offer comfortable accommodation, with oak beams, chintz curtains and soft furnishings. **Restaurant:** Guests can enjoy the best of British cooking. Dinner, chosen from a three-course table d'hôte or à la carte menu, is taken in the candlelit pillared dining room and might include such dishes as fresh grilled sardines with lime butter sauce, followed by roast tenderloin of pork wrapped in smoked bacon with a blue cheese cream sauce. Light lunches are served in the bar or in the garden. On Sundays, a traditional three-course lunch is served. Packed lunches and hampers can be provided. **Nearby:** The inn is near the heart of the town, where guests can browse through antiques shops or laze by the waters of the River Windrush. Burford is within easy reach of Oxford, Cheltenham, Stow-on-the-Wold and the many attractive Cotswold villages. **Directions: Sheep Street is off the main street in Burford. Burford is 20 miles west of Oxford.**

THE HOSTE ARMS HOTEL

THE GREEN, BURNHAM MARKET, NORFOLK PE31 8HD
TEL: 01328 738777 FAX: 01328 730103

OWNER: Paul Whittome
MANAGER: Rebecca Mackenzie
HEAD CHEF: Stephen David

 S: £60
D: £84–£108

Inn: The Hoste Arms dates back to the 17th century, when it was known as The Pitt Arms, after William Pitt's cousin, a local landowner. Overlooking the green in the picturesque village of Burnham Market, the hotel has undergone extensive refurbishments, all 20 bedrooms are beautifully decorated, all en suite. Four rooms have four-poster beds and great care has been taken to preserve any original features. Despite being voted Johansens Inn of the Year and Egon Ronay Pub of the Year, Paul Whittome continues his quest constantly to improve and upgrade services and facilities to enhance the enjoyment of his guests. A panelled function room is available for private parties and conferences. **Restaurant:** The menus are created by head chef Stephen David who creates an excellent menu using British, French and Oriental influences on his menu. The Hoste offers an outstanding wine list personally selected by Paul offering a good selection on the bar wines along with exceptionally well priced fine wines on the main list. **Nearby:** The Hoste Arms is well situated to cater for most interests. There are several stately homes in the area, including Holkham Hall and Sandringham. For nature lovers there are four bird sanctuaries in the area and boat trips can be arranged to Scolt Head Island. Golf enthusiasts are also well catered for at Hunstanton, Brancaster and Cromer. **Directions: Burnham Market is about two miles from the A149 between Brancaster and Wells-next-the-Sea.**

FENCE GATE INN

WHEATLEY LANE ROAD, FENCE, NR BURNLEY, LANCASHIRE BB12 9EE
TEL: 01282 618101 FAX: 01282 615432

OWNER: Kevin Berkins
MANAGER: Stephen Pope
CHEF: Erik McRobbie

Inn: Set within a collection of small villages a short distance from Pendle Hill in the picturesque village of Fence. The Fence Gate was originally a house used as a collection point for cotton delivered by barge and distributed to surrounding cottage dwellers to be spun into cloth. Owner Kevin Berkins has redesigned and refurbished the house into a stylish inn and an extensive banqueting centre for all occasions with two versatile suites and a brasserie. A large, restful conservatory overlooks beautifully landscaped gardens that incorporate waterfalls and fountains. **Brasserie:** The Brasserie menu boasts a variety of tempting dishes including Breast of Cressingham Duck cooked Pink, with a Gooseberry sauce and an Apple Chutney. English Leg of Lamb Steak marinated and cooked in Honey, flavoured with spices and Garlic served on a bed of Flageolet Beans, Grilled medallion of Salmon presented on a bed of Mange Tout flavoured with a Saffron and Sweet Pepper Butter Sauce. There are house specialities and a wide selection of vegetarian dishes. For Fence Gate Diners new to the area there are numerous places to visit, wether it be for shopping at the Boundary Mill Shop or other Leisure facilities available nearby. **Directions: From the M65 exit junction 13, take first left along the Padiham by-pass for 1½miles. Turn right at brown signs to Barley Picnic site then first left, the Fence Gate is set back on right.**

In association with MasterCard

In association
with MasterCard

BOAR'S HEAD HOTEL

LICHFIELD ROAD, SUDBURY, DERBYSHIRE DE6 5GX
TEL: 01283 820344 FAX: 01283 820075

OWNERS: John and Gail Crooks
CHEFS: Ralph Skripek and Gail Crooks

22 rms | 22 ens

S: from £39.50
D: from £49.50

Inn: This 17th century house was lost from the famous Vernon estate through a game of cards! It is now a well known local hostelry, having been run by the Crooks family for many years. Guests arriving will be welcomed by the architectural beauty of this very old building. There is a warm bar, with natural brick walls, horse brasses and hunting horns. The residents' lounge looks onto a pretty patio where drinks are served in summer months. Much thought has been given to furnishing the delightful bedrooms which have every possible facility, including teletext and Sky television. Visitors enjoy a choice of real ales and excellent home-cooked dishes with the chef's specials listed on a blackboard. **Restaurant:** There are two restaurants, the elegant Royal Boar with an imaginative à la carte menu and the less formal Hunter's Table Carvery and Bistro offering fresh fish, pasta dishes and splendid roasts, both at lunchtime and in the evening. The Royal Boar is closed on Sunday evenings, but is famous for its Sunday lunch. A fascinating wine list covers vineyards worldwide, with 70 entries that include 6 house wines and a selection of 10 half-bottles! **Nearby:** Alton Towers and Uttoxeter Racecourse are lively attractions nearby. Other guests will enjoy Chatsworth House, Sudbury Hall, Tutbury Castle and the Bass Museum. **Directions: The hotel is on the A515, just south of the A50 from Stoke on Trent to Derby.**

BURTON UPON TRENT (Branston)

THE OLD VICARAGE RESTAURANT

MAIN STREET, BRANSTON, BURTON–UPON–TRENT, STAFFORDSHIRE DE14 3EX
TEL: 01283 533222 FAX: 01283 540258

OWNERS: David and Eileen Boodie
CHEFS: David Boodie and Mark Alexander

Restaurant: Run by the chef-patron and his wife this excellent restaurant offers an extensive variety of superb dishes to cater for every taste. In addition to classic recipes there are gourmet specialities, these include warm salad of peppered chicken livers with a sherry and shallot sauce, topped with a soft poached egg; baked fillet of turbot served with a scallop soufflé and a champagne sauce; pot-roasted supreme of guinea-fowl stuffed with apricots and thyme served with a Maderia sauce; and monk fish and scallops with vermicelli. There are numerous delicious sweets to chose from, including cappuccino mousse with sable biscuits and steamed double ginger pudding with home-made honey and vanilla ice cream. Vegetarian dishes are always available. The price of the three course lunch menu is £13.95, while the dinner menu is priced at £23.95. Prices are inclusive of VAT. **Wine:** There are over 150 wines available to complement the cuisine, priced between £7 and £150 with some reasonably priced half bottles. The Restaurant is closed for the first two weeks of August and on every Sunday evening and Monday. **Nearby:** Bass Museum of Brewing, Tutbury Castle and glassworks, Calke Abbey and Sudbury Hall. Visits, which must be pre-booked, can be arranged to the Bass, Marstons and Ind Coope breweries. **Directions: The Old Vicarage Restaurant is 400 yards from the A38 Burton South junction in the centre of Branston village and next to the church.**

CHEFS' SPECIALITIES
●●●●●●●

salad roasted sea scallops
*with a puree of minted garden peas
and a balsamic vinegar dressing*

pan fried fillet of english lamb
*with provençal vegetables
and a light tomato jus*

assiette of chocolates
*on a compote of apples and blackcurrants
finished with spicy mocca ice-cream*

In association with MasterCard

THE CHEQUERS INN

FROGGATT EDGE, NR CALVER, DERBYSHIRE S30 1ZB
TEL: 01433 630231

OWNER: Bob Graham
MANAGER: Maggie Wheelden
CHEF: Julie Presland

6 rms   6 ens

S: £44–£51
D: £55–£66

Inn: A Grade II listed building. The Chequers Inn originally comprised four 16th century houses, rebuilt in the 18th century and now extensively refurbished. It is situated on an old pack horse road in the heart of the Peak district National Park. Visitors will see plenty of reminders of the inn's history; a horse-mounting block still stands outside the main building and the old stables house the logs that fuel today's open fires. Behind the inn, acres of unspoiled woodland lead up to Froggatt Edge, with its panoramic views. Each of the six cottage-style bedrooms has its own identity, and for an extra touch of romance one room has a four poster bed. **Restaurant:** Local chef Julie Presland creates a wide variety of European and British meals, with several fish dishes and local game in season. The menus are original, exciting and reasonably priced. As an alternative to the restaurant, a choice of hearty bar meals is served every day. Bakewell pudding, the local speciality, is a favourite dessert here – delicious served hot with cream. **Nearby:** This is wonderful walking country: you can leave your car and follow the Derwent River or the Peak trails. Chatsworth House, Haddon Hall, the caverns of Castleton and the market town of Bakewell are all closeby. **Directions: The inn is situated on the old pack horse road, now the B6054 which links Bakewell and Sheffield, 6 miles from Bakewell on Froggatt Edge.**

In association
with MasterCard

TYACKS HOTEL

27 COMMERCIAL STREET, CAMBORNE, CORNWALL TR14 8LD
TEL: 01209 612424 FAX: 01209 612435

OWNERS: St Austell Brewery & Co Ltd
MANAGERS: Terence and Elizabeth Davidson
CHEF: Stuart Illston

S: £42–£44
D: £75–£80
Suites: £100–£110

Inn: This charming 18th century coaching inn set in the heart of Camborne is just three minutes drive from the main A30 road or less than five minutes from the bus or railway stations. The Tyacks is used by business men and women as well as tourists as a base for travelling in the west of Cornwall. Re-opened in 1992, having been totally refurbished to AA and RAC 3 Star standard, the inn has become popular with visitors from all over the world as is reflected in the restaurant's imaginative menus. Adjacent to the restaurant is an attractive lounge bar, ideal for a quiet drink or bar snack. For those who enjoy a lively pub atmosphere there is the Coach Bar. Beside the hotel entrance, opposite the old stables is a patio and beer garden where drinks and snacks can be enjoyed on a sunny day. **Restaurant:** The à la carte, table d'hôte and vegetarian menus offer a splendid choice of English and Continental fare using fresh Cornish fish, vegetables and meats. **Nearby:** Camborne School of Mines and Geology Museum, Tehidy Country Park and Golf Club, St Ives Tate Gallery, Penzance and Lands End. The Engines Museum at Poole, the house of William Murdoch, founder of gaslighting, in Redruth. **Directions: From A30 turn off at the sign for Camborne West then follow signs for town centre. Tyacks Hotel is on the left-hand side.**

PANOS HOTEL AND RESTAURANT

154-156 HILLS ROAD, CAMBRIDGE, CAMBRIDGESHIRE CB2 2PB
TEL: 01223 212958 FAX: 01223 210980

OWNER: Genevieve Kretz

S: £50
D: £70

Inn: This small unpretentious and friendly hotel is managed by Genevieve Kretz. It is close to the centre of town and to the railway station, and has a regular clientèle who return again and again, treating it as Cambridge's best kept secret. Guests enter the hotel through the attractive conservatory bar, which like the other reception rooms, is filled with fresh flowers arranged by Genevieve. The six bedrooms are comfortable and well appointed, all with en suite shower facilities, colour television, a radio alarm, writing desk and mini-bar. Full breakfast is included in the price. **Restaurant:** The restaurant is recognised to be one of the best in Cambridge, with menus supervised by the owner. The famous Panos charcoal-grilled steaks and flambé dishes are listed beside mezze and sword-fish kebabs. An excellent wine list is available too. **Nearby:** The River Cam for those guests who wish to try their hand at punting, and for those preferring dry land the famous Cambridge Botanical Gardens. There are the historic colleges to admire, also the Fitzwilliam Museum. Ely Cathedral is not far away and for those who like more activity, there is the racing at Newmarket. **Directions: From city centre follow signs to station and hospital as far as Hills Road. Once on Hills Road carry straight on to traffic lights and railway bridge avoiding fork to station. Panos is immediately on your right. Private car park at the rear.**

 In association with MasterCard

THE TARN END HOUSE HOTEL

TALKIN TARN, BRAMPTON, CUMBRIA CA8 1LS
TEL: 016977 2340 FAX: 016977 2089

OWNERS: David and Vivienne Ball
CHEF: David Ball

S: £35–£49
D: £55–£72

Inn: The Tarn End House Hotel has idyllic surroundings at any time of year. This former estate farm house is over 100 years old and is set in its own grounds, with lawns running down to the shores of Talkin Tarn. A very warm welcome and traditional hospitality are guaranteed. The nicely furnished bedrooms have every modern facility and offer exceptional views. This is an ideal spot in which to escape from the world and there is a good choice of leisure activities. Long walks can be taken over the surrounding fells, or the more active can take advantage of rowing, wind-surfing or sailing on the tarn. There are good golf courses nearby and river fishing and rough shooting can be arranged. **Restaurant:** The inn enjoys a very good reputation for its cuisine. Guests can savour a meal chosen from two menus – à la carte or table d'hôte. Bar snacks are also available at lunchtime. **Nearby:** Hadrian's Wall, Lanercost Priory, and the City of Carlisle with its historic castle. The River Gelt is an ideal place to visit for birdwatchers and the Scottish borders are within easy reach. **Directions: From M6 junction 43 take A69 to Brampton. From the centre of Brampton take B6413 towards Castle Carrock and Talkin Tarn. Go over the railway and past Brampton Golf Club and take second left to Talkin village – the hotel is on the left.**

 CASTLE ASHBY

THE FALCON HOTEL

CASTLE ASHBY, NORTHAMPTON, NORTHAMPTONSHIRE NN7 1LF
TEL: 01604 696200 FAX: 01604 696673

OWNERS: Neville and Jo Watson
CHEF: Neil Helks

S: £70
D: £77.50

Inn: Six miles south of Northampton, in the heart of the Marquess of Northampton's estate, The Falcon is a delightful country cottage hotel, secluded and tranquil, minutes away from the rambling acres of Castle Ashby House. Proprietors Neville and Jo Watson, both committed professionals, have invested energy and enthusiasm into transforming this once modest place into a haven of comfort, excellent food and attentive service. Bedrooms are beautifully furnished, cosy cottage style and the bathrooms have been recently upgraded. There are fresh flowers, French, Spanish and German are spoken, and dogs are welcome. **Restaurant:** Lunch and dinner, which are created where possible from seasonal, home-grown produce, are served in the intimate restaurant which overlooks a lawn with willow trees. The excellent value-for-money cuisine, modern English in flavour, is prepared by chef Neil Helks. A fixed-price menu costs £19.50, including coffee and *petits fours*. There is also an interesting à la carte selection. The extensive wine list can be studied by guests at their leisure over pre-prandial drinks by a glowing log fire. **Nearby:** Walk in the grounds of Castle Ashby estate. Further afield, visit Woburn, Althorp, Silverstone, Bedford and Stratford. **Directions: Exit M1 junction 14 northbound or 15 southbound. Follow the signs to A428 where Castle Ashby and The Falcon are clearly signposted, six miles south-east of Northampton.**

In association with MasterCard

CASTLE COMBE

THE CASTLE INN

CASTLE COMBE, NR CHIPPENHAM, WILTSHIRE SN14 7HN
TEL: 01249 783030 FAX: 01249 782315

OWNERS: Hatton Hotels Group
MANAGER: Philip Brumfitt
CHEF: Jamie Gemmell

11 rms   11 ens

S: £60–£90
D: £90–£110

Inn: This famous inn can trace its origins back to the 12th century, and the restoration completed in 1994 reflects the owners' determination to combine history with discreet modernisation, creating an elegant small hostelry by the market place of this pretty village. The bedrooms are delightful, filled with all modern amenities and luxurious accessories that include towelling robes, fresh fruit, mineral water and homemade cookies. Attention to detail is also reflected in the en suite bathrooms with their antique style gold fittings, two having a whirlpool bath and one a Victorian style slipper bath. **Restaurant:** The inn is open daily for lunch and dinner. Oliver's Restaurant, awarded two Rosettes by the AA, has built up a reputation for outstandingly good food and fine wine, at affordable prices. Guests can dine in the oak beamed restaurant, the conservatory or the bar which offers an excellent selection of real ales, premier beers, wines and spirits. A member of Hatton Hotels Group. **Nearby:** Castle Combe is ideally situated for exploring Bath, Bristol and the Cotswolds. Golf and motor racing are local sports. **Directions: Castle Combe is on the A420 south of the M4 at junction 17 from London, or junction 18 from South Wales.**

CASTLE DONINGTON

THE DONINGTON MANOR HOTEL

HIGH STREET, CASTLE DONINGTON, DERBYSHIRE DE74 2PP
TEL: 01332 810253 FAX: 01332 850330

OWNER: Nigel Grist
CHEF: Bernard Bradley

24 rms
24 ens

S: £65
D: £80

Inn: Although it has been considerably extended this historic, 18th century former coaching inn has retained much if its erstwhile Regency splendour, highlighted by magnificent wide, bowed, curved glass windows. It is a comfortable and friendly hostelry offering good and tastefully furnished accommodation, with satellite television and all the usual modern amenities. Most of the bedrooms and bathrooms are of exceptional appointment and several provide the comfort of a traditional four-poster bed. The hotel also has two purpose-built and fully equipped conference rooms. **Restaurant:** The gastronomic skills of chef Bernard Bradley can be sampled in three dining rooms - the lovely, 18th century Adam Room with its intricate offset plasterwork ceiling, the small, oak-panelled Gun Room which was formerly the kitchen of the coaching inn, and the 120-seater, Regency-style Rawdon Room, spectacularly lit by six crystal chandeliers and where weddings and dinner dances are regularly held. Both food and wine are very reasonably priced. **Nearby:** Calke Abbey, Donington Park motor racing circuit and car museum, Nottingham castle and racecourse, canal cruising on the Trent and Mersey Canal. Closed 24-31 December. **Directions: From M1, exit at junction 24 and follow signs for Donington Park then Castle Donington. The hotel is situated on the B6540 road next to the traffic lights in the centre of the village.**

KINGSHEAD HOUSE RESTAURANT

BIRDLIP, GLOUCESTERSHIRE GL4 8JH
TEL: 01452 862299

OWNERS: Warren and Judy Knock
CHEF: Judy Knock

   D: £66

Judy and Warren Knock have now been running their restaurant, a stone-built former coaching inn on the edge of the Cotswolds, for over ten years. In the welcoming oak-beamed dining-room Judy provides excellent modern English cooking. Her menu changes twice-weekly, offering up to four courses with perhaps five delicious choices for each course. She uses only fresh ingredients; fish is delivered from South Wales, meat is from a local butcher and vegetables from a nearby farm. Main courses range from fillet of brill with chives and broad beans to rack of lamb with garlic fritters, while starters may include a splendid brandade of smoked haddock in puff pastry.

Puddings are equally appealing, with such delights as fresh poached pear with an elderflower sabayon and home-made sorbet. There is one en suite bedroom well proportioned and comfortably furnished. The restaurant opens for lunch Tuesday to Sunday and for dinner Tuesday to Saturday. Smoking is discouraged but not entirely banned. **Wine:** The wine list, compiled by Warren Knock, offers over seventy different wines and has a particularly useful selection of half-bottles. **Directions: Kingshead House stands at the top of Birdlip Hill with its famous view. Birdlip is situated just off the A417 on the B4070, 8 miles from Gloucester and Cheltenham.**

CHEF'S SPECIALS
•••••••

fettuccini
with fennel, asparagus and a rocket sauce

Saumon en civet
salmon fillet cooked in red wine, with French beans and a purée of red beans

summer fruits
in limeflower syrup with a sorbet of fromage blanc

THE SWAN HOTEL

50 HIGH STREET, TARPORLEY, CHESTER CW6 0AG
TEL: 01829 733838 FAX: 01829 732932

OWNER: Christine Pickering
MANAGER: Chris Sharp
CHEF: Jason Pullinger

  S: £52.50–£62.50
D: £68.50–£80

Inn: The Swan Hotel was built in the 1560s as a coaching inn and is now a listed building. Its bedrooms are attractively furnished in an individual style, with a range of modern comforts to make life as luxurious as possible. In the bar, guests are spoilt for choice – five cask ales, 4 lagers, over 100 continental and British bottled beers and 50 single malt whiskies are served. **Restaurant:** There is a choice of two restaurants – the Cynet and the informal Brasserie – offering a selection of interesting and varied dishes. Starters on the Table d'Hote menu might include chicken and sage rissoles served with polenta chips or smoked salmon and spinach pancake glazed with a rich cream sauce. To follow, try the crostini of aubergine and field mushrooms with olives, herbs and garlic or pan fried fillet of grey mullet served on tomato concass and topped with deep fried spinach leaves. Delicious desserts include brandy snap basket filled with strawberry romanoff and bread and butter pudding layered with chocolate and served with fresh custard. **Nearby:** The Roman city of Chester and Chester Zoo. Manchester, North Wales, The Potteries and The Peak District are all within an hours' drive. **Directions: From Chester take the A51 towards Nantwich. Go into the centre of Tarporley and the Swan Hotel is on the left hand side, with a car park at the rear.**

In association with MasterCard

THE WILD BOAR HOTEL AND RESTAURANT

WHITCHURCH ROAD, NEAR BEESTON, TARPORLEY, CHESHIRE CW6 9NW
TEL: 01829 260309 FAX: 01829 261081

GENERAL MANAGER: Tony Cadman
CHEF: Andrew Griffiths

S: £50-£70
D: £75-£99

Inn: The Wild Boar Hotel, a 17th century hunting lodge, is built in the style of the dramatic and 'typically Cheshire' black and white half timbered tudor buildings. It stands beneath the ruins of 12th century Beeston Castle, overlooking the beautiful surrounding countryside. The individual bedrooms all overlook Vale Royal farm land and offer guests every comfort – including trouser press, hairdryer, minibar and complimentary sherry. **Restaurant:** The hotel has enjoyed an unrivalled reputation for its gourmet restaurant through the ages and this fine tradition is carried on today. High levels of culinary skills are used to produce a tempting menu which utilises only the freshest produce. An excellent wine cellar complements the dishes and guests will experience a friendly and efficient level of service. **Nearby:** The historic walled Roman city of Chester is only 10 miles away. Beeston and Peckforton Castles are also within easy reach, along with a candle factory and Stapeley Water Gardens. There are several golf courses, including Portal Golf Club, motor racing at Oulton Park and horse racing at Chester. The international airport at Manchester and Liverpool are a relatively short drive away. **Directions: From Chester take the A51 towards Nantwich. After bypassing Tarporley turn right onto the A49 at 'Red Fox' pub traffic lights. The Wild Boar is on the left on the brow of the hill after about 1¹/₂ miles.**

THE NOEL ARMS

CHIPPING CAMPDEN, GLOUCESTERSHIRE GL55 6AT
TEL: 01386 840317 FAX: 01386 841136

OWNER: Noel Hotels Ltd
MANAGER: Paul Rees

 S: £65 D: £92

Inn: A long tradition of hospitality awaits you at the Noel Arms Hotel. In 1651 the future Charles II rested here after his Scottish army was defeated by Cromwell at the battle of Worcester and for centuries the hotel has entertained visitors to the ancient and unspoilt, picturesque Cotswold Village of Chipping Campden. Many reminders of the past; fine antique furniture, swords, shields, and other mementoes can be found around the hotel. There are 26 en suite bedrooms in either the main house or in the tastefully constructed new wing, some of which boast luxurious antique four poster beds and all offering the standards you expect from a country hotel. **Restaurant:** The impressive oak panelled, award winning restaurant offers an excellent menu, including a seasonal selection of fresh local produce. You may be tempted to choose from the extensive range of bar snacks available in the conservatory or Dovers Bar. Your meal may be accompanied by wine from the fine selection from around the world. Try some of the traditional cask ales and keg beers. **Nearby:** Browse around the delightful array of shops in Chipping Campden or many of the enchanting honey-coloured Cotswold Villages, Hidcote Manor Gardens, Cheltenham Spa, Worcester, Oxford and Stratford-upon-Avon which are all close by. **Directions: The Noel Arms is in the centre of Chipping Campden, which is on the B4081, 2 miles east of the A44.**

For hotel location, see maps on pages 183-189

CIRENCESTER (Meysey Hampton)

THE MASONS ARMS

MEYSEY HAMPTON, NR CIRENCESTER, GLOUCESTERSHIRE GL7 5JT
TEL: 01285 850164 FAX: 01285 850164

OWNERS: Andrew and Jane O'Dell

8 rms — 8 ens

S: £34
D: £52

Inn: Located beside the village green, this 17th century inn is situated on the southern edge of the Cotswolds. It provides a perfect haven for travellers or holidaymakers seeking peace and tranquility. There are eight comfortable and individually decorated bedrooms and all offer en suite facilities, tea and coffee trays and remote control colour TVs. The heart of the Masons is the bar, still a centre of village life where locals and guests enjoy a convivial atmosphere. Golf, fishing, windsurfing and jet skiing are all available locally, with cycle routes and nature walks ensuring that there is something for every guest to enjoy. **Restaurant:** Excellent home cooked food is served in the separate dining room or the bar. The menus are varied and interesting and include daily 'specials' catering for all tastes. Why not try Cotswold chicken with stilton and bacon, or breast of duck with a black cherry sauce, topped with honey and almonds? Or perhaps more traditional fare such as homemade steak mushroom'n'ale pie or tikka kebabs for the vegetarian? **Nearby:** Cirencester, originally the centre of Roman Britain, is six miles to the west and Bibury, with its famous Arlington Row, four miles to the north. **Directions:** Meysey Hampton is six miles east of Cirencester on A417. Nearest motorway M4 junction 15, M5 junction 11A

In association
with MasterCard

THE NEW INN AT COLN

COLN ST-ALDWYNS, Nr. CIRENCESTER, GLOUCESTERSHIRE GL7 5AN
TEL: 01285 750651 FAX: 01285 750657

OWNERS: Brian and Sandra-Anne Evans
CHEF: Stephen Morey

14 rms   14 ens

S: £65
D: £90–£120

Inn: In days of yore, when Queen Elizabeth I was giving royal assent to the import of tobacco from the new-found Americas, she was also patronising a travel boom in England, by instigating a network of coaching inns after the pattern already set on the Continent. One of the Cotswold inns that her initiative helped to create was The New Inn at Coln St-Aldwyns on Akeman Street, the old Roman Road, leading North East out of Cirencester. The New Inn, though old in years, is today utterly new in spirit, winning ever fresh awards for food and hospitality – its two rosettes being in permanent flower as a second Queen Elizabeth reigns. **Restaurant:** Since Brian and Sandra-Anne Evans took over six years ago The New Inn has blossomed and

Stephen Morey's skills in the kitchen have added a gastronomic dimension to the charm and comfort of the ancient but cleverly modernised bedrooms – perfect accommodation for an idyllic week in the Cotswolds, a useful stop-over or as a timely resting place after an exceedingly fine dinner when driving home might prove a lesser option. For those whose minds may be more focussed on business, there is a charming meeting room. **Nearby:** Stratford-upon-Avon, Bath, Oxford and Cheltenham, plus, of course, the Cotswolds, and within healthy walking distance of Bibury with its photogenic Arlington Row. **Directions: From Burford (A40), take B4425 towards Bibury, then** turn left after Aldsworth.

THE CRICKETERS

CLAVERING, NR SAFFRON WALDEN, ESSEX CB11 4QT
TEL: 01799 550442 FAX: 01799 550882

OWNERS: Trevor and Sally Oliver
MANAGER: Philip Waldron
CHEF: Christopher Hill

6 rms   6 ens

S: £60
D: £80

Inn: This attractive 16th century freehouse in the Essex countryside, just ten minutes from Stansted Airport, has responded to its popularity and reputation for good food by purchasing an adjacent residence to provide increased accommodation for guests. Known as The Pavilion, this new house provides six charming bedrooms, two with four-posters – one on the ground floor suits those with mobility problems. All are en suite, colourful and well appointed. Breakfast is served in the main building. The oak-beamed bar, serving real ale, and restaurant have cricket memorabilia on the walls. There is a non-smoking area. Guests enjoy the big log fire in the winter and alfresco refreshments in the garden in summer.

Restaurant: The Restaurant menu, changing seasonally, has ten appetizing starters and ten succulent main courses, interesting interpretations of classic English cooking and the puddings are of the same calibre. A salad bar pleases slimmers. The wine list is diverse, from house wines through to champagnes, European vineyards alongside many New World names, and many half-bottles. **Nearby:** Guests enjoy visiting Audley End with its renowned house and park, going racing at Newmarket, or exploring Cambridge, Saffron Walden and Duxford Air Museum. **Directions: Leave M11 at junction 8, heading west, then right onto B1383, signed Newport and left at the B1038 to Clavering.**

In association
with MasterCard

THE CROWN AT HOPTON

HOPTON WAFERS, CLEOBURY MORTIMER, WORCESTERSHIRE DY14 0NB
TEL: 01299 270372 FAX: 01299 271127

OWNERS: John and Mavis Price

| 8 rms | 8 ens |

 S: £47.50
D: £75

Inn: This enticing 16th century inn is situated in a hamlet dating back to the Norman Conquest, surrounded by the lush farmland, tumbling streams and wooded valleys of South Shropshire. Exposed beams and wooden floors characterise the bedrooms, which are decorated in a welcoming cottage style. All are spacious and most attractive. The bar, which offers a selection of cask-conditioned beers, adjoins an open terrace and, like all the rooms, has many original features including an inglenook fireplace. **Restaurant:** Originally a 15th century smithy, the traditionally furnished restaurant – known as The Hopton Poacher – makes a fine setting in which to relax over dinner. There is a fixed-price menu offering a choice of imaginatively cooked dishes prepared from fresh, seasonal ingredients. The wine list is well compiled and dessert wines are available by the glass. A good selection of ports, cognacs and armagnacs is available. **Nearby:** Apart from exploring the beautiful countryside, guests can visit Stokesay Castle, many National Trust properties and historic Ludlow. Another option is to take a romantic trip aboard a steam locomotive on the Severn Valley Railway. Ironbridge Gorge Museum is about 30 minutes drive away. **Directions: The Crown Inn is by the A4117 between Ludlow and Kidderminster, two miles west of Cleobury Mortimer.**

In association with MasterCard

THE REDFERN HOTEL

CLEOBURY MORTIMER, SHROPSHIRE DY14 8AA
TEL: 01299 270395 FAX: 01299 271011 E-MAIL: jon@red–fern.demon.co.uk

OWNERS: Jon and Liz Redfern
CHEF: Jamie Bailey

11 rms   11 ens

S: £45–£60
D: £70–£85

Inn: This country town hotel provides good value accommodation and a warm welcome in the heart of England. The Redfern Hotel stands in an attractive setting in Cleobury Mortimer – a market town dating back to the *Doomsday Book*. Crisply decorated bedrooms have white-painted walls and floral fabrics, in keeping with the country house style. Real ale is served in the cosy bar where memorabilia and pictures depicting the town's history are displayed. For parents' peace of mind, a baby-listening service is available. **Restaurant:** Redfern's English Kitchen Restaurant has a homely, welcoming atmosphere, with its home-cured hams and cider flagons hanging from the beams. The menu is changed daily to offer a variety of home-cooked dished such as Shropshire chicken stuffed with Lymeswold cheese and breadcrumbs, or fillet of pork in orange and ginger sauce. **Nearby:** Golf is available at a local course with concessionary green fees. For the more adventurous the Redfern also has its own canal narrowboat for hire. Local attractions include the Ironbridge Museum, famous for its archaeological records of the Industrial Revolution. A trip on the Severn Valley Railway takes you on a scenic route through riverside towns. Other sights close by are Ludlow Castle and the beautiful countryside of the Welsh Marches. **Directions: Cleobury Mortimer is on the A4117 midway between Kidderminster and Ludlow, 11 miles from each.**

NEW INN HOTEL

HIGH STREET, CLOVELLY, DEVON EX39 5TQ
TEL: 01237 431303 FAX: 01237 431636

OWNERS: Clovelly Estate Co Ltd
MANAGER: Alan Cook
CHEF: Alan Cook

8 rms   8 ens

 S: £33–£39
D: £66–£78

Inn: Discover for yourself the magic that attracts visitors from all over the world to this historic and picturesque fishing village, where quaint, flower strewn cottages seem to tumble over one another down the steep hill to the ancient, tiny harbour. The fascinating 17th century New Inn can be found in the heart of the village. Within, the skill of a talented interior designer can be seen everywhere. The hotel has been awarded 2 stars and 73% for quality by the AA, 2 crowns and 'highly commended' by the English Tourist Board. There are luxurious bedrooms with lovely views of the village or the sea. The cosy lounges are just right for enjoying a Devon Cream Tea. Try sitting in the Bar supping real ale whilst listening to ripping yarns told by local fishermen. And guests visiting the new Inn have always been charmed by the fact that their luggage arrives by sledge and is portered back up to their cars by donkey. **Restaurant:** Home made dishes are served in a delightful restaurant whose exposed heavy beams give it a medieval feel. The menu changes daily and always includes fresh fish and local produce. Nearby: Coastal walks, fishing, shooting, riding, Lundy, Hartland Point, Arlington Court, Rosemoor Gardens and Westward Ho! **Directions: Exit M5 at junction 27 and follow A361 to Barnstaple. Then take A39 and 10 miles after Bideford turn right at sign for Clovelly.**

THE RED LION HOTEL

HIGH STREET, COLCHESTER, ESSEX CO1 1DJ
TEL: 01206 577986 FAX: 01206 578207

OWNERS: Brook Hotels PLC
CHEF: Gary Neale

24 rms   24 ens

S: £67.50
D: £75

Inn: The Red Lion is a uniquely elegant example of Tudor England. It stands majestically tall and rambling in the heart of Colchester whose heritage dates back through the centuries to when it was the capital city of "Old King Cole", the ancient chieftain Cunobelin who ruled over much of the south-east of England. Built in 1465, the Grade I listed Red Lion, bearing the sign of the House of Lancaster, is one of the oldest inns in East Anglia and retains much of the original character and atmosphere of those bygone years. There are heavy beams, fine antiques a four-poster bed, lattice windows and deep, richly coloured furnishings. Each of the 24 bedrooms has en suite facilities and all modern comforts. Conference and banqueting facilities are available in The Tudor Room. The hotel has no car park but there is a voucher arrangement with the nearby NCP park. **Restaurant:** Set in the impressive old banqueting hall, the restaurant has an excellent reputation for its à la carte menu with dishes prepared from fresh local produce, complemented by an extensive selection of quality wines. **Nearby:** Colchester's Roman walls and Norman castle keep, the largest in Britain, 12th century St Osyth's Priory, Flatford Mill, Stanway Hall and zoo. **Directions: From the M25, exit at junction 28 and take the A12 to Colchester.**

WINSTON MANOR

BEACON ROAD, CROWBOROUGH, EAST SUSSEX TN6 1AD
TEL: 01892 652772 FAX: 01892 665537

OWNER: Chasley Hotels Limited
CHEF: Freddie Jones

54 rms   54 ens

 S: £72
D: £90–£100

Inn: Set on the edge of Ashdown Forest, Winston Manor lies in the heart of English wine growing country. This charmingly traditional hotel has 54 tastefully decorated bedrooms, fully equipped to meet the needs of today's guests. The elegant Edwardian lounge, warmed by a blazing log fire in the colder months, is the perfect place to read and relax after a day's business or pleasure. The beautifully restored deerstalker bar offers excellent pub food, including local specialities such as the famous Cheese Gorge. Guests are invited to take advantage of the excellent facilities offered by the Oasis Leisure Club. These include a swimming pool with jetstream, sauna, Jacuzzi, fully equipped state-of-the-art gym, sunbed and Beauty Room. **Restaurant:** An award-winning team of chefs provides a superb range of dishes, complemented by an extensive range of fine wines. Sample the delicious roasted sea bream and grey mullet served with couscous and sun-dried tomato and coriander butter sauce or be tempted by the grilled Scottish sirloin steak au poivre, accompanied by a shallot brandy and green peppercorn sauce. **Nearby:** Glyndebourne, Chartwell, Hever and Leeds Castles and Penshurst Place. Golf enthusiasts are spoilt for choice with five first-class courses within easy reach. **Directions: From the M25, junction 5 via Tunbridge Wells. Winston Manor is set back from the A26, between Tunbridge Wells and Uckfield.**

THE VICTORIA HOTEL

VICTORIA ROAD, DARTMOUTH, DEVON TQ6 9RT
TEL: 01803 832572 FAX: 01803 835815

OWNER: Annie Glarfield
GENERAL MANAGER: Nigel Thorpe

10 rms   10 ens

S: £40–£55
D: £70–£100

Inn: The Victoria Hotel is situated just 150 yards from the River Dart and harbour in Dartmouth, a town steeped in history in an area of unspoilt natural beauty. In the elegant bedrooms, great attention has been paid to the quality of furnishings and lighting to provide an environment of total comfort and luxury. All rooms include an en suite shower or bathroom and full range of modern amenities. Two lounge bars offer excellent food, traditional beers and fine wines. The range of leisure activities offered in this locality include sailing, boat trips to Totnes, sea fishing and golf. **Restaurant:** Every sumptuous meal produced in this intimate and inviting restaurant is cooked to order using first class local produce. A full à la carte menu is available for lunch and dinner and includes an excellent range of seafoods such as local lobsters and crabs. There is also a good choice of prime meats all prepared with flair. Over two dozen carefully selected wines are available to complement any meal. **Nearby:** Dartmoor, Dartmouth Castle and South Hams. **Directions: From the M5 join the A38, leave at the A384 signposted to Totnes and follow the signs to Dartmouth.**

THE GEORGE HOTEL

HIGH STREET, DORCHESTER-ON-THAMES, OX10 7HH
TEL: 01865 340404 FAX: 01865 341620

OWNER: Brian Griffin
MANAGER: Michael Pinder

18 rms | 18 ens

S: £60
D: £75–£90

Inn: In the heart of the Thames Valley lies The George. Dating from the 15th Century, it is one of the oldest inns in the country. In the days of the stage coach it provided a welcome haven for many an aristocrat including the first Duchess of Marlborough, Sarah Churchill. However, more recent times have seen famous guests of a different hue such as author D.H. Lawrence. The buildings of the George Hotel have changed little since their heyday as a coaching inn. It retains all the beauty and charm of those days, whilst offering every modern amenity. All the rooms are en suite and furnished with fine antiques and the owners have created a decor which suits the requirements of our age whilst maintaining the spirit of another.

Restaurant: The menu changes daily allowing the chef to ensure that only the freshest and finest produce reaches your table. The dishes are imaginative, beautifully presented and delicious. The beamed dining room provides a delightful setting in which to enjoy an excellent meal, served by friendly, professional staff. **Nearby:** Dorchester-on-Thames provides easy access to the Cotswolds, Blenheim Palace and Oxford. Stratford-upon-Avon, Henley, Windsor and an inexhaustible source of beautiful walks and cultural and sporting activities. Excellent meeting facilities for up to 36 in the Stable Suite and two smaller rooms each for up to 8 people. **Directions: On A4074 nine miles south of Oxford.**

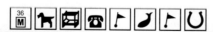

THE ANCHOR COUNTRY INN AND HOTEL

EXEBRIDGE, NR DULVERTON, SOMERSET TA22 9AZ
TEL: 01398 323433 FAX: 01398 323808

OWNERS: John and Judy Phripp
CHEF: Stephen Rickard

 S: £38
D: £70–£75

Inn: The Anchor Inn, a lovely 16th century coaching inn, is mentioned in R.D. Blackmore's *Lorna Doone*. It has been expertly modernised to provide the highest standards of comfort, while retaining its old world charm and atmosphere. A warm and sincere welcome awaits guests. There are six most attractive en suite bedrooms, all offering modern facilities and one boasting a four poster bed. The inn enjoys a superb location on the bank of the River Exe. The comfortably furnished residents' lounge looks towards it over the beautiful lawned gardens. **Restaurant:** The resident chef provides a delicious array of home cooked cuisine, with several local specialities including venison and trout. Vegetables are carefully selected from the best local suppliers. The superb quality and presentation of the food are complemented by first class service and an excellent selection of wines. Lighter meals are offered on the bar menu. **Nearby:** All year long brown trout swim under the bridge and in the deep pools alongside the Inn's gardens. Dry and wet fly fishing are available in season. Riding, shooting and golf can all be enjoyed locally and guided tours of the moor to see the elusive red deer can also be arranged. Walkers will enjoy Exmoor National Park, just 2 miles away, and there are many National Trust properties and gardens within 25 miles. **Directions: Exebridge is south of Dulverton on the B3222, just off the A396 Minehead–Tiverton road.**

THE WOODCOCK INN AND RESTAURANT

WOODCOCK HILL, FELBRIDGE, WEST SUSSEX RH19 2RE
TEL: 01342 325859 FAX: 01342 318340

OWNER: Valerie Jones
CHEF: Valerie Jones

In association with MasterCard

4 rms   2 ens

S: from £35
D: £45–£75

Inn: A thoughtful mix of old and new is the distinguishing feature of this friendly, traditional West Sussex inn. Attractively furnished in cottage style, the Woodcock has a warm, cosy and hospitable atmosphere that makes it popular with locals and travellers to and from the south coast and Gatwick airport. Professionally run for the past ten years it offers many comforts and facilities. Furnishings and decor are of a high standard and there are many special little touches that add to the welcome. Two of the bedrooms are en suite and are extremely stylish – one having a distinctive and unusual Oriental theme. **Restaurant:** The inn has a high reputation locally for its cuisine. Valerie Jones uses the best local produce in season and changes her good value menus daily. Beams, brasses, antique tables, white linen and lace tablecloths are features of the ground floor, cottage-style restaurant. Upstairs, approached by an attractive spiral staircase, there is a smaller dining room which offers visitors superb views through a huge, wall-length leaded window. Less formal meals can be had in a cheerful brasserie and the bar whose real ales are changed monthly. **Nearby:** The Woodcock is conveniently close to Gatwick and easily accessible from London. It is also well placed for visiting Tunbridge Wells and the stately homes and gardens of Surrey and Sussex. **Directions: From the M25, exit at junction 6 and then travel south on the A22.**

THE BLUE LION

EAST WITTON, NR LEYBURN, NORTH YORKSHIRE DL8 4SN
TEL: 01969 624273 FAX: 01969 624189

OWNERS: Paul and Helen Klein
CHEF: Chris Clarke

12 rms   12 ens

S: £45–£50
D: £75–£85

Inn: Heather moorlands, waterfalls, limestone scars and remote valleys surround the picturesque village of East Witton – the gateway to Wensleydale and Coverdale. The Blue Lion, a 19th century coaching inn, has much to entice visitors to its doors – lovely individually furnished bedrooms, welcoming public rooms with original flag-stone floors and open fires, plus delicious food. Private functions for up to 45 people can be accommodated. **Restaurant:** A frequently changing menu provides an ample selection of well-compiled, innovative dishes. Some interesting choices such as red mullet, monkfish or wild boar served with a rich port wine sauce are regularly available. The wine list that accompanies the menus offers a vast array of excellent wines from all over the world. The dining room is attractively decorated with candle-light creating an intimate atmosphere. In the bar there is a fine selection of hand-pulled traditional beers as well as an extensive menu of freshly prepared meals served at lunchtime and dinner. **Nearby:** The spa towns of Ripon and Harrogate are within easy driving distance and well worth a visit. Jervaulx Abbey and many castles are in the area. There is an all-weather tennis court in the village. **Directions: A6108, eight miles north of Masham and five miles south of Leyburn.**

THE GEORGE HOTEL

CASTLE STREET, ECCLESHALL, STAFFORDSHIRE ST21 6DF
TEL: 01785 850300 FAX: 01785 851452

OWNERS: Gerard and Moyra Slater
CHEF: Andrew Ward

S: £55
D: £90

Inn: This charming family-run 17th century coaching inn is set in the quaint Staffordshire market town of Eccleshall. Its nine bedrooms have been tastefully decorated in sympathy with the age and character of the building and are equipped with a full range of modern amenities. Freshly made teas and coffees are served throughout the day in the bar. With its oak beams, dried hops and inglenook fireplace, this is also the place to enjoy fine traditional ales, malt whiskies and a selection of light lunches. The hotel also boasts its own micro brewery, producing four different ales for guests to sample. **Restaurant:** George's Bistro offers an impressive range of imaginative dishes. Tempt your palate with pan-fried breast of chicken, stuffed with a pork and capsicum mousseline and coated with a cream of onion sauce or maybe try the pot-roasted poussin, marinated in a chillied sweet and sour wild berry sauce. There is also an excellent range of fish, pasta and rice dishes to choose from, as well as various omelettes and mouth-watering grills. **Nearby:** Shugborough Hall, Weston Park, Bridgemere Garden World, Wedgwood Visitor centre and Lichfield Cathedral. The hotel also lies within easy reach of Alton Towers and Ironbridge. **Directions: From the M6 junction 14 turn left towards Eccleshall on the A5013. From junction 15 turn left towards Stoke, then right towards Eccleshall via the A519.**

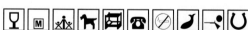

THE WHEATSHEAF INN

EGTON, NR WHITBY, NORTH YORKSHIRE YO21 1TZ
TEL: 01947 895271 FAX: 01947 895271

OWNERS: Albert, Susan and Michael Latus

S: £30–£40
D: £40–£50

Inn: This traditional, stone-built inn is situated in a delightful part of North Yorkshire in the small village of Egton, just five miles from the sea. Proprietors of The Wheatsheaf, Albert, Susan and Michael Latus, create a welcoming atmosphere. With the emphasis on attentive service, guests receive good hospitality and excellent value for money. In the public rooms the original character has been maintained and the small, cosy bedrooms have been furnished in keeping with the style of an old country inn. **Restaurant:** Stone walls, oak beams and attractively laid tables are the setting for dinner. A varied à la carte menu offers a good selection of starters, including several seafood choices: herring, fresh sardines, fish pâté and smoked trout. Main courses range from country pies to international dishes such as Cajun chicken. A good selection of bar meals is available. There is also a special dish-of-the-day. **Nearby:** The surrounding North York Moors National Park provides ample scope for walking, fishing, riding, canoeing, sailing and trips on steam trains. Captain Cook's birthplace at Great Ayton, Robin Hood's Bay, Staithes and Whitby, with its abbey, are a short drive away. **Directions: Egton is close to Whitby. From Pickering, turn off the A169 to Grosmont and Egton in Esk Dale.**

THE CHRISTOPHER HOTEL

HIGH STREET, ETON, WINDSOR, BERKSHIRE SL4 6AN
TEL: 01753 811677/852359 FAX: 01753 830914

OWNER: Mrs Carol Martin

S: £79
D: £88–£99
(room only)

Inn: Half way between Eton College and Windsor Bridge, in Eton's High Street, The Christopher Hotel is an old coaching inn which for many years enjoyed somewhat of a racy reputation. The hotel, which dates from 1511, has comfortable and elegantly furnished bedrooms in both the main building and courtyard. A range of modern amenities includes colour TV with cable channels, tea and coffee making facilities, trouser press, hairdryer and direct-dial telephone. Guests may choose between having a continental breakfast served in their room or taking a full traditional English breakfast in the restaurant. **Restaurant:** Excellent food, which has a good local reputation, can be enjoyed in the relaxed atmosphere of the hotel's welcoming restaurant. The cuisine is prepared from the freshest produce and complemented by a fine selection of wines to suit all pockets. A traditional atmosphere and friendly service are the hallmarks of the Victoria Bar, which offers a wide variety of bar food and a wide variety of drinks. **Nearby:** Windsor Castle, Eton College, Legoland and Cliveden; The many outdoor attractions available in the locality include trips on the Thames, golf at Sunningdale and the Berkshire, the Windsor Royal Horse Show and Driving Championships, Ascot and Windsor races. **Directions: Leave M4 at junction 5 and follow signs to Eton. The hotel is in the High Street with its own car park through a carriage entrance.**

RIVERSIDE RESTAURANT AND HOTEL

THE PARKS, OFFENHAM ROAD, NR EVESHAM, WORCESTERSHIRE WR11 5JP
TEL: 01386 446200 FAX: 01386 40021

OWNERS: Vincent and Rosemary Willmott
CHEF: Rosemary Willmott

S: £60
D: £80

Inn: The Riverside may not be a big hotel, but it has great style and a superb position, being perched high above the River Avon in the original Evesham Abbey's 15th century deer park. Three cleverly converted 17th century cottages blend with the main house to create an elegant 1920's residence. There are just seven enchanting bedrooms, all thoughtfully appointed. Lovely chintz fabrics and views over the gardens to the river add to guests' pleasure on arrival. **Restaurant:** Having a Chef-Patronne, the restaurant is extremely important, and a designated non-smoking area. The three menus are reasonably priced for the exceptional range and style of choices offered. Interesting starters are followed by a selection of traditional and innovative dishes, including fresh monkfish and local pheasant. The tempting dessert list is shorter. The cellar holds 60 wines from £9 to £60. The restaurant is closed on Sunday evenings and all day Monday. The bar has big sofas, deep armchairs and large windows overlooking the river, the ambience being that of a country house drawing room. **Nearby:** Guests may fish in the Avon, take a small boat out or visit the Royal Worcester Porcelain factory, go to Stratford-upon-Avon, or relax watching county cricket at Worcester. **Directions:** Take M5/ junction 7 or M40/junction 16 to Evesham and approach the hotel from the B4510 to Offenham down a private drive through market gardens.

THE ROYAL OAK INN

WITHYPOOL, EXMOOR NATIONAL PARK, SOMERSET TA24 7QP
TEL: 01643 831506/7 FAX: 01643 831659

OWNERS: Dick and Jo Howard
CHEF: Jill Tapp

S: £33–£59
D: £66–£88

Inn: The Royal Oak Inn has a reputation for good food and hospitality spanning 300 years. Set in the pretty village of Withypool, it is ideal for exploring Exmoor. Today's visitors are offered comfortable accommodation in individually furnished bedrooms. A two bedroomed self-contained cottage is also available. The Residents' and Rod Room Bars, with their beamed ceilings and crackling log fires, epitomise the character of an old country inn. **Restaurant:** The restaurant, open in the evenings, offers guests table d'hôte and à la carte menus. Dishes of the highest calibre are cooked to order with particular emphasis on preparation and presentation. To complement the meal, choose from a list of over 70 carefully selected wines. Extensive lunch and supper menus are available in the Rod Room Bar. **Nearby:** The inn specialises in organising country sports for either groups or individuals. Arrangements can be made for riding, hunting, stabling, game shooting, fly-fishing, and Exmoor Safaris. **Directions: Withypool is seven miles north of Dulverton – just off the B3223 Dulverton–Exford road, or 10 miles off North Devon Link road A361 via North Molton.**

THE BULLS HEAD INN

FOOLOW, EYAM, HOPE VALLEY, DERBYSHIRE S32 5QR
TEL: 01433 630873 FAX: 01433 631738

OWNERS: Dorothy and Mike Hall
CHEF: Jeremy Hall

S: £45
D: £60

Inn: This welcoming, family-run inn, located in a traditional old limestone village, is one of the prettiest pubs in the Peak District. Open log fires, oak beams and a charming inglenook, create a cosy and welcoming milieu. There are three bedrooms, each offering a TV and tea/coffee making facilities. In the bar, visitors can enjoy a meal or savour one of the traditional cask beers or fine malt whiskies. With its elevated position, Foolow offers wonderful views over the surrounding countryside. For any outdoor pursuits enthusiast, Hope Valley is a paradise. Opportunities for walking, gliding, caving, pot-holing and climbing abound. **Restaurant:** Main courses include delicious dishes such as leek, chestnut and cheddar crumble and collops of fresh monkfish marinated in ginger, lime juice and a little sesame oil, flash-fried and presented on a bed of cous cous, napped with a warm, red pepper and coriander coulis. Follow this with a one of the restaurant's fine home-made desserts and freshly filtered coffee and mints for a truly satisfying gastronomic experience. For residents only, The Bulls Head has rods available on the Derbyshire Wye which is populated with both brown and Rainbow trout. **Nearby: Villages celebrated for well-dressing.** Haddon Hall, Chatsworth, Eyam and Castleton. **Directions: From M1 Junction 29 via Baslow and A623 west (towards Stockport) Foolow is signposted after Eyam.**

FALMOUTH (Constantine)

TRENGILLY WARTHA COUNTRY INN AND RESTAURANT

In association with MasterCard

NANCENOY, CONSTANTINE, FALMOUTH, CORNWALL TR11 5RP
TEL: 01326 340332 FAX: 01326 340332 E-MAIL: trengilly@compuserve.com

OWNERS: The Logan and Maguire Families
CHEF: Michael Maguire

5 rms 5 ens

  S: £34–£42
D: £48–£62

Inn: Trengilly Wartha is in "an area of outstanding natural beauty" near the village of Constantine close to the Helford River. The location is romantic and famous. Daphne du Maurier's novel "Frenchman's Creek" could have been written here about the local creek Polpenwith. The ambience is like staying in a private house that happens to be the local inn – there are newspapers in the attractive lounge and the Logan and Maguire families are very hospitable. The 'cottage' bedrooms are pristine, furnished in pine. Trengilly's Bar is is cheerful, frequented by the locals. Being a freehouse a good range of real ales is available, together with farm ciders. The Beer Garden overlooks the valley, and vine shaded pergola offers escape from the sun. In winter a big fire blazes! **Restaurant:** The bar food is delicious. The restaurant has a Gallic theme, both in appearance and having an ever-changing inspired Prix Fixe menu – local fish included – and the wines are superb (180 listed!) The substantial breakfast is very English. **Nearby:** Energetic guests sail, golf, ride or surf off the beaches. Cornish gardens, little harbours, the seal sanctuary, Falmouth harbour and the Lizard Peninsula must be explored. **Directions: A39 to Falmouth, then head for Constantine on B3291, where the inn is signed.**

FORDINGBRIDGE (New Forest)

THE WOODFALLS INN

THE RIDGE, WOODFALLS, FORDINGBRIDGE, HAMPSHIRE SP5 2LN
TEL: 01725 513222 FAX: 01725 513220

OWNERS: Michael and Amanda Elvis
CHEF: Paul Boyland

10 rms   10 ens

S: from £49.95
D: £59.95–£95

Inn: Standing alongside the old coaching route from the beautiful New Forest to historic Salisbury, The Woodfalls Inn has provided rest and relaxation for travellers since 1870. Its welcome, hospitality, quality of service and traditional English ambience is such that owner Michael Elvis was honoured with the prestigious Innkeeper of the Year award by the British Institute of Innkeeping last year. All the bedrooms, named after flowers of the forest, are en suite, extremely comfortable, and are tastefully and individually decorated in typically English fashion. Some have four posters. The inn also has a purpose-built conference and meetings suite with a capacity for up to 150 delegates. **Restaurant:** The standard of cuisine served in the intimate Lovers' Restaurant will satisfy every palate. Chef Paul Boyland produces excellent French dishes and interesting ethnic touches on his frequently changing table d'hôte and à la carte menus. More informal meals can be enjoyed in the conservatory or bar which has an extensive selection of properly stored cask conditioned ales. Picnic baskets can be arranged. **Nearby:** Walking and riding in the enchanting New Forest, sailing on the Solent and golf. Salisbury with its cathedral is within easy reach. **Directions: From the M27, exit at junction 1. Take the B3079, fork left at Brook onto the B3078, then fork right at Telegraph Corner onto the B3080 for Woodfalls.**

 **FULBECK (Lincoln)**

HARE & HOUNDS

THE GREEN, FULBECK, LINCOLNSHIRE NG32 3SS
TEL: 01400 272090 FAX: 01400 273663

OWNERS: The Riley and Freeman Families
CHEF: Michael Savil

 S: £35
D: £45-£50

Inn: The Hare and Hounds, a Grade II listed 17th century building, was a maltings until 1910. It is set on one of the two greens in the village of Fulbeck on The Ridge and offers splendid views of Newark, nine miles away. The inn's new owners have undertaken an extensive refurbishment programme, improving the bedrooms' decor and furnishings and upgrading the public areas using attractive pine panelling. Open fires and fresh flowers create an attractive and inviting environment in which to relax and forget the cares of the world. **Restaurant:** Monthly changing menus offer good food, which is both freshly prepared and well presented. Sample the delights of 'fillet of pork rösti', pork fillet wrapped in a lattice potato shell with a stem ginger and piquant sauce, mushrooms and served on a crouton of bread with Madeira sauce, or choose from an excellent range of fish dishes. The meals are complemented by a small but inexpensive wine list and for those who enjoy real ale, the proprietors plan to build a mini brewery within the grounds. A function room and full conference facilities are now available. 3 Crowns Commended. **Nearby:** The inn is ideally placed for guests wishing to expore Lincoln, Newark or Rutland Water. There is no shortage of interesting places in close proximity and they include Fulbeck Hall, Belton House and Harlaxton Manor. **Directions: On the A607 between Grantham and Lincoln, near the point where A607 crosses A17.**

MALLYAN SPOUT HOTEL

GOATHLAND, NR WHITBY, NORTH YORKSHIRE YO22 5AN
TEL: 01947 896486 FAX: 01947 896327 E-MAIL: peter_heslop@msn.com

OWNERS: Peter and Judith Heslop
CHEFS: Peter Heslop and David Fletcher

S: £50–£65
D: £65–£135

Inn: Set in excellent walking country, this is a perfect spot from which to explore the beautiful North York Moors National Park, to cast for trout or salmon on the River Esk and to enjoy many country pursuits such as riding. The hotel occupies a fine position in the picturesque village and takes its name from the waterfall flowing through the wooded valley, just a short walk away. Behind the stone-built, ivy-clad exterior are comfortable rooms with a relaxing atmosphere. Three spacious lounges command views of the two acre garden and Esk valley beyond. Cottage-style bedrooms, decorated with lovely fabrics, provide every convenience. Mini-breaks available all year. **Restaurant:** Chef-patron Peter Heslop takes pleasure in creating fine cuisine. An impressive table d'hôte menu offers guests an extensive choice of dishes, making it easy to see why this restaurant is so popular locally. Freshly caught seafood from Whitby is a house speciality. An AA Rosette has been awarded for cooking. Special breaks available. **Nearby:** Take a scenic trip on the North York Moors Railway. Whitby Abbey – once a burial place for kings, Easby Abbey, a 12th century monastery. Magnificent Castle Howard is just 20 miles away. **Directions: The hotel is situated nine miles from Whitby and 38 miles from York. From the A169 Pickering–Whitby road, turn off to Goathland. The nearest railway station is Whitby.**

Inn On The Lake

OCKFORD ROAD, GODALMING, SURREY GU7 1RH
TEL: 01483 415575 FAX: 01483 860445

OWNERS: Martin and Joy Cummings
MANAGER: James Ginders MMCIMA MCFA(SG)
CHEF: Wayne Hatenboer

 21 rms 21 ens

S: from £45
D: £80–90

Inn: Part Tudor, part Georgian, part modern, this country house inn stands in two acres of landscaped gardens overlooking a reed-fringed lake. Proprietors Martin and Joy Cummings make the comfort of guests their priority, and as a result were recipients of the Innkeeper of the Year Award 1987. The warmth of welcome visitors receive here is matched by the efficient service provided by the staff. The fully equipped bedrooms are individually designed and furnished to a high standard. The comfortable public rooms include a cosy real ale bar and several rooms for conferences and functions. **Restaurant:** Seasonal à la carte providing superb international dishes is offered in the attractively decorated Lake View Restaurant which has been awarded an AA Rosette. The wine list, although modest, seeks to represent the classic wine regions of Europe. For private functions, quotations can be given for outside catering. **Nearby:** The Royal Horticultural Society headquarters at Wisley is a short drive away, as is the Winkworth Arboretum. Several historic houses can be found in the vicinity while the North Surrey Downs are good for walks. Three theatres, six museums and an art gallery are all within easy reach. **Directions: Take the A3 Guildford–Portsmouth road from London. Then A283 towards Milford. At Milford, turn left at the lights on the A3100. Go under the railway bridge; the inn is situated on the right, beside the mini-roundabout.**

In association with MasterCard

THE LEATHERNE BOTTEL RIVERSIDE INN & RESTAURANT

THE BRIDLEWAY, GORING-ON-THAMES, BERKSHIRE RG8 0HS
TEL: 01491 872667 FAX: 01491 875308

OWNER: Keith Read

Dinner for Two including Wine: £70–£90

Winner of the Johansens 1996 Most Excellent Restaurant Award. The setting is unique, on the banks of the Thames in a nature conservation area, overlooking water meadows and the Berkshire Downs. Self-taught chef-patron Keith Read has become widely acclaimed. *The Times* has awarded him a six-star rating and includes him among today's most accomplished chefs. *Egon Ronay* describes him as unpretentious and imaginative, relying on fresh, quality produce. In summer, dine in the riverside terrace garden, which is ablaze with colour and scented with wild herbs. The menu may include sea bass with virgin olive oil, samphire and sweet ginger, or tuna with apple mint and a stew of plum tomatoes and basil. In winter huge log fires glow and the smell of simmering game stock fills the air. Local pheasant flavoured with lemon thyme and pancetta, or local wood pigeon with red chilli, chick peas and coriander, are among the choices. Puddings are simple and mouthwatering: ginger brandy snap baskets full of summer berries, or steaming cappuchino pudding with Mount Gay sauce. The two dining rooms reflect the style and taste of the owner: strong colours, fresh flowers and faultless yet relaxed service. Each table has a view of the river and the bar is filled with cookery books and exquisite marble sculptures. **Directions: Signposted off the B4009 Goring –Wallingford road. From M4 junction 12: 15 minutes; from M40 junction 6: 15 minutes. Oxford is 30 minutes drive and London 60 minutes.**

In association
with MasterCard

THE BLACK HORSE INN

GRIMSTHORPE, BOURNE, LINCOLNSHIRE PE10 0LY
TEL: 01778 591247 FAX: 01778 591373

OWNERS: Brian and Elaine Rey

S: £40–£49
D: £55–£69
Suite: £80

Inn: The Black Horse lies within a short detour off the A1. Skilful restoration work has preserved the charm of the old inn while upgrading the accommodation to a high standard of modern comfort. The traditional character of the bar creates a welcoming area for guests and local residents alike. The original beams, stone walls and open fires all add to the considerable charm of the inn. There is a delightful honeymoon/executive suite with its own small sitting room and a spa bath. **Restaurant:** Guests can chose between the innovative bar and dining room menus. Sample baked St Peter's fish in a cream sauce, flavoured by essence of peach, apricot and exotic fruits; tender pieces of pork in a mild curry and coconut cream sauce accompanied by fresh fruit; or perhaps tomato chicken with sun-dried tomato and basil butter with wild mixed mushrooms. There's something to tempt the most discerning of palates – with game and fish as in season – and the dishes are complemented by a very reasonably priced fine wine list. **Nearby:** Grimsthorpe Castle, with its attractive park and nature trail around the lake. Burghley House, famous for its horse trials, Belvoir Castle and Belton House. Golf, fishing and swimming are all within a 20 minute drive. **Directions: Leave A1 between Grantham and Stamford, taking A151 at Colsterworth heading towards Bourne.**

68

In association with MasterCard

THE MAYNARD ARMS

MAIN ROAD, GRINDLEFORD, DERBYSHIRE S32 2HE
TEL: 01433 630321 FAX: 01433 630445

OWNERS: Bob and Thelma Graham
MANAGERS: Jonathan and Joanne Tindall
CHEF: Brian Holloway

10 rms · 10 ens

S: £59
D: £69

Inn: The owners of this Victorian inn have transformed its ambience and image into a very stylish small hostelry at this superb location overlooking the beautiful Derbyshire Peak National Park. The en suite bedrooms, which include two suites, are charming, comfortable and well equipped. Guests booking Friday and Saturday nights may stay in their room free on the Sunday night (except before Bank Holidays). **Restaurant:** The excellent restaurant offers a primarily traditional English fare featuring local game when in season, together with a carefully selected wine list. An extensive range of bar food is served at lunchtime and in the evenings in the Longshaw Bar – the busy hub of the inn. The second, quieter, bar is ideal for a drink before dinner, and has a big log fire in winter months. There is a peaceful lounge with a view of the pretty gardens and the Dales. **Nearby:** Chatsworth, Haddon Hall and Castleton are spectacular reminders of the architectural heritage of the region. The market town of Bakewell is fascinating. Walkers have an endless choice of directions to take, fishing is on the Derwent. Golf, ponytrekking, even gliding can be arranged locally. Regional theatres abound. **Directions: Leaving Sheffield on the A625, The Maynard Arms is on the left just before reaching Grindleford.**

In association
with MasterCard

THE ROCK INN HOTEL

HOLYWELL GREEN, HALIFAX, WEST YORKSHIRE HX4 9BS
TEL: 01422 379721 FAX: 01422 379110 E-MAIL: the.rock@dial.pipex.com

OWNER: Robert Vinsen
CHEF: James Pardon

S: £45–£85
D: £64–£94

Inn: Situated in a tranquil valley, yet mid-way between the commercial centres of Halifax/Huddersfield and Manchester/Leeds, this superb hostelry offers all the attractions of a traditional wayside inn as well as the sophistication of a first-class hotel. AA, Egon Ronay and Les Routiers recommended, ETB 4 Crowns commended, all double-glazed bedrooms are equipped to luxurious standards being en suite with baths and showers, remote-control satellite TV, mini-bar and tea/coffee making facilities. The Victorian-style bar serves a range of hand-pulled ales and is open all day, every day, for meals and drinks. Superb conference facilities are available for up to 200 persons. **Restaurant:** Churchill's is a spacious restaurant, with a dance floor and a light and airy conservatory, opening out on to a large patio, overlooking a delightful rural aspect, where one can dine 'alfresco'. A variety of menus is available all day in any of the dining areas including the two conservatories, ranging from snacks to an 'East meets West' selection and daily blackboard specials. **Nearby:** Romantic Brontë country and the spectacular Yorkshire countryside. The award-winning Eureka! Museum is a great favourite with families and the immediate area is a golfer's paradise. **Directions: Take junction 24 off M62 and follow signs for Blackley for approximately one mile, at the crossroads turn left for Holywell Green. The hotel is ½ mile along on the left.**

THE CHEQUERS AT SLAUGHAM

SLAUGHAM, NR HANDCROSS, WEST SUSSEX RH17 6AQ
TEL: 01444 400239/400996 FAX: 01444 400400

OWNERS: Paul and Sue Graham
CHEF: Wayne Hall

S: £55–£60
D: £75–£80

Inn: Situated in the 1996 award-winning Best Kept Village in Sussex, The Chequers at Slaugham is a delightful hostelry offering a good welcome, superior accommodation and acclaimed cooking. All six of the de luxe guest rooms have four-poster beds and are appointed to a high standard, each with a host of amenities that include remote-control television, trouser press, radio alarm, hairdryer and refreshments. All have four poster beds and some have spa or double baths. The public rooms are given over mainly to dining areas, however, there is a comfortable residents' lounge. **Restaurant:** The Chequers' culinary reputation has gone from strength to strength. The menu caters for all tastes but it reflects a special emphasis on seafood dishes as proprietor Paul Graham purchases fresh fish from the new Billingsgate Market. Depending upon availability, the menu may include wing of skate, halibut, monkfish, fresh crab, plaice, lemon sole, scollops, salmon and richly flavoured fish soups. Guests can also dine in the conservatory restaurant with outstanding views of the Sussex countryside. **Nearby:** The Chequers is conveniently located just ten minutes from Gatwick and is easily accessible from London. It is also well placed for visiting the stately homes and gardens of Surrey and Sussex. **Directions: From the main London– Gatwick–Brighton road (A23), exit 2 miles south of Handcross.**

THE BOAR'S HEAD HOTEL

THE RIPLEY CASTLE ESTATE, HARROGATE, NORTH YORKSHIRE HG3 3AY
TEL: 01423 771888 FAX: 01423 771509

OWNERS: Sit Thomas and lady Emma Ingilby
MANAGER: Paul Tatham

S: £90–£110
D: £110–£125

Inn: Imagine relaxing in a four star hotel at the centre of a historic 1700 acre private country estate in England's incredibly beautiful North Country. The Ingilby family who have lived in Ripley Castle for 28 generations invite you to enjoy their hospitality at The Boar's Head Hotel. There are 25 luxury bedrooms, individually decorated and furnished, most with king-size beds. **Restaurant:** The restaurant menu is outstanding, presented by a creative and imaginative kitchen brigade, and complemented by a wide selection of reasonably priced, good quality wines. There is a welcoming bar serving traditional ales straight from the wood, and popular bar meal selections. When staying at

The Boar's Head, guests can enjoy complimentary access to the delightful walled gardens and grounds of Ripley Castle, which include the lakes and a deer park. A conference at Ripley is a different experience – using the idyllic meeting facilities available in the castle, organisers and delegates alike will appreciate the peace and tranquility of the location which offers opportunities for all forms of leisure activity outside meeting hours. **Directions: Ripley is very accessible, just 10 minutes from the conference town of Harrogate, 20 minutes from the motorway network, and Leeds/Bradford Airport, and 40 minutes from the City of York.**

THE LOW HALL HOTEL

RIPON ROAD, KILLINGHALL, HARROGATE, NORTH YORKSHIRE HG3 2AY
TEL: 01423 508598 FAX: 01423 560848

OWNERS: Richard and Maureen Stokes
CHEF: Maureen Stokes

7 rms   7 ens

S: £45–£79
D: £55–£89

Inn: The Low Hall is a lovely Grade II listed building circa 1672 with views of seven miles over beautiful Nidderdale. To the rear are lovely spacious gardens. Heavy beams, stone walls, open fires and ancient beams all add to The Low Hall's character and cosy atmosphere. The seven bedrooms, created from the mainly Georgian part this former family home are snug and comfortable, all en suite with modern facilities. A delightful, low ceiling bar/restaurant leads onto a patio and the gardens beyond. **Restaurant:** The hotel's original coach house is now an attractive, beamed dining area where the accent is on a high standard of cooking, quality and presentation that should please the most discerning palate. Floor-to-ceiling wine racks house a vast variety of choice for guests to consider before sitting down for dinner. The Barn Suite is a large room for parties and meetings for as many as 90 people. **Nearby:** Harrogate is only 2 miles away, Ripon 9. The historic city of York, Skipton and Leeds are within easy reach. There is trout and coarse fishing on the River Nidd, boating, horseriding, shooting on the moors and several golf courses close by. **Directions: The Low Hall Hotel is on the edge of the village of Killinghall, two miles north of Harrogate on the A61.**

THE GEORGE HOTEL

MARKET STREET, HATHERLEIGH, DEVON EX20 3JN
TEL: 01837 810454 FAX: 01837 810901

OWNERS: Christine and David Jeffries
CHEF: Rafael Aunon

| 10 rms | 8 ens |

S: £30–£55
D: £50–£80

Inn: A century prior to the Reformation, The George Hotel was a rest house and sanctuary for monks of Tavistock, then in later years it served as a brewery, tavern, law court and coaching inn, its structure having been virtually unchanged over the passage of time, The George Hotel has an atmosphere of English heritage which guests will sense upon arrival. The thatched roof, blackened beams and huge open fireplaces all add to the inn's character, while the bedrooms – which vary in size – are in the process of being modernised and upgraded. As well as the three bars, there is a well-furnished residents' lounge upstairs. Among the facilities, the inn has a games room plus an outdoor swimming-pool. **Restaurant:**

Whether choosing from the à la carte menu, savouring a bar snack or enjoying cream tea, guests will be presented with Devon's finest produce. The à la carte menu features Cornish seafood, prime local beef and fresh garden vegetables, prepared with flair and finesse. On the bar menu traditional dishes like steak and ale pie appear next to vegetarian choices such as spinach, mushroom and cheese roulade. **Nearby:** Ideal for Dartmoor and the coastlines of Devon and Cornwall. Riding, tennis, golf and the newly completed Tarka Trail are all nearby. **Directions: Approaching from Exeter on A30, turn right at Okehampton on to the A386 signposted to Hatherleigh, about 7 miles to the north.**

For hotel location, see maps on pages 183-189

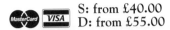

THE PLOUGH INN

LEADMILL BRIDGE, HATHERSAGE, DERBYSHIRE S30 1BA
TEL: 01433 650319

OWNERS: Bob and Cynthia Emery
MANAGER: John Elliot
CHEF: Karl Cohen

S: from £40.00
D: from £55.00

Inn: Situated in nine acres of grounds, the 16th century Plough Inn has recently been restored to give visitors every modern facility and comfort. It is in an idyllic position, close to the meandering River Derwent and surrounded by magnificent countryside which is home to many species of wildlife. Cosy and tastefully decorated, The Plough Inn provides an ideal environment in which to unwind and is an ideal base from which to explore the heritage of the Peak District. The adjoining spacious bedrooms, which are are reached by an external staircase, are decorated in an attractive and welcoming cottage style and have satellite television, hairdryer and tea and coffee making facilities. All have countryside views. The inn is closed on Christmas Day. **Restaurant:** The owners have created a welcoming ambience complemented by attentive service. A good value menu offers a splendid choice of dishes. **Nearby:** Castleton with its caves and caverns and the ruins of Pevril Castle, Bakewell's 700 -year-old arched bridge and 17th century Bath House built for the Duke of Rutland, Haddon Hall and 18th century Chatsworth House, one of the great stately homes of England, the Blue John Mine, Speedwell Cavern and Treak Cliff. Potholing, riding, climbing, paragliding and golf can be enjoyed locally. **Directions: From the M1 exit 29 take the A617 west and then via the A619 and A623. Shortly after Baslow turn north onto the B6001 toward Hathersage.**

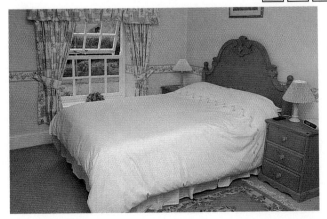

OLD WHITE LION HOTEL

HAWORTH, KEIGHLEY, WEST YORKSHIRE BD22 8DU
TEL: 01535 642313 FAX: 01535 646222

OWNERS: Paul and Christopher Bradford

14 rms	14 ens

 S: £60–£70
D: £85–£95

Inn: Situated on the cobbled main street in the village of Haworth, famous for being the home of the Brontë family, The Old White Lion is a 300-year-old inn. Resident owners Paul and Chris extend a warm and friendly welcome to guests. Relax in the oak-panelled residents' lounge or enjoy a drink in one of the two cocktail bars, which also serve a wide range of home-made hot and cold bar snacks, as well as an extensive range of real ales. There are 14 comfortable bedrooms with en suite facilities, including some family rooms. Most have magnificent views over the surrounding countryside. There is a self-contained function room which seats up to 100 people, with private bar and dance area. Special offers and weekend breaks are available. Price on application. **Restaurant:** Featured in many of the food guides, the candle-lit restaurant offers an extensive à la carte menu as well as a good value table d'hôte. All meals are freshly cooked to order. **Nearby:** Scenes of *Jane Eyre* and *Wuthering Heights*, Brontë Museum, Parsonage and Church; Keighley and Worth Valley Railway, Bradford, National Museum of Film, Photography and Television. Ideal for exploring the Yorkshire Moors and Dales, including the medieval city of York and the beautiful English Lake District, ten golf courses within 10 miles. **Directions: Leave the M62 at junction 24, then take the A629 through Halifax towards Keighley. Follow signs to Haworth.**

RHYDSPENCE INN

WHITNEY-ON-WYE, NR HAY-ON-WYE, HEREFORDSHIRE HR3 6EU
TEL: 01497 831262 FAX: 01497 831751

OWNERS: Peter and Pamela Glover
CHEFS: Michael Everleigh

S: £27.50–£35
D: £65–£75

Inn: This 14th century manor house is set in the heart of Kilvert country and features several times in the works of the celebrated diarist. A striking half-timbered building, it has been tastefully extended to create an attractive dining room overlooking a well-kept garden. The bedrooms are individually furnished in time honoured style and all afford scenic views of the Wye Valley and the Black Mountains. The two welcoming bars have exposed beams and open fires typical of traditional inns and both serve draught ale and cider on tap. Closed for two weeks in January. **Restaurant:** An exceptionally well-balanced à la carte menu offers the best of country fare and international cuisine. Advantage is taken of the abundance of fresh local produce – Hereford beef, Welsh lamb, fresh fish and seasonally available game are among the choices on the frequently changing menu. The sweet trolley offers a delicious array of puddings. Snacks, both the traditional and more unusual, are served in the bar. Private parties can be catered for. **Nearby:** The area is a paradise for nature lovers. Riding, pony-trekking, caving, wind-surfing and canoeing on the River Wye are all available and Hay-on-Wye, famous for its second-hand bookshops, is close by. For walkers Offa's Dyke Path passes near to the inn. **Directions: The Rhydspence stands above – and is well protected from – the A438 Brecon–Hereford road. OS map reference 243472.**

THE WALTZING WEASEL

NEW MILLS ROAD, BIRCH VALE, HIGH PEAK, DERBYSHIRE SK22 1BT
TEL: 01663 743402 FAX: 01663 743402

OWNERS: Lynda and Michael Atkinson
CHEF: George Benham

S: £45–£75
D: £65–£95

Inn: The Waltzing Weasel is a traditional country inn which, as its distinctive name suggests, offers a welcome alternative to the anonymous urban hotel. It is set within the heart of the Peak District, yet is only 40 minutes from Manchester and its international airport, Sheffield and Stockport. With its log fires, relaxed rustic character and country antiques, this is a civilised retreat for those looking for a restful break, be they tired executives, hardy walkers or confirmed slouches. They are guaranteed no jukeboxes nor fruit-machines here. Individually styled bedrooms offer comfortable accommodation and most of the rooms enjoy lovely views over the surrounding countryside. **Restaurant:** Acclaimed chef George Benham provides good, honest food in the intimate restaurant which overlooks the garden towards the dramatic landscape of Kinder Scout. Starters such as seafood pancakes, fresh asparagus and gravadlax promise good things to come. Main courses may include poached Scotch salmon, roast duck in tangy orange sauce and chicken cooked to order in white wine, tomatoes, mushrooms and crevettes. Excellent bar meals are served at lunchtime. **Nearby:** Shooting, fishing and golfing facilities are within easy reach, as are Chatsworth, Haddon Hall, Castleton, Bakewell and Buxton with its opera house. **Directions:** The Waltzing Weasel is near A624 on the A6015 New Mills–Hayfield road, ¹/₂ mile from Hayfield.

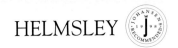

THE FEATHERS HOTEL

MARKET PLACE, HELMSLEY, YORK, NORTH YORKSHIRE YO6 5BH
TEL: 01439 770275 FAX: 01439 771101

OWNERS: Tony Fawcett and Graham Davies
CHEF: Robert Thompson

14 rms · 14 ens

S: £35–£40
D: £60–£70

Inn: This 15th century inn is set in the centre of Helmsley, a beautiful market town lying on the edge of the North Yorkshire Moors National Park. There are three bars – the Pickwick bar with its low beamed ceiling and open fire, the cosy Feversham lounge bar where bar meals are served, and the Stables Restaurant cocktail bar. Local Thompson 'Mouse Man' furniture is featured throughout the hotel. Its 14 bedrooms have been recently refurbished and redecorated to a high standard. **Restaurant:** The hotel has an excellent local reputation for good food and fine ales. The restaurant has an à la carte menu and a carvery and bar meals are served at both lunch time and in the evening. Delicious main courses include roulade of chicken filled with black pudding and Stilton cheese; pork fillet with a whisky and green peppercorn sauce; poached supreme of salmon set in a pool of lemon and chive butter sauce; and home-made steak pie. **Nearby:** Leisure activities in the area include golf at the Kirkbymoorside Golf Club, pony-trekking and racing at York. The East Coast resorts, Rievaulx Abbey, Byland Abbey, Duncombe Park and the historic city of York. **Directions: The Feathers is in the centre of Helmsley overlooking the Market Place. There is a private car park at the rear of the hotel.**

THE FEVERSHAM ARMS HOTEL

HELMSLEY, NORTH YORKSHIRE YO6 5AG
TEL: 01439 770766 FAX: 01439 770346

OWNERS: Gonzalo Aragues y Gaston and Rowan Bowie de Aragues
CHEF: David Brown

S: £55–£65
D: £80–£90

Inn: This historic coaching inn, rebuilt in 1855 of mellow Yorkshire stone by the Earl of Feversham, has been owned and managed by the Aragues family since 1967. Set in two acres of walled gardens, The Feversham Arms has been updated to a high standard to offer every modern amenity, while special care has been taken to preserve the character and charm of the older parts of the hostelry. The bedrooms are individually furnished and some have special features such as four-poster beds and de luxe bathrooms. Open fires blaze in the winter months. Dogs can be accommodated by arrangement. **Restaurant:** The attractive candle-lit Goya Restaurant serves English, French and Spanish cooking and, by relying on fresh local produce, offers seasonal variety. There is a delicious fish and seafood menu. To accompany dinner, an extenive wine list includes a wide selection of Spanish wines and clarets. **Nearby:** Situated in the North York Moors National Park and close to many golf courses, this comfortable and welcoming hotel is ideal for sporting pursuits as well as for touring the moors, dales, east coast and the medieval city of York. The ruins of Rievaulx Abbey in Ryedale (2½ miles) should not be missed. Special Bonanza Breaks available. **Directions: From the A1 take the A64, then take the York north bypass (A1237) and then the B1363. Alternatively, from the A1 take the A168 signposted Thirsk, then the A170.**

THE FOX COUNTRY HOTEL

IBSTONE, NR HIGH WYCOMBE, BUCKINGHAMSHIRE HP14 3GG
TEL: 01491 638289 FAX: 01491 638873

OWNER: Ann Banks

S: £45–£59
D: £58–£76

Inn: This attractive inn, in a country setting and dating back to the 17th century, is off the Chilterns Ridgeway. It is a haven for local businessmen from the busy High Wycombe area and equally much enjoyed at the weekend by those seeking a genuine country 'pub'. It is privately owned, and the pride of the proprietress is reflected throughout – first sight being the pretty hanging baskets enhancing the exterior – and once inside guests are instantly aware of the friendly ambience. There are nine charming pine-furnished bedrooms, all with en suite showers, looking out over the countryside. The bars are traditional, with oak beams and log fires. Well kept real ale is served. In summer guests enjoy their drinks on the patio and in the flower-filled garden. **Restaurant:** The restaurant is very inviting, with its fresh flowers and crisp table linen. Fish is a speciality on the appetizing menu and the wines have been carefully chosen. Excellent informal meals can be enjoyed in the lounge bar, which has a dedicated non-smoking area. **Nearby:** National Trust places to visit include Cliveden, and there is even a small vineyard and brewery in the valley. Families will enjoy Beckonskot Model Village or taking out a boat on the Thames at Henley or Marlow. **Directions: Leave the M40 at Junction 5, for Ibstone, and after one mile the hotel is on the left down a country lane. It is just 45 minutes from London and a useful stopover for Heathrow.**

In association
with MasterCard

BARNACLES RESTAURANT

WATLING STREET, NR HINCKLEY, LEICESTERSHIRE LE10 3JA
TEL: 01455 633220 FAX: 01455 250861

OWNER: David Freeman
CHEF: Carl Shardlow

Cuisine: The name of this excellent restaurant gives prospective guests a clue that fish plays an important part on the menu. It has its own smokery and trout lake in two acres of walled garden – an oasis for local business men and women, being open for both lunch and dinner, although closed all day Sunday and Monday lunchtime. The brick-walled restaurant is elegantly furnished and has a stylish small bar in which to enjoy apéritifs while studying the fascinating menu which gives translations for lobster, scallops and snappers in many languages! The selection of grilled fish includes tuna and 'house' trout, while the whole baked turbot and brill is a triumph. Carnivores enjoy specialities such as Carpet Bagger steaks, home-grown venison and roast Gressingham duck. The sweet dishes are exciting variations of traditional dishes, the bread and butter pudding served with honey ice cream and crème brûlée is accompanied by cherries in Kirsch! There are over 70 wines listed, including a good range of half bottles. House wines and dessert wines may be had by the glass, and the prices are very reasonable, with a choice at under £10-a-bottle through to premier cru white Burgundy below £30. **Directions: Leave the M69 at junction 1, taking the exit A5 south after leaving roundabout 100 yards on right hand side.**

CHEF'S SPECIALS
• • • • • • •

pan fried baby red mullet
cooked and served with herb butter

tail of monkfish
*grilled and finished in the oven with Pernod
and caviar butter*

roast Gressingham duck
half roast duck pan fried and served with cherry jus

steam toffee and apple sponge
with sticky toffee sauce and clotted cream

82

In association
with MasterCard

HOME FARM HOTEL

WILMINGTON, NR HONITON, DEVON EX14 9JR
TEL: 01404 831278 FAX: 01404 831411

OWNERS: Jim and Libby Cressy
CHEF: Barry Bingham

10 rms 10 ens

S: from £32
D: from £60

Inn: Home Farm is an attractive thatched farmhouse, set in four acres of beautiful grounds. A small hotel since 1950, which the owners have tastefully restored to create a charming and relaxing ambience. The staff are friendly, the public rooms have big bowls of flowers in summer and big log fires in the winter. Children are made welcome. The target is to offer value for money. The Residents' Lounge is comfortable, and there is a cosy, well-stocked bar serving light bar meals, draught beer and lager. **Restaurant:** The restaurant, oak-beamed and with an inglenook fireplace, offers a marvellous à la carte choice as well as a good 'home cooking' table d'hôte menu using local produce. The wine list is good. Bedrooms are in the main building or across a cobbled courtyard. All have private bathroom, telephone, colour television, hairdryer, radio alarm and tea/coffee making facilities. **Nearby:** Wilmington is in the heart of 25 National Trust properties and there are six golf courses within 15 miles. Riding, water sports and fishing can be arranged. Honiton is known for its lace, as is Axminster for its carpets. **Directions: Take the A303 to Honiton, join the A35 signposted to Axminster. Wilmington is three miles further on and Home Farm is set back off the main road on the right.**

 In association with MasterCard

WHOOP HALL INN

BURROW-WITH-BURROW, KIRKBY LONSDALE, CUMBRIA LA6 2HP
TEL: 015242 71284 FAX: 015242 72154

OWNERS: John and Dorothy Parr

S: £50–£60
D: £68–£78

Inn: Although over 350 years old this rambling, white-walled, 17th century coaching inn offers every modern comfort and has excellent facilities for families and disabled visitors. Log fires in the cooler months, heavy oak beams and traditional hand-pulled beers make this a popular rendezvous to soak up the friendly atmosphere or enjoy a quite game of darts or dominoes. All 20 bedrooms are en suite and well equipped. Most have views down the Lune Valley or over the Bourbon Fells. There are two four-poster bedrooms and the ground floor Lunesdale Suite has been specifically designed for the disabled. **Restaurant:** The unique galleried restaurant is in an imaginatively converted old barn and menus cater for all tastes. Specialities include freshly caught seafoods, crisply roasted duckling with orange and a variety of game in season. All dishes are cooked to order and there is a reasonably priced wine list. Lighter meals are served in the 40-seater buttery. In warm weather guests can enjoy an alfresco barbecue meal on the patio and orchard beer garden where there is a children's play corner. **Nearby:** Whoops Hall is well situated for visits to the Yorkshire Dales and Lake District. Kirkby Lonsdale has a traditional Thursday market and an 18-hole golf course. Ingleton waterfalls and caves and Leighton Hall are nearby. **Directions: From the M6, exit at junction 36 and take the A65. The hotel is half a mile south-east of Kirkby Lonsdale.**

LONGVIEW HOTEL AND RESTAURANT

51/55 MANCHESTER ROAD, KNUTSFORD, CHESHIRE WA16 0LX
TEL: 01565 632119 FAX: 01565 652402

OWNERS: Stephen and Pauline West
CHEF: James F. Falconer-Flint

23 rms	23 ens

S: £40–£73
D: £60–£85

Inn: This delightful house, once the home of a Victorian merchant, has been thoughtfully restored to create an elegant small friendly hotel a few minutes walk from the centre of this little market town, so accessible from Manchester and the airport. The house has been furnished to reflect its era, with well polished antiques, fresh flowers and pleasant chintzes. The bedrooms are very pretty, decorated in floral cottons and benefit from hairdriers, television and a hot drinks tray, as well as Victorian pin cushions! Ten bedrooms are in the modernised 19th century house next door. There are also six luxury service apartments in a house nearby and all overlook 'The Heath'. **Restaurant:** There is a well stocked cosy cellar bar where you can relax before being seated in the comfortable period restaurant. Noted for its cuisine throughout the area, you will certainly enjoy such delights as roast beef and Cheshire puddings made with a home-made horseradish mixture or Tatton Estate venison fillet. There are superb vegetarian dishes. Last of all treat yourself to some lovely desserts or some delicious home-made ice cream The wine list is international, and includes very reasonable house wines. **Nearby:** There are beautiful country house gardens to visit, and Tatton Park just round corner. Chester is within reasonable driving distance. **Directions: Leave M6 at junction 19 on A556 westbound towards Chester. Left at lights, left at roundabout in Knutsford and the hotel is 300 yards on the right.**

THE FEATHERS HOTEL

HIGH STREET, LEDBURY, HEREFORDSHIRE HR8 1DS
TEL: 01531 635266 FAX: 01531 632001

OWNER: David Elliston
CHEF: John Capaldi

11 rms   11 ens

S: £59.50–£65
D: £79.50–£95

Inn: The black and white timbered exterior of The Feathers Hotel stands out very clearly in Ledbury's main street. This traditional coaching inn, which dates back to the 1560s, is impressive even by the high standards of the area. The bedrooms retain their quaint character, with beamed walls and ceilings, yet are comfortably appointed. There are two bars and a comfortable lounge area in which to relax, all with log fires. Up to 100 people can be seated in the ballroom and conference suite, making it a popular venue for wedding receptions and private functions. Within the premises are two squash courts which guests can use. **Restaurant:** The Feathers' cooking has earned an AA rosette and a great reputation in the area. The main restaurant offers an à la carte menu with appetising dishes, many of which are prepared simply, to maximise the flavour of the ingredients. More informal meals are served in Fuggles, a bistro-style bar where hops hang from the rafters. A wide range of ales and over 60 international wines is offered, to accompany dishes such as sauté pork tenderloin with sage and calvados cream sauce. **Nearby:** Ledbury, with its narrow lanes and cobblestone streets, is ideally placed for the Malvern Hills, Hereford, Worcester and Gloucester. Also close are Eastnor Castle and the Falconry Centre at Newent. **Directions: Leave the M50 at junction 2 and take the A417 towards Hereford. The Feathers Hotel is in Ledbury High Street.**

THE THREE HORSESHOES INN & RESTAURANT

BUXTON ROAD, BLACKSHAW MOOR, NR LEEK, STAFFORDSHIRE ST13 8TW
TEL: 01538 300296 FAX: 01538 300320

OWNERS: William and Jill Kirk
CHEFS: Paul Knight, Chris Gordon and Mark Kirk

S: £45
D: £55–£65

Inn: A homely family run hostelry situated in the beautiful Staffordshire Moorlands on the edge of the Peak District National Park, the Three Horseshoes is a traditional farmhouse style inn providing comfortable accommodation and excellent food. It stands in its own large and beautiful garden, with patios, terraces and a children's play area. The six en suite cottage style bedrooms have been recently redecorated and furnished. **Restaurant:** Affording superb views, the restaurant serves fine food, fresh vegetables and a choice of over 200 wines. In the evening, candlelight and romantic music combine to create a peaceful and relaxing atmosphere. A Bar Carvery provides home cooked traditional dishes, as well as a roast of the day, accompanied by fresh market vegetables. On Saturday nights there is a dinner and dance with a cabaret and à la carte menu offering an extensive choice of food. The inn is closed from Christmas through to the New Year. **Nearby:** The area around the inn includes Rudyard Lake for sailing and walks (from which Kipling took his name), Tittesworth Reservoir for fishing, walking and bird watching, and the Roaches for climbing and walking. About 15 minutes away are the Manifold Valley, Dovedale, Berrisford Dale, Hartington, Alstonefield and Butterton. Alton Towers and Chatsworth are is just 20 minutes away. **Directions: Inn is on the A53 road to Buxton, easily reached by the M6 via the Potteries and the M1 via Derby.**

WHEELBARROW CASTLE

STOKE PRIOR, LEOMINSTER, HEREFORDSHIRE HR6 0NB
TEL: 01568 612219 FAX: 01568 612219

OWNERS: Valerie and Bryan Gardiner
CHEFS: Valerie and Emma Birchley

S: £35
D: £50

Inn: This has to be one of England's most pleasant inns, a 17th century grand farmhouse, surrounded by beautiful countryside. The front terrace and enclosed courtyard are lovely places to sit, if not seeking a shady spot in the pretty gardens. There are six comfortable double rooms, either with bathrooms or showers en suite and television. **Restaurant:** The kitchen is a family affair with chef Valerie Birchley being ably assisted by her daughter, Emma. À la carte lunch and dinner are served in the very pleasant restaurant, a traditional Sunday lunch is offered and there is an extensive bar menu. A set price menu, changing daily, now has become a regular feature. Conferences and private parties are catered for in a separate function room with its own bar. The inn has its own smokery, specialising in smoked fish, so guests may take home a delicious souvenir of their stay! **Nearby:** Hereford Cathedral and Hay-on-Wye, famous for its bookshops are nearby. Active guests may enjoy the heated outdoor pool, play golf at Leominster, attend Chepstow Races or walk down to the River Lugg. **Directions: One mile south-east of Leominster signed at a lane between the A44 and A49.**

In association
with MasterCard

THE COUNTRYMEN

THE GREEN, LONG MELFORD, SUFFOLK CO10 9DN
TEL: 01787 312356 FAX: 01787 374557

OWNERS: Stephen and Janet Errington
CHEF: Stephen Errington

S: £45–£65
D: £65–£95

Inn: Overlooking Melford's magnificent green, the Countrymen has received wide acclaim for its superb food and splendid accommodation. Recognised by all major guides, the Countrymen is enjoyed by visitors and locals alike. Stephen and Janet have earned much praise for their enthusiastic and generous hospitality. The bedrooms, individually furnished with country antiques, offer every modern amenity. If you are lucky or ask in advance you could be sleeping in one of the four-posters or in an antique brass bedstead in a room with panoramic views over Melford. The comfortable lounge leading out to an attractive walled courtyard garden offers scope to enjoy the many books and games. **Restaurant:** Stephen, who learnt his skills at The Dorchester, creates dishes to tempt even the most jaded palate. The Countrymen has several fixed price menus as well as full à la carte fare. All menus change regularly to give pride of place to seasonal dishes and Stephen's specialities. Adding another string to their bow Janet and Stephen have now opened a delightful bistro and wine bar, offering a selection of old and new world wines in an informal relaxed atmosphere. **Nearby:** Melford Hall, Kentwell Hall and a plethora of antique shops; Constable country, Gainsborough's birthplace, historic Bury St Edmunds, Lavenham, Newmarket and Cambridge. **Directions: On the village green on the A1092 and the A134.**

THE ROEBUCK INN

BRIMFIELD, NEAR LUDLOW, SHROPSHIRE SY8 4NE
TEL: 01584 711230 FAX: 01584 711654

OWNERS: Dave and Sue Willson-Lloyd

3 rms | 3 ens

S: £45
D: £60

Inn: This Grade II inn, parts of which date back to the 15th century, is easily accessible from both Ludlow and Leominster, and the fact that it is in capable new hands will be welcomed by racegoers and antique hunters alike. The young Willson-Lloyds are experienced innkeepers who truly understand the art of hospitality. Guests receive a cordial welcome, and are escorted to their charming bedrooms, which are fresh and pretty, with comfortable furniture, and supplied with many amenities, including ground coffee and homemade biscuits! **Restaurant:** Relaxing in the character lounges, enjoying traditional ales, or an aperitif is followed by a wide variety of aromatic dishes selected from an imaginative menu always supplemented by daily specials. As indicated on the joyously presented wine list, prices are reasonable. **Nearby:** Tenbury Wells – Queen Victoria's preferred spa town, Burford House – riverside home to the National Clematis Collection and Hereford with its Norman Cathedral and Cider Museum. Dinmore Manor should not be missed, nor Stokesay and Croft Castles. Historic Ludlow, always busy during the National Hunt Season, has a profusion of antique shops, as does Leominster, once an important wool town, which still has its weekly market. Riding, golf, tennis, fishing, flying and shooting are locally available. **Directions:** Brimfield is signed from the A49 between Ludlow and Leominster.

THE RISING SUN

HARBOURSIDE, LYNMOUTH, DEVON EX35 6EQ
TEL: 01598 753223 FAX: 01598 753480 E-MAIL: risingsunlynmouth@easynet.co.uk

OWNERS: Hugo and Pamela Jeune
CHEF: David Lamprell

S: £55
D: £79–£130

Inn: Recommended in every way, this award-winning 14th century thatched smugglers' inn is perfectly positioned on the picturesque harbour overlooking East Lyn River. The building is steeped in history: *Lorna Doone* was partly written here and the inn's adjacent cottage – now luxuriously equipped for guests' use and pictured below – was once the honeymoon retreat for the poet Shelley. The best of the inn's medieval character has been preserved: oak panelling, uneven floors, open fires and crooked ceilings, all enhanced by tasteful furnishings and modern comforts. The bedrooms lack nothing and, like the terraced gardens, have splendid views. Parking in Lynmouth can be difficult at the height of the season. **Restaurant:** The food served in the oak-panelled restaurant is of excellent quality. Classic modern English and French cuisine is provided on an à la carte menu, which also features local specialities such as freshly caught lobster and salmon. All this is accompanied by a superb wine list. Good value bar meals are also available. **Nearby:** The inn owns a 1/2 mile stretch of river for salmon fishing and there are opportunities for sea angling. The hills and combes of Exmoor National Park, the North Devon coastline and the hunting country of Doone Valley are also near. **Directions: Leave the M5 at junction 23 (signposted Minehead) and follow the A39 to Lynmouth. Or take the A361, exit 27 (Tiverton) to South Molton, then the B3226 in the direction of Ilfracombe and then the A39 at Blackmoor Gate to Lynmouth.**

In association
with MasterCard

BOULTERS LOCK HOTEL

BOULTERS ISLAND, MAIDENHEAD, BERKSHIRE SL6 8PE
TEL: 01628 21291 FAX: 01628 26048

S: £70–£95
D: £85–£150

Inn: Originally built as a miller's house in 1726, this privately owned hotel stands on its own island, next to the famous Boulters Lock, which is the longest, deepest and for many the loveliest lock on the River Thames, where E.J. Gregory painted his famous picture "Boulters Lock – Sunday Afternoon 1895". There are panoramic views from both the Riverside Restaurant and Terrace Bar. The bedrooms are in converted lock-keepers' cottages, and have been individually designed and furnished, some with authentic Victorian baths and ornate showers. The honeymoon suite has a carved four-poster bed. **Restaurant:** The food is modern English with seasonal dishes. It features local fresh produce and fresh fish delivered daily. Dinner dances are organised on some Saturday nights throughout the year and traditional Sunday lunch is served from 12.00 noon until 3.00pm. Dining also in the Terrace Bar from a Bistro menu. **Nearby:** Windsor Castle, Legoland, Cliveden, former home of Nancy Astor, Cookham and Burnham Beeches are nearby. **Directions: Leave M4 at exit 7, take A4 to Maidenhead, over bridge turn right at mini roundabout into Ray Mead Road, signposted Cookham, under a mile to Boulters Lock Hotel.**

92

THE HARROW AT WARREN STREET

WARREN STREET, NEAR LENHAM, KENT ME17 2ED
TEL: 01622 858727 FAX: 01622 850026

OWNERS: Alan Cole and Sheila Burns
CHEF: Richard Arter

S: £39.50
D: £49.50

Inn: High on the North Downs of Kent stands this attractive hostelry, amid rolling farmland in the hamlet of Warren Street. Once the forge and rest house for travellers en route to Canterbury via the nearby Pilgrims' Way, it has now been converted into a comfortable country inn. Refurbishments have ensured that all the guest accommodation is designed to a high standard. For guests who wish to enjoy a leisurely lie-in, a Continental breakfast can be brought to the bedroom. The traditional character and atmosphere of the public rooms are enhanced by open log fires in the winter and exposed oak beams. **Restaurant:** The Harrow enjoys a reputation locally for its good cooking. There is a superb conservatory restaurant with views over a delightful floodlit water garden and patio. The à la carte menu features a delicious choice of seasonal dishes. For an appetiser perhaps try the *terrine de poireaux* – a terrine of leeks and langoustines served with tarragon vinaigrette, followed by pot-roasted guinea fowl with Madeira sauce. An excellent range of meals is also presented on the bar menus. The inn's facilities can be tailored to accommodate special functions. **Nearby:** Convenient for Canterbury, Maidstone and the Cinque Port of Rye. Leeds Castle is just 10 minutes' drive. **Directions: Leave the M20 at junction 8 or 9. Warren Street is signed from the A20 between Harrietsham and Charing.**

In association
with MasterCard

RINGLESTONE INN

'TWIXT' HARRIETSHAM AND WORMSHILL, NR MAIDSTONE, KENT ME17 1NX
TEL: 01622 859900 FAX: 01622 859966

OWNER: Michael Millington-Buck

S: £85
D: £95

Inn: Truly traditional is the welcome that awaits visitors as they step back in time into this delightfully unspoilt, medieval, lamplit tavern. Built in 1533 as a hospice for monks, the Ringlestone became one of the early Ale Houses around 1615 and little has changed since. Its delights include original brick and flint walls and floors, massive oak beams, inglenooks, old English furniture and eight acres of idyllic gardens. Recent additions are three en suite bedrooms in a charming farmhouse just a few steps opposite the inn. They are furnished in style and totally in keeping with expectations for a stay in this beautiful escapists' spot. The spacious farmhouse dining and reception rooms are also available for private and corporate functions. **Restaurant:** Full of character and candlelight ambience with sturdy, highly polished tables made from the timbers of an 18th century Thames barge, The Ringlestone has a reputation for excellent English cooking and features in many food guides. A help yourself 'hot and cold' buffet lunch offers a seasonal variety of traditional country recipes. The varied evening menu includes unusual and interesting pies and local trout. All complemented by their exclusive House Wines imported directly from France and a wide range of English Country Fruit Wines. **Nearby:** Leeds Castle. **Directions: From M20, exit at junction 8. Travel north off A20 through Hollingbourne, then turn right at the water tower crossroads towards Doddington.**

THE HORSE AND GROOM INN

CHARLTON, NEAR MALMESBURY, WILTSHIRE SN16 9DL
TEL: 01666 823904 FAX: 01666 823390

MANAGERS: Nichola King and Philip Gilder
CHEFS: Neil Lowthian and Robert Bieniasz

S: from £60
D: from £75

Inn: In the small village of Charlton in the heart of Cotswold country, the Horse & Groom Inn possesses a unique rustic charm. Inside, this 16th century coaching inn has been sensitively reinterpreted, with no loss of its period atmosphere; careful thought and attention has been invested in each of the three bedrooms, resulting in peaceful, relaxing rooms with all modern conveniences (plus extra touches like mineral water, fresh fruit, flowers and bathrobes). Décor is muted, in elegant shades like sage green, jasmine and peach; windows look out over the beautiful Cotswold countryside. A full English breakfast is included in the tariff. **Restaurant:** The Horse & Groom has a fine reputation for its cuisine, which has attracted the attention (and recommendation) of such connoisseurs as Egon Ronay. There are simple bar snacks such as ploughman's lunches and jacket potatoes, or more elaborate meals such as half a locally smoked chicken with a creamy sherry sauce, guinea fowl with rich game sauce or monkfish fillets with a dill and lemon sauce. The Horse & Groom is a free house serving real ales from Wiltshire breweries. In summer, drinks and meals may be enjoyed in the private garden. In winter guests choose to relax by log fires crackling in the grates. **Nearby:** Bath, Cotswolds, Malmesbury. **Directions: Exit M4 junction 17. Horse & Groom is two miles east of Malmesbury on B4040.**

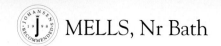

THE TALBOT INN AT MELLS

HIGH STREET, MELLS, NR BATH, SOMERSET BA11 3PN
TEL: 01373 812254 FAX: 01373 813599

OWNER: Roger Elliott
MANAGER: James Finch
CHEF: Mark Jones

S: £40–£50
D: £60–£70

Inn: This beautiful coaching inn is set in the picturesque village of Mells on the edge of the Mendips. Parts of the building date back to the 15th century and the bedrooms have been individually furnished and decorated in keeping with an old 'traditional style' inn. However, character and charm are combined with every modern amenity to ensure that guests can relax in total comfort. The cobbled courtyard and pretty cottage garden are ideal places to sit and enjoy an early evening drink on a warm summer day or to take an alfresco meal. **Restaurant:** In the oak-beamed Oxford and Snug bar restaurant guests can enjoy a quick snack or a superb à la carte meal. Freshly prepared dishes include game from the local shoot and fresh fish which is delivered daily. Sample the poached fillet of salmon with linguini pasta, vermouth and fresh herb sauce; oven baked breast of chicken with a fresh sage mousse and port wine sauce; or oven roasted breast of guinea fowl with potato rosti, oyster mushrooms and rosemary cream sauce. An excellent wine list is also available. **Nearby:** The historic cities and towns of Bath, Wells, Cheddar, Glastonbury and Longleat. **Directions: Exit M4 at Junction 18 to Bath and then take A36 towards Warminster. Turn right onto A361 into Frome and then take A362 towards Radstock. Within ½ mile turn left to Mells and follow signposts.**

THE DIFFERENT DRUMMER

HIGH STREET, STONY STRATFORD, BUCKINGHAMSHIRE MK11 1AH
TEL: 01908 564733 FAX: 01908 260646

OWNER: Mairead Keswani
CHEF: Micheal Hanlon

10 rms   10 ens

S: £40–£60
D: £65–£85

Inn: This charming hostelry dates back to 1470. During its long and interesting history, it passed through the hands of Bradwell Abbey and the de Longueville family before being leased to Lord Grey of Wilton by Queen Elizabeth 1. Following damage during the Great Fire of 1742, the present Georgian facade was added. In 1982 a programme of refurbishment was completed, bring this ancient coaching inn up to a superb standard of comfort. Elegant antique furniture sits comfortably alongside every modern accoutrement. Several en suite bedrooms are set in the seclusion of The Courtyard - including one with a four poster bed for that special occasion. **Restaurant:** Original ideas, top-class ingredients, generous portions

and a real enthusiasm for classic Italian food are all much in evidence in the Different Drummer's beautiful 'Al Tamborista' oak-panelled restaurant. As well as a profusion of pasta dishes, accompanied by imaginative sauces, chicken, veal, steak, lamb, beef and venison are all well represented on the menu. The dessert trolley offers a selection of deliciously tempting sweets, while a modestly-priced wine list is available to complement any meal. **Nearby:** The historic town of Stony Stratford is just 10 minutes' drive from central Milton Keynes. Bletchley and Newport Pagnell are also within easy reach. **Directions: From M1 junction 15A follow A421 to Stony Stratford. The hotel is in the High Street.**

THE RAGGED COT

HYDE, MINCHINHAMPTON, NR STROUD, GLOUCESTERSHIRE GL6 8PE
TEL: 01453 884643/731333 FAX: 01453 731166

OWNER: Nicholas Winch

S: £35
D: £50–£70

Inn: This charming inn, built in traditional Cotswold stone and steeped in history, is in the heart of the Cotswolds, surrounded by delightful small villages and adjacent to 580 acres of National Trust pastures where cattle wander. The pine-furnished bedrooms are separated by just a few feet from the main building and include a romantic bridal suite with a four-poster bed. These are comfortable, with en-suite bathrooms, and guests appreciate the hospitality trays and teletext television. **Restaurant:** The congenial bar is well stocked with real ales and over 30 malt whiskies. It has a welcoming log fire on cool evenings. Delicious snack meals are available, but many visitors prefer dining in the intimate restaurant, lingering over the excellent à la carte menu and enterprising wines introduced by the new owner. Reservations are recommended. **Nearby:** The Ragged Cot, which has its own conference room, is the perfect base for visitors or businessmen with meetings in Bath, Stroud or Cheltenham and garden enthusiasts will enjoy the Rococo Gardens at Painswick. Badminton, Gatcombe, 3 golf courses, watersports, gliding and fishing are nearby. **Directions: From M5 J13 take the A419. Pass through the village of Minchinhampton into Hyde; the Ragged Cot is on the Minchinhampton – Cirencester Road.**

THE KING'S ARMS INN & RESTAURANT

MONTACUTE, SOMERSET TA15 6UU
TEL: 01935 822513 FAX: 01935 826549

OWNERS: Jonathan and Karen Arthur
CHEF: Mark Lysandrou
MANAGER: Guillaume Lesage

15 rms   15 ens

S: £53–£62
D: £69–£105

Inn: This charming inn in the picturebook village of Montacute dates back to the 16th century. The discreet modernisation has preserved the mullioned windows and stone walls. The bedrooms recently decorated and comfortably furnished provide every amenity for today's discerning traveller. All rooms are en suite and include a four-poster and a half tester rooms. ETB 4 crowns highly commended and AA 2 stars. The traditional Pickwick Bar welcomes guests, with real ales and an interesting selection of snacks and light meals – the popular cold buffet is available at lunchtimes. **Restaurant:** The Abbey Restaurant has established a fine reputation for its modern English cuisine with 2 AA rosettes and commendations from Michelin and Egon Ronay. Salmon mousse is studded with truffles and pistachio nuts, while pork fillet is served with a cumin and coriander potato timbale. Asparagus, goats' cheese and mushroom strudel with a red and green pepper sauce will appeals to non-vegetarians as well. The wine list reflects a particular emphasis on the New World wines. Special mini-breaks and room upgrades are usually available. **Nearby:** Montacute House, of 'Sense and Sensibility' fame a magnificent Elizabethan mansion with superb gardens, Sherborne Castle and Abbey, Yeovil Air Museum, Cricket St Thomas Wildlife Park and Dorset beaches. **Directions: Just off A303, take A3088. Montacute is clearly marked. The inn is in the centre of the village by the church.**

THE WHITE HART HOTEL

THE SQUARE, MORETONHAMPSTEAD, DEVON TQ13 8NF
TEL: 01647 440406 FAX: 01647 440565

CHEF: Neville Wilkinson

S: £30–£35
D: £60–£70

20 rms
20 ens

Inn: Ornamented by colourful window boxes, a tall pillared entranceway and with a grey slated roof contrasting grandly with its gleaming white facade, the White Hart is the epitome of a friendly, welcoming Devon hostelry. A former Post House for coach travellers between Plymouth and London, this listed hotel has stood in the centre of the little market town of Moretonhampstead for over 300 years. Standing on the eastern slopes of the Dartmoor National Park it is an ideal base for exploring the surrounding rugged countryside scattered with beautiful, densely wooded hills, remote villages and reminders of the moor's earlier inhabitants. Three of the hotel's bedrooms are in an attractive courtyard. All are en suite, very well equipped and extremely comfortable. **Restaurant:** Old world and highly acclaimed locally. Chef Neville Wilkinson's finely balanced table d'hôte and à la carte menus are based on the best seasonal produce from local suppliers. More informal meals, and snacks can be enjoyed in the cheerful bar and lounge. **Nearby:** Granbrook Castle, an Iron Age hill-fort 1,100 ft above the River Teign and a wealth of National Trust properties. Golf, fishing on the River Teign and Hennock lakes, riding and horse racing at Newton Abbot, Devon and Exeter. **Directions: From Exeter travel on the M5 (A38) to the Newton Abbot/Bovey Tracey/Moretonhampstead junction, then join the A382 Bovey Tracey bypass to Moretonhampstead.**

THE WILLOW TREE INN

BARNBY-IN-THE WILLOWS, NEWARK, NOTTINGHAMSHIRE NG24 2SA
TEL: 01636 626613 FAX: 01636 626060

OWNERS: Steve and Rosemary O'Leary
CHEF: Steve McLeavy O'Leary

S: £35
D: £45

Inn: Some parts of this traditional country inn date back 300 years, with lovely beamed ceilings recalling a bygone age. The seven en suite bedrooms are cosy and comfortable, while the bathrooms are all well equipped. The other public rooms have been recently upgraded to create more space. During the cooler months guests can warm themselves in front of roaring fires and savour the friendly and relaxed atmosphere. **Restaurant:** A wide range of excellent cuisine is expertly prepared on the premises using only the best ingredients available. Meals are created to suit all tastes and include English, French and Italian dishes. Sample tempting main courses such as medallions of beef sauteed with mushrooms and onions, wrapped in puff pastry and served with stilton cream sauce; pan fried halibut steak with garlic and rosemary and served with a rich gravy; and wild mushroom and roquefort strudel placed on a pool of tomato and olive concasse. Choose from a selection of home-made desserts and complete the meal with coffee and truffles. Great emphasis is placed on providing good food, cask conditioned ale and fine wines from around the world. **Nearby:** Historic Newark, Nottingham and Lincoln are only a short drive away. **Directions: On the A46 near Newark follow signs for the A17 Sleaford road. Barnby in the Willows is just off this road.**

THE SWAN HOTEL

SWAN STREET, KINGSCLERE, NR NEWBURY, BERKSHIRE RG20 5PP
TEL: 01635 298314

OWNERS: Alistair and Sarah McLaren
CHEF: Alistair McLaren

9 rms | 9 ens

S: £47.50–£55
D: £55–£65

Inn: Whether you have just one drink or stay for several nights, you will receive a warm welcome at the Swan Hotel. Much of the building dates back to the 15th century, local parish records show that in 1459 the house was owned by farmer Thomas Bladon who bequeathed two cows and six sheep to the village church which stands opposite the hotel today. In 1485 it was purchased by Winchester College and owned by them for the next 300 years, by 1830 the hotel was being used as a posting house for coaches and offering accomodation to the many weary travellers. Today it provides the amenities of a modern hotel in a setting rich in original features. The bedrooms are all en suite with up-to-date facilities framed in the character of the inn's historic past. **Restaurant:** The cosy beamed restaurant offers a good variety of dishes always prepared with the freshest of ingredients, including the chef's specialities such as lemon marinaded chicken. Bar meals are served along with a selection of traditional ales **Nearby:** The cathedral city of Winchester, Basingstoke, and Newbury with its racecourse. Local places of interest include Watership Down and trainer Ian Balding's stables. **Directions: From Basingstoke follow A339 for 5 miles to Kingsclere, continue to the church, turn left into Swan Street.**

In association with MasterCard

THE SWAN HOTEL

NEWBY BRIDGE, NR ULVERSTON, CUMBRIA LA12 8NB
TEL: 015395 31681 FAX: 015395 31917

MANAGER: Brian Crewes
CHEF: Philip Gorton

36 rms   36 ens

S: £50–£85
D: £80–£135
Suite: £144

Inn: At the southern end of Lake Windermere, The Swan Hotel undoubtedly has one of the most picturesque locations in the whole of the Lake District, with superb views over the water and surrounding countryside. Comfort is the declared first priority of the management. The 36 en suite bedrooms, ranging from suites and deluxe doubles to high standard doubles and singles, are traditional in character yet offer every modern amenity. The public rooms are attractively decorated, with comfortable bars as well as an elegant lounge which adjoins the restaurant. **Restaurants:** Choose from the traditional Tithe Barn (non-smoking) or less formal Mailcoach. Imaginative menus are complemented by a carefully compiled wine list. Local produce such as potted Morecambe Bay shrimps, Lakeland char, venison and Esthwaite trout are freshly cooked to order. Special diets can be catered for. A special children's menu is available. Smaller conferences may be accommodated and special breaks are available. ETB 4 Crowns Highly Commended and AA 3 stars. **Nearby:** The Lake District National Park, Holker Hall and Stott Park. There are facilities for many sports close by and the hotel has its own fishing rights and boat moorings. **Directions: Newby Bridge is on the A590. Leave the M6 at junction 36 and follow the A590 to Barrow. The Swan is just across the bridge at Newby Bridge.**

In association
with MasterCard

THE GARDEN HOUSE HOTEL

SALHOUSE ROAD, RACKHEATH, NORWICH, NORFOLK NR13 6AA
TEL: 01603 720007 FAX: 01603 720019

OWNERS: John and Jill Smart

7 rms	6 ens

S: £40
D: £60

Inn: This small modern, family owned, hotel, with its reputation for extremely good food, falls into the category, long recognised in France, of a restaurant with rooms. Its name is justified, nonetheless, as it has extensive and well-kept gardens, guests appreciating the mass of colour in the summer. The lounge has large windows, big inviting chairs, and a small bar which is available only to residents and those dining that evening. The light bedrooms are immaculate and extremely comfortable, the double rooms en suite and the singles with private shower rooms. **Restaurant:** The very popular restaurant consists of two dining rooms, one overlooking the gardens. The fixed price menu offers a wide choice. It always includes locally caught fish, seasonal game and shellfish. Extremely fresh vegetables, delicious tarts and puddings all emphasise the quality of the ingredients used. The wine list is small but well balanced and reasonably priced. **Nearby:** The Norfolk Broads for boating, and the coast with its bird sanctuaries. Norwich City has its cathedral and museum and The Garden House is an ideal base for exploring the county's fascinating villages, historic houses and parks, such as Blickling Hall near Aylsham. **Directions: From Norwich take the A1151 for Wroxham. At Rackheath turn right at sign for Salhouse Station. On reaching T-junction turn right and Garden House is mile on the left.**

HOTEL DES CLOS

OLD LENTON LANE, NOTTINGHAM, NOTTINGHAMSHIRE NG7 2SA
TEL: 0115 9866566 FAX: 0115 9860343

OWNER: John Abbey
CHEF: John Abbey

10 rms   10 ens

 D: £75–£90
Suite: £100–£125

Inn: An attractive conversion of Victorian farm buildings, this quiet privately run hotel retains the atmosphere of its origins while offering guests every modern comfort. The hotel benefits from its location on the banks of the River Trent, yet its close proximity to Nottingham and the motorway network ensures its convenient suitability for the traveller. Each designed around an individual theme, the en suite bedrooms and suites are well-equipped with colour TV, trouser press and refreshment facilities. Conference amenities enable executives to stage small meetings and a wide choice of weekend breaks is also on offer. **Restaurant:** Since the opening of the French restaurant in 1990, chef-proprietor John Abbey has established a reputation for cuisine and fine wines and has been rewarded this year with his first AA rosette. A choice of lunch and evening menus is presented and during the summer guests may dine alfresco in the courtyard garden. An admirable list of French wines includes over 50 half-bottles and 60 different Chablis labels. **Nearby:** The city of Nottingham is home to the National Watersports Centre, Trent Bridge Cricket Ground and a large market. Other notable landmarks are Nottingham Castle, Sherwood Forest and Southwell Minster. **Directions: Take exit 24 from M1 and take A453 signposted Nottingham (10 miles). Cross River Trent and follow signs to Lenton. Turn left at roundabout and immediately left again, down the lane to the river.**

In association with MasterCard

THE WHIPPER-IN HOTEL

THE MARKET PLACE, OAKHAM, RUTLAND, LE15 6DT
TEL: 01572 756971 FAX: 01572 757759

OWNERS: Brook Hotels PLC
MANAGER: Lisa Butterfill
CHEF: James Butterfill

24 rms   23 ens

S: £59
D: £71

Inn: This impressive 17th-century former coaching inn stands proudly in the market square of historic Oakham, county town of Rutland. Just two miles away is magnificent Rutland Water, whose 26 miles circumference makes it the largest man-made lake in Europe. The area is hunting country and this is reflected in the hotel through old pictures and prints decorating the walls. The country atmosphere is enhanced by exposed oak beams, log fires, antiques and rich fabrics in warm hues. All 24 bedrooms – four in the courtyard – are individually and comfortably furnished and some have interesting views over the busy market square with its ancient set of stocks and old butter cross. The hotel's two bars are popular meeting places for locals who come to enjoy the lunchtime food as well as the real ale which is brewed just two miles away. A private dining room and an air-conditioned conference room are available. **Restaurant:** Imaginative English country cooking is offered in the rustic surroundings of this beamed restaurant, which has recently been awarded for its food an AA rosette. **Nearby:** Sailing, windsurfing, water sports and trout fishing at Rutland Water. Golf and facilities for a variety of country sports are nearby. The area has many stately homes and castles, such as Belvoir Castle, Burghley House and Grimsthorpe Castle. **Directions: From the A1 take the A606 to Oakham.**

THE WHEATSHEAF INN AT ONNELEY AND LA PUERTA DEL SOL – RESTAURANTE ESPAÑOL

BARHILL ROAD, ONNELEY, STAFFORDSHIRE CW3 9QF
TEL: 01782 751581 FAX: 01782 751499

OWNERS: Mark and Milagros Bittner
CHEFS: Milagros Bittner and Trevor Smits

S: £45
D: £50–£60

Inn: This traditional inn, located in the North Staffordshire countryside – yet close to the Potteries, welcomes business travellers and tourists alike. Attractively refurbished and professionally run by the congenial resident proprietors, The Wheatsheaf Inn offers many comforts and facilities. Furnishings and décor are of a high standard throughout, and special touches like a basket of fruit on arrival and a complimentary morning paper add to the welcome. Popular Champagne Breaks and Golfing Breaks (using the amenities of the adjoining Onneley Golf Club) offer excellent value for money. **Restaurant:** Recently refurbished, the hotel's restaurant, La Puerta del Sol, offers the best traditional Spanish cooking – prepared by authentic methods – along with a wide range of popular English dishes. Guests are given a choice from the extensive à la carte menu and daily three-course table d'hôte menu. **Nearby:** The Wheatsheaf Inn at Onneley is just a short drive from the Potteries, the heart of Britain's ceramic industry. Also nearby are Bridgemere Garden World, Stapeley Water Gardens, the Dorothy Clive Gardens and the University of Keele. Alton Towers and Chester can be easily reached by car. **Directions: Located on the main A525 between the villages of Madeley and Woore just a 10 minute drive from Newcastle-under-Lyme and 15 minutes from Crewe, Nantwich, Market Drayton and Stoke-on-Trent. Easy access to the M6 motorway is available at junctions 15 and 16.**

For hotel location, see maps on pages 183-189

HOLCOMBE HOTEL

HIGH STREET, DEDDINGTON, NR. WOODSTOCK, OXFORDSHIRE OX15 0SL
TEL: 01869 338274 FAX: 01869 337167

OWNERS: Carol and Chedly Mahfoudh
HEAD CHEF: Alan Marshall

17 rms   17 ens

S: £65–£78
D: £92.50–£110.50

Inn: Conveniently located a few miles north of the university city of Oxford, this delightful 17th century high quality hotel is family run and set in a pretty Cotswold village. It offers personalised attention and traditional hospitality and has a relaxed and friendly atmosphere. Each of the 17 tastefully appointed bedrooms has its own distinctive character and one boasts a water bed. Every amenity, including ionisers, is provided for the comfort of guests. **Restaurant:** Holcombe Hotel is known locally for its superb French, classical and traditional English cuisine. It is highly recommended and is recognised with an AA Red Rossette and RAC awards. Great care is taken in creating original and beautifully presented food. Real ale and excellent bar meals are served in the oakbeamed cottage bar. The Holcombe has been in the resident ownership of Chedley and Carol Mahfoudh since 1988, during which time they have received 5 awards, including the AA Courtesy and Care Award 1993, one of only 15 hotels out of 4,000. **Nearby:** The Cotswolds, Stratford, Woodstock and Oxford and Bicester Shopping Village "Bond Street at a 50% discount" and many National Trust Properties. Golfing arranged at two excellent, 18-hole golf courses. **Directions: Deddington is on the A4260, 6 miles south of Banbury M40 J11. Follow A4260 to Adderbury; hotel is on the right at traffic light. M40 J10: follow A43, then B4100 to Aynho, then B4031 to Deddington**

THE JERSEY ARMS

MIDDLETON STONEY, OXFORDSHIRE OX6 8SE
TEL: 01869 343234 FAX: 01869 343565

OWNERS: The Livingston Family

16 rms | 16 ens

S: £69
D: £85

Inn: Near Oxford, the city of dreaming spires, in the country of sparkling streams and gentle green pastures, The Jersey Arms occupies a site rich in history. As far back as 1241, the inn was listed as providing William Longsword 'for 25 men of Middleton, necessaries as food and drink'. It thrived in the days of coach-and-horse long-distance travel, and in 1823 was a key posting house for cross-country traffic. Today, The Jersey Arms has been honed into a retreat of comfort and peace. An informal air is created with old beams, antique flintlocks and simple, elegant furnishings. Bedrooms, all with private access, vary in size, while blending the charm of the past with modern décor. Facilities include hairdryers, colour TV and telephone.

Restaurant: Cuisine of exceptional quality is prepared from the freshest local ingredients, and the menu is changed according to season. Diners can sit in the Bar or Restaurant or, in fine weather, in the secluded courtyard garden. Relax first with an apéritif in the elegant lounge. **Nearby:** Oxford, Woodstock, Blenheim Palace with its gardens, Towcester and Cheltenham racecourses and Silverstone Racetrack. Heathrow airport is an hour away by car. **Directions:** Between junctions 9 & 10 of the M40 on the B430 10 miles north of Oxford. From junction 9 take the Oxford Road, Middleton Stoney is signposted 1 mile down. From junction 10 Middleton Stoney is signposted as you leave the slip road.

In association
with MasterCard

THE MILL AND OLD SWAN

MINSTER LOVELL, OXFORDSHIRE OX8 5RN
TEL: 01993 774441 FAX: 01993 702002

OWNERS: Style Conferences
GENERAL MANAGER: Ian Conder
SALES & MARKETING MANAGER: Gráinne Moore

S: £50–£80
D: £80–£140

Inn: The Old Swan stands in the historic village of Minster Lovell, a small Oxfordshire village lying in the valley of the River Windrush, on the edge of the Cotswolds. According to the *Doomsday Book*, three mills were at Minster Lovell, two of which existed on the present site and now constitute part of these historic properties. A wealth of oak beams, glowing fires, four-poster beds and antique furnishings welcome you to The Old Swan, which has been carefully restored to luxury standards. King Richard III was a regular guest at The Old Swan – his original crest 'The Sun in Splendour' can be found emblazoned in one of the bedroom walls.

The Mill: Attached to The Old Swan is The Mill, set in a 60 acre estate by the River Windrush (which was the inspiration for Kenneth Grahame's children's book 'The Wind in the Willows'. It is a charming location for relaxing, walking through the gardens or enjoying a choice of sporting activities including tennis, punting and fly-fishing. The Mill was awarded the European Architecture Heritage Award for its design in bringing modern facilities into a historic building. **Directions: From the A40 (Oxford/Burford road), take B4047 signposted to Minster Lovell. Once in the village follow the signs for Minster Lovell Hall.**

THE TALKHOUSE

WHEATLEY ROAD, STANTON ST JOHN, OXFORDSHIRE OX33 1EX
TEL: 01865 351648 FAX: 01865 351085

OWNERS: Johnny Chick and Alan Heather
MANAGERS: Shane Ellis and Leanne Grieveson
CHEF: Mark Skidmore

4 rms   4 ens

S: £45.50
D: £59.50

Inn: The Talkhouse is a 17th century inn which once housed the local blacksmith. In a country village on the London side of Oxford, it has been carefully and tastefully refurbished under its new owners, Johnny Chick and Alan Heather, who also own the Mole & Chicken near Thame. A friendly and courteous staff are happy to attend to their guests' every need. **Restaurant:** An extensive and interesting menu is provided in the restaurant. For a starter try a chicken breast satay with garlic bread and chilli dip, or perhaps a plate of the best smoked Scottish salmon. Follow with home made steak and kidney pie, grilled calves' liver with bacon and sage or chargrilled chicken breast with a delicious five-spice sauce. The house specialities are irresistible puddings with orange sauce and cream, and just being there dining in the Talkhouse. **Nearby:** The Talkhouse is ideally situated for guests who wish to visit the famous university city of Oxford. There are six premier golf courses within a 20 minute drive, along with opportunities locally for fishing, shooting and walking. Blenheim Palace, William Kent's garden at Rousham House, Cliveden, the Cotswolds, Henley and Silverstone are all within easy reach. **Directions: M40 junction 8, then the A40 to Wheatley and pick up the B4027.**

THE OLD CUSTOM HOUSE HOTEL

SOUTH QUAY, PADSTOW, CORNWALL PL28 8ED
TEL: 01841 532359 FAX: 01841 533372

OWNERS: St Austell Brewery & Co Ltd
MANAGER: Linda Allen
CHEF: Neil Markram

24 rms	24 ens

S: £49–£71
D: £60–£96

Inn: Miles of golden sands, rugged cliffs topped with wild flowers and numerous old harbours make Cornwall's north coast one of Britain's most scenic areas. Padstow, a town of narrow, crooked streets lined with quaint inns and shops, is an ideal touring base. Originally built in the 1800s as the Customs and Excise building, this listed house occupies a fine position on Padstow's quayside. Most of the bedrooms overlook the harbour and the Camel estuary; all are decorated and equipped to a high standard. The bars are decorated in keeping with the building's character, and there is also a pleasant conservatory lounge. **Restaurant:** Situated in the old grain warehouse, the dining room offers à la carte and table d'hôte menus. There is an extensive choice of fresh fish and seafood dishes as the hotel makes good use of the local produce available. AA 3 star and RAC 3 star. **Nearby:** Guests can walk the Coastal Path which passes through Padstow, discover the legend of King Arthur at Tintagel or visit the beautiful stately homes and gardens in the vicinity. Water sports can be enjoyed locally including golf at Trevose and St Enodoc, surfing at Polzeath and sailing in the estuary. **Directions: Entering Padstow, follow the signs for the quay.**

JUBILEE INN

PELYNT, NR LOOE, CORNWALL PL13 2JZ
TEL: 01503 220312 FAX: 01503 220920

OWNERS: Tim and Judith Williams
P.A: Pam Dawson
HEAD CHEF & GENERAL MANAGER: Peter Catnach

S: £36
D: £59

Inn: The Jubilee has been an inn since the 16th century, changing its name from The Axe in 1887 to mark the 50th anniversary of Queen Victoria's accession. The low beamed ceilings, open hearths and old prints create an air of tradition and charm throughout. The bedrooms are tastefully furnished in a cottage style; three are for families and one is a bridal suite with a spiral staircase designed by Stuart Armfield, the well-known artist. With a residents' lounge, three bars, a beer garden, plus a large garden with a children's play area and volley-ball net, there are plenty of places to relax. Barbecues are held in the summer. Special breaks arranged. **Restaurant:** An impressive à la carte menu and friendly, professional service are offered in the dining room. The inn's speciality is fish and shellfish, which come straight off the boats in nearby Looe. An extensive bar menu and traditional Sunday lunches are also on offer. **Nearby:** The Duchy of Cornwall nurseries, several National Trust Properties and Dobwalls Adventure Park and Monley Sanctuary are a selection of the many interesting places to visit. Bodmin Moor, numerous picturesque villages and beautiful coastline are all to be explored. **Directions: From Plymouth, cross Tamar Bridge and follow the main road to Looe. Leave Looe on the Polperro road and turn right for Pelynt.**

In association with MasterCard

BADGERS

COULTERSHAW BRIDGE, PETWORTH, WEST SUSSEX GH28 1JE
TEL: 01798 342651 FAX: 01790 343649

OWNER: Jules Arlette

3 rms   3 ens

 D: £70

Inn: This glorious Georgian inn, just outside Chichester in the beautiful countryside from which Turner derived so much inspiration, has a fascinating history. It was built in conjunction with the railway in 1860, with horse and carts from the inn transporting passengers and goods into Petworth. The bore hole dug to provide water is today a trout stream and pond. The interior of the inn is immaculate, the furnishings and decorations appropriate, and the ambience in the bar is wonderfully relaxing, enhanced by open fires in winter. The spacious bedrooms, each different, are exquisite. The beds are king-size, with attractive en suite bathrooms. **Restaurant:** The stylish restaurant has a fine reputation, the menu a Mediterranean influence. Zarzuela, a Spanish fish casserole, is a house speciality. It also includes delicious interpretations of classical English dishes. The wine list makes good reading. The Inn has a charming secluded sunny cobbled courtyard, perfect for al fresco aperitifs and summer dining. **Nearby:** Sporting guests will enjoy golf at Cowdray Park and Goodwood. The former also is famous for polo and the latter for racing. Fly fishing, ballooning and speed festivals are alternatives. Petworth House and Arundel Castle should be visited, and Chichester with its sailing harbour and theatre is a 'must'. **Directions:** Badgers is south of Petworth on the A285.

THE WHITE HORSE INN

SUTTON, NR PULBOROUGH, WEST SUSSEX RH20 1PS
TEL: 01798 869221 FAX: 01798 869291

OWNERS: Howard and Susie Macnamara
MANAGERS: Joslyn and Valerie Maude

S: from £48
D: £58–£68

Inn: This privately owned inn has offered rest and comfort to both travellers and locals since 1746. Howard and Susie Macnamara have restored the traditions of the inn by making available six pretty rooms which are comfortably furnished and appointed with modern amenities. The double-bedded rooms have king-size beds and all rooms have well-kept en suite bathrooms. All bedrooms are 'non-smoking' – all have tea & coffee facilities and colour TV. There is also an attractive garden cottage; however, unlike the other bedrooms this does not have a direct-dial telephone. Joss and Val Maude are always on hand to offer a friendly welcome.

Restaurant: The White Horse is a popular place to eat, both with locals and patrons from further afield. Fresh wholesome food is always featured on the menu. The three-course table d'hôte dinner with coffee is very reasonably priced. **Nearby:** Amberley Chalk Pits, horseracing at Goodwood, the harbour town of Chichester, Arundel Castle, Petworth House, Parham House and Gardens, and the Roman Villa at Bignor. **Directions: Sutton is a little hamlet situated between A29 (Pulborough to Arundel road) and A285 (Petworth to Chichester road). Look for brown sign to Roman Villa at Bignor – Sutton is a mile further west.**

THE WHITE SWAN

THE MARKET PLACE, PICKERING, NORTH YORKSHIRE YO18 7AA
TEL: 01751 472288 FAX: 01751 475554

OWNERS: The Buchanan Family

12 rms   12 ens

 S: £45–£58
D: £65–£95
Suite: £90–£110

Inn: A charming hotel, centrally located in an energetic market town, originally a 16th century coaching inn. The White Swan provides an ideal base to explore the surrounding area, or the perfect country retreat. Warm yourself in front of a log fire in the welcoming bar or relax in one of the twelve bedrooms each with its own individual character. **Restaurant:** Critically acclaimed, the menu offers a delicious range of imaginative and innovative dishes using local fresh produce. Duck, venison, fresh lobster and shellfish in season together with vegetarian dishes. The wine list is unusually extensive with a choice of over 200 bins. Some extremely rare, all excellent value. Special 2-3 day breaks, golf holidays, shooting parties, walking, riding, fishing and wine weekends. Microlyting available. Many other activities are on offer and can easily be arranged. **Nearby:** The moors, the coast, North York Moors Steam Railway, historic castles, museums, craft villages, abbeys and stately homes. **Directions: From York: take the A64 to the Malton bypass and the A169 to Pickering. From the A1 North (or the A19), go via the A170 from Thirsk (up Sutton Bank).**

THE PORT GAVERNE HOTEL

NR PORT ISAAC, NORTH CORNWALL PL29 3SQ
TEL: 01208 880244 FAX: 01208 880151 FREEPHONE 0500 657867

OWNER: Midge Ross
CHEF: Ian Brodey

S: £47.50–£51.50
D: £95–£103

Inn: Port Gaverne Hotel is situated on the North Cornwall Coastal Path in a secluded cove half a mile from the old fishing village of Port Isaac. Much of the surrounding area is supervised by the National Trust. The 350-year-old hotel is owned and managed by Midge Ross and its character owes as much to the skills and materials of local tradesmen as it does to the dedication of its proprietress. Bedrooms are cosy and well appointed, with direct dial telephone and TV. The residents' lounge never fails to woo guests with its old-world personality.
Restaurant: At Port Gaverne Hotel chef Ian Brodey and his staff have built up an international reputation for fine cuisine with delicious seafood dishes and a vegetarian menu. It was recently awarded an AA rosette. The hotel is also noted for its 'Breather' weekends in autumn and winter and its self-contained 18th century cottages.
Nearby: Walk the coastal path in either direction for National Trust countryside in abundance. There is safe, sheltered swimming within seconds of the hotel door. Visit: Delabole Slate Quarry, Boscastle, Tintagel Castle (King Arthur's birthplace), Bodmin and Polzeath.
Directions: Port Gaverne is signposted from the B3314 south of Delabole and is reached along the B3267. Follow the signs for Port Gaverne only (not Port Isaac).

For hotel location, see maps on pages 183-189

 PORTHLEVEN (Nr Helston)

 In association with MasterCard

THE HARBOUR INN

COMMERCIAL ROAD, PORTHLEVEN, NR HELSTON, CORNWALL TR13 9JD
TEL: 01326 573876

OWNERS: St Austell Brewery & Co Ltd
MANAGERS: David and Wendy Morton
CHEF: Brian Mortimore

| 10 rms | 8 ens |

   S: £33
D: £63

Inn: Overlooking Porthleven's picturesque quayside, The Harbour Inn is popular with locals and visitors alike. Characterised by flag-stoned floors, beams and wood panelling, the bar retains the atmosphere of an old fishermen's pub. Good-value accommodation, friendly service and traditional surroundings are assured. Most bedrooms overlook the harbour and all have pastel décor with stripped pine furnishings. On the first floor there is a comfortable lounge. ETB 3 Crowns Commended, AA 2 Stars, Egon Ronay recommended. **Restaurant:** Not surprisingly, imaginative seafood dishes are a speciality. Starters include squid, king prawns and poached scallops, followed by main courses such as swordfish, sharksteak or monkfish flamed with brandy in a cream sauce. All meals are well presented and complemented by a good choice of wines and ales. Bar meals are also available. Live entertainment on some Wednesdays and most Saturdays. **Nearby:** Fine beaches, open moorland, wooded estuaries, undulating sand dunes and rugged cliffs can all be found in the area. For skin-divers King Arthur's sword is said to be lying at the bottom of Loe Pool near Penrose. Penzance, Falmouth, the north coast and the beauty spots of The Lizard peninsula are a short car journey away. Facilities for riding, tennis, fishing and many types of water sport are nearby. **Directions: Via Truro take the A39 to Falmouth, then follow signs to Helston. Porthleven is signposted.**

118

In association with MasterCard

YE HORN'S INN

HORN'S LANE, GOOSNARGH, NR PRESTON, LANCASHIRE PR3 2FJ
TEL: 01772 865230 FAX: 01772 864299 E-MAIL: yehornsinn@msn.com

OWNERS: Mark Woods and Elizabeth Jones

6 rms 6 ens

S: £45
D: £70

Inn: A striking black-and-white timbered building standing at a crossroads in lovely rolling countryside, Ye Horn's radiates charm and atmosphere. Built in 1782 as a coaching inn, the hotel has been run by the Woods family for 40 years. Today it is expertly managed by Elizabeth Jones, her brother Mark Woods and his wife Denise, offering first-rate accommodation for both business visitors and the holiday-maker. The 6 spacious bedrooms, all en suite, are in the adjoining barn – a recent conversion – and are stylishly furnished as well as spotlessly clean. All offer tea and coffee-making facilities, trouser press and hairdryer. Oak beams, sumptuous carpets and, in winter, open fires, combine to create a mood of cosy, relaxed hospitality throughout. **Restaurant:** The restaurant has earned a fine reputation for its delicious traditional cuisine, prepared wherever possible from fresh, local produce and served in the main dining room or the 'snug' next to it. Specialities include home-made soup, roast duckling, roast pheasant and a truly addictive sticky toffee pudding. Full English or Continental breakfasts are also available daily. **Nearby:** Chingle Hall, a haunted house, Beacon Fell Country Park, the Ribble Valley, the Forest of Bowland and Blackpool. **Directions: Exit M6 junction 32, take A6 north to first traffic lights. Turn right onto the B5269 signposted Longridge, to just past Goosnargh village shop. Where the road veers sharply right, continue straight ahead into Camforth Hall Lane: the hotel is signposted after a few minutes.**

THE OLD BREWERY HOUSE HOTEL

MARKET SQUARE, REEPHAM, NORWICH, NORFOLK NR10 4JJ
TEL: 01603 870881 FAX: 01603 870969

OWNER: Derek Lloyd
MANAGER: Iain Wilson
CHEF: Mark Snelling

21 rms   21 ens

S: £39.95
D: £67.50

Inn: As a family-run business, the Old Brewery House Hotel prides itself on offering friendly hospitality in relaxing surroundings. Set in the market square of the old village of Reepham, it retains the atmosphere of a past age. The bedrooms are quiet and comfortable – the furniture in the original part of the building is French antique, while newer rooms are styled in country pine. Energetic guests may like to take advantage of the Old Brewery's sports centre. Here there are opportunities to swim, take part in aerobics classes, work out in the new hi-tech fitness suite or relax in the sauna. **Restaurant:** Only the best local produce is used to create the dishes served in the warm atmosphere of the hotel's restaurant. The menus are constantly changing and it is well worth looking out for 'specials of the day'. Some of the culinary delights guests may sample include finest fish pie, thai crispy lamb, pigeon and raspberry and oriental duck. An excellent range of vegetarian dishes is also available. **Nearby:** The vast expanse of salt marshes and sandy beaches which make up the Norfolk Coast and Broads is a haven for nature lovers and bird-watchers. The beautiful city of Norwich, Holt, Sandringham and Blickling Hall. **Directions: The hotel is off the A1067 Norwich to Fakenham road. Take the B1145 signposted Aylsham.**

The Golden Lion Inn Of Easenhall

EASENHALL, NR RUGBY, WARWICKSHIRE CV23 0JA
TEL: 01788 832265 FAX: 01788 832878

OWNERS: James and Claudia Austin

   S: £40
D: £60

Inn: The Golden Lion, dating back to the 16th century, is set back from the main road through Easenhall, a delightful English village not far from Rugby, and ideal for parents visiting the celebrated boarding school. It has low oak beamed ceilings, narrow doorways and uneven floors which all add to its charm, and guests receive a traditional warm welcome. The small bar is proud of its best ales, fine wines and wide range of spirits. Delicious snacks are available both at lunchtime and in the evening. The bedrooms are extremely comfortable, quite spacious, with attractive cottage furniture. **Restaurant:** The restaurant is divided into two rooms and specialises in country cooking. In summer guests can eat al fresco in the garden and patio, where barbecues are often held, sometimes joined by the pet donkey. **Nearby:** Guests can enjoy village cricket or go further afield to Coventry Cathedral, Coombe Abbey or Warwick Castle. The NEC Birmingham and Stoneleigh Agricultural Centre are in easy reach too. There are excellent golf courses in the neighbourhood. **Directions:** Easenhall is reached from the M6 junctions 1/2, taking the B4112 off the A426 for Rugby or the B4027 from the Coventry by-pass.

THE RISING SUN

THE SQUARE, ST MAWES, CORNWALL TR2 5DJ
TEL: 01326 270233 FAX: 01326 270198

OWNER: St Austell Brewery & Co Ltd
MANAGERS: Norman and June Gilbert
CHEF: Graeme Fryett

8 rms 8 ens

S: £45
D: £62–£95
D: £90–£100

Inn: At the Rising Sun, guests can enjoy a waterside location overlooking the harbour in the heart of St Mawes. The newly refurbished bedrooms are a delight, offering total comfort, all individually furnished, and the sea-facing rooms command fine views. With two choices of bar – a conservatory lounge bar and a public bar – and a beautiful residential lounge, The Rising Sun has plenty of places for relaxation. Special Christmas and New Year breaks are available. **Restaurant:** Emphasis on seafood. The chef makes good use of the area's rich supply of seafood when compiling the à la carte menu. Lunchtime snacks and evening meals are also available from the bar menu. An extensive wine list carries a varied selection of French, German and New World wines. **Nearby:** St Mawes is situated on the tip of the picturesque Roseland Peninsula, overlooking the estuary of the River Fal. The Rising Sun makes a good base for exploring Cornwall's dramatic coastline and picturesque villages. **Directions: Take A30, then follow signs to Truro via A39 when leaving at Fraddon. Soon after joining A390 turn left to A3078 to St Mawes.**

THE OLD BELL INN HOTEL

HUDDERSFIELD ROAD, DELPH, NR OLDHAM, SADDLEWORTH, GREATER MANCHESTER OL3 5EG
TEL: 01457 870130 FAX: 01457 876597

OWNERS: Philip and Judith Grew
MANAGER: Susan Doherty

10 rms | 10 ens

S: £35–£50
D: £55–£70

Inn: Many famous figures from the past, including Queen Victoria and Charles Dickens, have visited this stone-built, 18th century inn, which acquired its current name under the tenancy of William Bell. Today's guests are offered attractive accommodation in furnished and well-equipped bedrooms. A number of rooms have four-poster beds – perfect for a romantic weekend. Old beams, open fires and lead lattice windows create a cosy atmosphere in the bar and comfortable residents' lounge. Private parties for up to 40 can be catered for. **Restaurant:** An imaginative menu is changed seasonally to offer plenty of choice and variety. Guests can try, for example, venison steak on a croûte topped with pâté coated in port wine sauce. A separate vegetarian menu is always provided. For less formal occasions, meals are also served in the bar.
Nearby: The village of Delph, with its weavers' cottages, and cobbled side-streets still a reminder of its cloth-making history, lies on the edge of the Peak District National Park and Saddleworth Moor – an area of great natural beauty. Places to visit include Castle Shaw Roman Fort, Huddersfield canal where boat trips can be taken, Dovestones Reservoir with its watersports and the art and craft centre at Uppermill. Various golf courses are nearby. Special weekend rates are available on request. **Directions:** The Old Bell Inn is on the A62 Oldham–Huddersfield road, in the village of Delph.

NEW INN

CLAPHAM, NR SETTLE, NORTH YORKSHIRE LA2 8HH
TEL: 015242 51203 FAX: 015242 51496

OWNERS: Keith and Barbara Mannion
CHEFS: Andrew Whaley and Jonathan Mannion

16 rms 16 ens

S: £43–£48
D: £63–£73

Inn: Keith and Barbara Mannion have owned this lovely listed Yorkshire Inn since 1987. Over the years they have lovingly refurbished it with a fine blend of old and new, carefully retaining its original 18th century character while adding every modern comfort. All the cosy bedrooms are en suite and some feature antique or four poster beds. The two comfortable bars have open fires in winter and serve hearty bar meals. **Restaurant:** On the à la carte menu there is a selection of starters including Yorkshire pudding and mussels provençale, followed by a variety of steaks, local game and a good choice of vegetarians meals. In the bar, 'light bites' and children's meals are served. Main dishes include pork in cider casserole; Stilton, butterbean and leek bake; steak in ale pie, deep fried jumbo haddock; and Cajun chicken. There is no shortage of leisure activities for guests of the New Inn Hotel. Trout fishing is available across the road in Clapham Beck and the area is an ideal resort for walking, caving and climbing. Four golf courses are within a ten mile radius. **Nearby:** There are many castles, abbeys and stately homes in the area. The Settle to Carlisle Railway is also within easy reach. **Directions: The New Inn is in the village of Clapham which is off the A65 midway between Skipton and Kendal.**

In association with MasterCard

SEVENOAKS

THE ROYAL OAK

HIGH STREET, SEVENOAKS, KENT TN13 1HY
TEL: 01732 451109 FAX: 01732 740187

OWNERS: Brook Hotels PLC

37 rms | 37 ens

    S: £79
D: £85

Inn: The Royal Oak is located just a short walk from Sevenoaks town centre and its many shopping opportunities. Built in the 17th century, the hotel is an ideal base from which to explore the surrounding countryside of Kent, Surrey and Sussex and visit the area's many famous castles, houses, gardens and National Trust properties. The hotel has 37 comfortable en suite bedrooms, all attractively decorated and furnished and with 24-hour service. Guests may enjoy morning coffee or afternoon tea in the conservatory which opens out onto a delightful, paved patio with small tables and shady sun umbrellas. Two ground floor rooms are available for conferences, meetings and private functions. **Restaurant:** The light and airy Sycamore Restaurant plays an important role in the hotel. The head chef prepares a blend of modern English and French dishes making full use of Kent's abundance of natural produce. A good range of hot and cold dishes is also served in the bistro and bar. **Nearby:** Leeds and Hever Castles, Chartwell, the 14th century manor house Igtham Mote, the Elizabethan village of Chiddingstone, Penshurst Place and Knole. Royal Tunbridge Wells and its excellent shops are within easy reach. **Directions: Sevenoaks is only a short drive from junction 5 of the M25.**

For hotel location, see maps on pages 183-189

125

In association with MasterCard

COPPLERIDGE INN

MOTCOMBE, SHAFTESBURY, DORSET SP7 9HW
TEL: 01747 851980 FAX: 01747 851858

OWNERS: Goodinge, Newell and Horsley
CHEFS: Chris and Claire Goodinge

S: £40
D: £70

Inn: The Coppleridge nestles in 15 acres of superb meadow, woodland and gardens, overlooking the Blackmore Vale. This 18th century farmhouse offers simply furnished and spacious en suite bedrooms in the tastefully converted farm buildings in the courtyard. The welcoming bar and flagstoned lounge with its warming log fire are the places to relax with a drink. The inn's magnificent 18th century barn has been converted into a function and conference room, a perfect setting for weddings, parties and business meetings. A wide range of leisure facilities is available in the villge. **Restaurant:** In the cosy candelit restaurant, guests can choose from the à la carte menu which utilises only the freshest ingredients from local suppliers. Alternatively, an excellent range of home-cooked bar meals is available, incorporating traditional favourites, as well as a number of interesting ethnic dishes. Game and a daily changing fresh fish selection are both also featured on the menu. A good choice of wines is available to complement any meal. **Nearby:** There are many places of interest within easy reach, including Stourhead, Kingston Lacy, Gold Hill in Shaftesbury, Stonehenge, Longleat and Yeovilton Fleet Air Arm Museum. **Directions: Exit Shaftesbury to the north on the Gillingham Road. Watch for sign to Motcombe. Drive through village and then turn left to Mere. Coppleridge Inn is on left after 100 yards.**

In association with MasterCard

S: £42.95–£45
D: £59.95–£80

5 rms | 5 ens

SHERBORNE (West Camel)

THE WALNUT TREE

WEST CAMEL, NR SHERBORNE, SOMERSET BA22 7QW
TEL: 01935 851292 FAX: 01935 851292

OWNERS: Peter and Georgina Ball

Inn: Just over the border from Dorset in a delightful Somerset village with its tranquil setting stands The Walnut Tree. The charming newly renovated en suite bedrooms will satisfy the demanding criteria of today's traveller, with finishing touches of toiletries, hairdryers, trouser-presses, colour TV and telephones. **Restaurant:** Imaginative food is served in the charming candle-lit dining room, which has a marvellous ambience. Alternatively, relax and eat in the delightful lounge bar. The Walnut Tree has a fine reputation for its cuisine and has been in the Egon Ronay's guide for three successive years, also in the 'Which' guide for inns. For the discerning walker the 'Leyland Trail' passes through the village of West Camel. For the golfer there are six courses within the area. There are plenty of places to visit locally. The Fleet Air Arm Museum at Yeovilton, Haynes Motor Museum at Sparkford and historic the town of Sherborne and its Abbey Church. **Nearby:** Cheddar Gorge, Wookey Hole, Longleat House Safari Park, Glastonbury, Stourhead Gardens, the ancient city of Wells, Montacute House, Stonehenge and Cricket St Thomas' Wildlife Park. The Inn is also very convenient for visiting the old Dorset coastal towns of Weymouth and Lyme Regis. **Directions: From Wincanton follow A303 westward. Cross A359 at Sparkford. West Camel is the next village you come to. Take the first turning left**

For hotel location, see maps on pages 183-189

In association
with MasterCard

THE LAMB INN

SHIPTON-UNDER-WYCHWOOD, OXFORDSHIRE OX7 6DQ
TEL: 01993 830465 FAX: 01993 832025

OWNERS: Michael and Jennifer Eastick
CHEF: John McGarrigle

S: £58
D: £68–£95

Inn: Although it has been a hostelry for several hundred years, this inviting inn has lost none of its charm. It is situated on the outskirts of a delightful Cotswold village and has much to recommend it. The Lamb Bar has log fires and serves real ales, a carefully selected range of single malted whiskies, plus a choice of apéritifs and liqueurs. Bar meals are served during the day and evenings, and there is a lunchtime buffet. The bedrooms, which offer every comfort, are tastefully furnished with character in traditional period style. The proprietors offer everyone a friendly welcome, making this a most pleasant place to stay. **Restaurant:** Chef John McGarrigle has a fastidious approach to quality and presentation. The restaurant offers fresh fish from Cornwall, ducks from Minster Lovell, seasonally available game and carefully chosen beef, lamb and fresh vegetables. Specialities include Wychwood chicken – boned chicken stuffed with asparagus, sliced and served with tarragon mayonnaise. There is a wine list of over 50 bins. Private parties and receptions for up to 30 people can be accommodated. Open 7 days a week all year. **Nearby:** The Cotswolds, Blenheim Palace, Oxford and Cheltenham are just a few of the places to see. **Directions: The Lamb is on the A361 near Shipton-under-Wychwood, between Burford and Chipping Norton.**

THE SHAVEN CROWN HOTEL

HIGH STREET, SHIPTON-UNDER-WYCHWOOD, OXFORDSHIRE OX7 6BA
TEL: 01993 830330 FAX: 01993 830330

OWNERS: Mr and Mrs J. Brookes
MANAGER: Justin Brookes

 S: £33
D: £66–£82

Inn: Built of honey-coloured stone around an attractive central courtyard, The Shaven Crown Hotel dates back to the 14th century, when it served as a monks' hospice. The proprietors, the Brookes family, have preserved the inn's many historic features, such as the medieval hall with its ancient timbered roof. This is now the residents' lounge. Each of the bedrooms has en suite facilities and has been sympathetically furnished in a style befitting its own unique character. Rooms of various style and sizes are available, includeing a huge family room and ground-floor accommodation. **Restaurant:** Dining in thr intimate, candle-lit room is an enjoyable experience, with meals served at the tables beautifully laid with fine accessories.

The best ingredients are combined to create original dishes with a cosmopolitan flair. The table d'hôte menu offers a wide and eclectic choice with a daily vegetarian dish amoung the specialities. An imaginative selection of dishes is offered every lunchtime and evening in the buttery bar. **Nearby:** The Shaven Crown is ideal for day trips to the Cotswolds, Oxford, Stratford-upon-Avon and Bath. There are three golf courses and tennis courts close by. Trout fishing and antiques hunting are popular activities in the area. **Directions: Take the A40 Oxford–Cheltenham road. At Burford follow the A361 towards Chipping Norton. The inn is situated directly opposite the village green in Shipton-under-Wychwood.**

In association
with MasterCard

THE NESSCLIFFE

NESSCLIFFE, SHREWSBURY, SHROPSHIRE SY4 1DB
TEL: 01743 741430 FAX: 01743 741104

OWNER: Mr T.E.Jones
MANAGER: Alan Crossley

7 rms · 7 ens

S: £45
D: £55
S: from £65

Inn: The Nescliffe's friendly, courteous staff make sure that guests at this substantial and handsome Grade II listed rural hotel are warmly welcomed. The village is imbued with history. It was a turnpike on the old stagecoach route from Shrewsbury to Holyhead and just behind the hotel is a hill that was a defensive site in Roman times and a lookout point for Oliver Cromwell's soldiers during the Civil War. The Nescliffe Hotel dates back to the early 19th century and has been completely refurbished to a high standard. The bedrooms are tastefully furnished, decorated on a traditional theme and have every modern amenity. A family room features a four-poster bed and has panoramic views over the rolling Shropshire countryside. **Restaurant:** Bar style and enjoying a growing reputation for varied lunches and dinners ranging from hearty steaks through to creative cuisine, with interesting 'specials'. The wine list is thoughtfully selected and reasonably priced. **Nearby:** The historic country town of Shrewsbury with its pink sandstone castle and many superb black-and-white buildings in plaster and weatherboard timber, Oswestry, Chester and the Meres, Shropshire's lake district. The hotel is an ideal base for touring and for those interested in active pursuits such as golf, fishing, clay pigeon shooting, riding and walking. **Directions: Nesscliffe is on the A5 road from Shrewsbury to Oswestry.**

TREE TOPS COUNTRY HOUSE RESTAURANT AND HOTEL

SOUTHPORT OLD ROAD, FORMBY, NR SOUTHPORT, LANCASHIRE L37 0AB
TEL: 01704 879651 FAX: 01704 879651

OWNER: Mrs Lesley Winsland
CHEF: David Oaks

S: £48–£65
D: £85

Inn: The Former Dower House of Formby Hall, Tree Tops, still retains all the elegance of a bygone age, set in five acres of lawns and woods. Over the last 15 years, the Winsland family have restored the house to its true glory and have installed all the modern conveniences sought after by today's visitor. Spacious accommodation is available in well-appointed en suite chalets with all the facilities a discerning guest would expect. An outdoor-heated swimming pool has direct access to the sumptuously decorated Cocktail Lounge. Rich, dark leather seating, oynx-and-gilt tables, and subtle lighting all contribute to the overall ambience, complemented by a truly welcoming and friendly staff. **Restaurant:** Highly polished Regency furnishings, silver tableware and crystal chandeliers set the scene for culinary delights involving only the finest fresh ingredients. The new conservatory resturant has a totally relaxed atmosphere with a superb new à la carte menu serving modern and interesting dishes together with a special snack selection. **Nearby:** Tree Tops is only seven minutes' drive from Southport with its sweeping sands, and 20 minutes from Liverpool. Ten golf courses can be found within a five mile radius, including six championship courses. **Directions: From M6 take the M58 to Southport to the end of motorway. Follow the signs to Southport on A565. Bypass Formby on dual carriageway and as it changes to single carriageway, turn right at bollards to Tree Tops.**

THE DOWER HOUSE

INGESTRE PARK, GREAT HAYWOOD, STAFFORDSHIRE ST18 0RE
TEL/FAX: 01889 270707

OWNERS: Richard and James Froggatt
CHEF: Malcom Matthews

S: £40–£60
D: £75–£100

Inn: A homely, family run little hotel surrounded by mature, colourful gardens in the beautiful Royal parkland of Ingestre, The Dower House was formerly owned by the Earl of Shrewsbury and in the 17th century was used as a hunting lodge. It was converted into a Dower House during the 18th century with no expense being spared on the lavish pitch pine staircase and interior woodwork. After generations of farming, the Froggatt family have combined their talents to restore the house to its former Victorian glory and to introduce every modern comfort. There are open fires in the lounge and bar and the beautifully styled bedrooms include a honeymoon suite with four-poster bed. **Restaurant:** A large, pleasant dining room serving traditional country food using fresh local produce in season. This is augmented by a good selection of wines. A Sunday lunch with a minimum choice of three roasts is offered and there is an extensive bar menu. Afternoon cream teas and light lunches are available on the garden terrace. **Nearby:** Stafford, a charming county town with a history dating back to before the Norman conquest, the old, mellow town of Stone with ruins of an ancient priory, 17th century Shugborough Hall and gardens, and Cannock Chase, remnant of the vast hunting ground which covered much of Staffordshire in Norman times. **Directions: M6, exit at junction 14 and join A34 north from Stafford. Ingestre Park if off the Great Haywood to Milford Road.**

THE HORSE AND GROOM INN & RESTAURANT

UPPER ODDINGTON, MORETON-IN-MARSH, GLOUCESTERSHIRE GL56 0XH
TEL: 01451 830584 FAX: 01451 870494

OWNERS: David and Jill South
CHEF: Mark Hillyard

S: £40
D: £55-£65

Inn: This delightful, heavy stoned 16th century village inn stands serenely in the heart of the Cotswolds surrounded by honey coloured cottages, lush greenery and meandering rivers. Charming, traditional bars with old oak beams, Cotswold Stone walling and a large inglenook fireplace, combined with tasteful furnishings, create a relaxing atmosphere which tempts guests to return again and again. The Horse and Groom is excellent value for money with all the recently refurbished bedrooms having every convenience to ensure that your stay is comfortable. On warm days and evenings there is nothing more enjoyable than lounging in the hotel's large garden with its tinkling stream and fish ponds. **Restaurant:** Activities in the kitchen are supervised by a new chef/partner Mark Hillyard whose talents have already enhanced the inn's reputation for superbly prepared and presented cuisine backed up by a selection of fine wines. **Nearby:** The Horse and Groom is ideally situated for exploring picturesque Cotswold villages such as Broadway, Bourton-on-the Water, Upper and Lower Slaughter, Broadwell and Chipping Campden. Blenheim Palace, Berkeley Castle, the Cotswold Wildlife Park, Oxford, Cheltenham, and Gloucester are within easy reach. **Directions: From the A40, exit to Burford and take the A424 to Stow-on-the Wold. Then join the A436 towards Chipping Norton. Upper Oddington is on the right 2¹/₂ miles east of Stow-on-the-Wold.**

THE KINGS HEAD INN & RESTAURANT

THE GREEN, BLEDINGTON, NR KINGHAM, OXFORDSHIRE OX7 6XQ
TEL: 01608 658365 FAX: 01608 658902

OWNERS: Michael and Annette Royce
CHEFS: Stephen Coots-Williams and Stephen Jones

S: £40–£45
D: £60-£75

Inn: The award-winning Kings Head Inn and Restaurant is peacefully located beside a traditional village green, complete with a babbling brook inhabited by friendly ducks. During the summer months Morris dancers and musicians can regularly be seen in action on the green performing the Bledington Dances. The building has always served as a hostelry and much of its medieval character remains. With its exposed stone walls, original beams, inglenook fireplace and old settles, the Kings Head fulfils everyone's anticipations of a traditional English inn. The attractive timbered bedrooms, are well furnished to complement the full facilities. **Restaurant:** Activities in the kitchen are supervised by Annette Royce, who has earned the reputation for superbly prepared English and Continental dishes with the 'personal' touch. The carefully compiled à la carte menu is changed daily and is backed up by a selection of fine wines. Excellent inventive bar food is served at lunchtimes and in the evenings together with a changing selection of real ales. **Nearby:** The Kings Head Inn is situated in the heart of the Cotswolds, within easy reach of Oxford, Stratford-upon-Avon, Cheltenham and Blenheim. **Directions: Take the A44 Oxford– Woodstock road to Chipping Norton, then the B4450 to Bledington; or take the Oxford–Burford road to Stow-on-the-Wold and join the B4450. Nearest motorway M40 junction 11.**

THE ROYALIST HOTEL

DIGBETH STREET, STOW-ON-THE-WOLD, GLOUCESTERSHIRE GL54 1BN
TEL: 01451 830670 FAX: 01451 870048

OWNERS: Graham and Marie-France Clark

12 rms   12 ens

S: £45–£55
D: £60–£85

Inn: Reputed to be the oldest building in Stow-on-the-Wold, The Royalist Hotel, Grade II* listed, constructed in AD 947, is also credited in the Guinness Book of Records as being the Oldest Inn in England. The original oak framework is still there behind the 17th-century Jacobean façade (carbon-dating testing has established the timbers to be over 1,000 years old) and the 'houris' frieze from Crusading times is one of only two left in the UK. Within this venerable exterior, modern comforts have been judiciously introduced. The hotel is family run and service is friendly and helpful. It is excellent value for money. Bedrooms are spotless, comfortable and centrally heated. The restaurant and bar have log fires in winter and are open all day, offering snacks and Buffet (£7.95) at lunch time, and an à la carte menu with an emphasis on fresh seafood and local farm produce in the evening. Classic ales and wine list to match. **Nearby:** the Cotswolds countryside offers year-round opportunities for walking and hiking. Also visit Blenheim Palace, Woodstock, Bourton-on-the-Water, Cirencester and Sudeley and Warwick Castles. **Directions: Stow-on-the-Wold is where the A436, A429 and A424 all intersect. Approaching from Chipping Norton on the A436, The Royalist is on the right in the village centre.**

In association
with MasterCard

THE COACH HOUSE HOTEL AND CELLAR RESTAURANT

16/17 WARWICK ROAD, STRATFORD-UPON-AVON, WARWICKSHIRE CV37 6YW
TEL: 01789 204109/299468 FAX:01789 415916 E-MAIL: kiwiavon@aol.com.uk

OWNERS: Geoff and Judy Harden
MANAGER: Rosemarie Moss

22 rms | 21 ens

S: £50–£55
D: £68–£75
Suite: £85–£98

Inn: For lovers of Shakespeare country the Coach House Hotel is an ideal base from which to explore the Bard's birthplace and the beautiful surrounding countryside. Consisting of two splendid adjacent buildings, one Georgian style dated 1843 and the other Victorian dating from 1857, the Coach House is just a five minutes walk from Stratford town centre and seven minutes from the Royal Shakespeare Theatre. Family owned and run it has a relaxed, friendly atmosphere. Careful thought and attention have been invested in the decor and furnishings of all the rooms. Guests may stay in a beautiful Victorian suite, a luxury Regency four-poster room with whirlpool bath, or one of the well appointed single, double or family rooms situated either on ground or first floor level. All have a good range of facilities. Close by the hotel there is a sports and leisure centre of which guests have free use. Golf enthusiasts have the choice of four local courses. Special breaks are available throughout the year. **Restaurant:** The Chef creates superb Continental and English dishes to tempt even the most jaded palate in the intimate Cellar Restaurant beneath the Victorian building. There are two dining areas and a cosy bar. **Nearby:** The Royal Shakespeare Theatre and the delights of Stratford-upon-Avon, Warwick Castle, Ragley Hall, Blenheim Palace and the Cotswolds. **Directions: Five miles from exit 15 of the M40, on A439.**

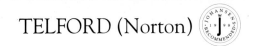
THE HUNDRED HOUSE HOTEL

BRIDGNORTH ROAD, NORTON, NR SHIFNAL, TELFORD, SHROPSHIRE TF11 9EE
TEL: 01952 730353 FAX: 01952 730355

OWNERS: The Phillips family

S: £65
D: £79–£100

Inn: Character, charm and a warm, friendly atmosphere are guaranteed at this family-run, award-winning inn, situated only 45 minutes' drive from Birmingham International Airport. The bedrooms are attractively furnished with antiques and feature country-style patchwork bed linen and drapes; all guest rooms are fully equipped. There are pretty gardens with a pond, gazebo and herb garden. A special tariff is offered for mid-week and weekend breaks and extra accommodation is available in two cottages in the Ironbridge Gorge. **Restaurant:** The inn enjoys a growing reputation for its varied, interesting à la carte and table d'hôte menus. Home-made English fare such as steak pies and game is offered alongside continental dishes, and sweets range from delicate sorbets to traditional favourites like treacle tart. Bar meals are served daily, alongside a number of real ales. Early booking is recommended as the restaurant is very popular locally. **Nearby:** Severn Valley Railway, Midland Motor Museum, Weston Park, Ironbridge Gorge and Telford are within easy reach. Shifnal's cottages inspired Charles Dickens's *Old Curiosity Shop*. **Directions: Norton is on the A442 Bridgnorth–Telford road.**

THELBRIDGE CROSS INN

THELBRIDGE, NR WITHERIDGE, DEVON EX17 4SQ
TEL: 01884 860316 FAX: 01884 861318

OWNERS: Bill and Ria Ball
CHEF: Ria Ball

S: £35
D: £50–£70

Inn: An attractive, picturesque family run, country inn situated in glorious mid-Devon. Built of stone and cob with oak beams and log fires it is the perfect base for exploring the Devonshire countryside. Exmoor and Dartmoor are only a short drive away. For those of you who are unashamedly romantic, this inn will definitely appeal. Legend relates it that Lorna Doone passed through Thelbridge in her carriage after being shipwrecked at Porlock. As a former coaching inn, it still fulfils that role today, for it is the only inn left where the original Lorna Doone stage coach still calls, with passengers who stop off to savour Ria's outstanding cuisine. The accommodation is in eight en suite bedrooms all of which are extremely clean and comfortable. The inn boasts wonderful views over both Exmoor and Dartmoor, and for walkers is only a short distance away from the famous Two Moors Way. **Restaurant:** First-time diners soon recognise the reason for the restaurant's popularity, and why it is recommended by Egon Ronay. **Nearby:** From the front of the inn there are views towards Dartmoor while from the rear Exmoor can be seen in the distance. Many outdoor activities can be arranged locally. **Directions: Thelbridge Cross Inn is two miles west of Witheridge on the B3042, reached from M5 junction 27 via A361 and B3137.**

THE LIFEBOAT INN

SHIP LANE, THORNHAM, NORFOLK PE36 6LT
TEL: 01485 512236 FAX: 01485 512323

OWNERS: Charles and Angie Coker
CHEF: Martin Bosco Kelly

 S: £40–£55
D: £60–£70

Inn: The Lifeboat Inn has been a welcome sight for travellers for centuries, offering roaring open fires on a frosty night, real ales and hearty meals. The summer brings its own charm with scenic views over open meadows to the harbour and rolling white horses breaking on Thornham's sandy beach. The original character of this former 16th century smugglers' ale house has been sympathetically restored and modernised. Sitting in the cosy Smugglers' Bar under the warm glow of the hanging paraffin lamps it is easy to drift back through the years. The old English game of "Pennies" is still played here regularly. A vine-hung conservatory backs onto a delightful walled patio garden which is a perfect sun trap. All bedrooms are en suite and have tea and coffee-making facilities, television, telephone and hairdryer. Most of them have sea views. **Restaurant:** Chef Martin Bosco Kelly offers a splendid choice of traditional country dishes using local produce, game, fish and meat. The bar menu is enhanced by daily specials to bring the best from each catch or shoot. **Nearby:** Several stately homes are in the area, including Holkham Hall, Sandringham House and Nelson's birthplace at Burnham Thorpe. There are six nature reserves, beach, clifftop and woodland walks, excellent sailing and windsurfing. Golf enthusiasts have the choice of five courses. **Directions: Thornham is approximately four miles north east of Hunstanton on the A149 coast road to Wells-next-the-Sea.**

GREEN FARM RESTAURANT AND HOTEL

NORTH WALSHAM ROAD, THORPE MARKET, NORFOLK NR11 8TH
TEL: 01263 833602 FAX: 01263 833163

OWNERS: Philip and Dee Dee Lomax

S: £52.50–£55
D: £60–£85

Inn: Green Farm is a delightful 16th Century Farmhouse Inn. A warm, friendly welcome awaits all guests be it business or pleasure from proprietors Philip and Dee Dee Lomax and their staff. All rooms are fully en suite with television, tea and coffee facilities, fresh fruit, flowers and homemade chocolates. Some of the rooms are on ground floor level and are ideal for elderly and less able bodied guests. **Restaurant:** The Restaurant and Bar are open 7 days a week and the Chef-patron has built up an excellent reputation for the food which is all home made, and uses local produce such as Cromer Crab, SHellfish, Sea Trout, and Holkham Vension when in season, many of the dishes are unique to Green Farm; subtle variations on well loved themes. Try the brie wrapped in filo pastry, served with apple and peppercorn sauce, the Norfolk Duckling with Rhubarb Compote followed by the Pillow of Pear on a Raspberry Coulis. The terraced Marquee offers an ideal location for a wedding or family function. Midweek and weekend breaks are available and special rates for Winter House parties available on request. **Nearby:** Green Farm is an excellent base for the Coast, Broads National Trust Properties and Historical Norwich. Ideal for those interested in Walking, Cycling, Golfing and Birdwatching. **Directions: On the A149 four miles from Cromer and from North Walsham.**

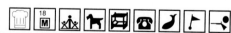

TINTAGEL (Trebarwith Strand)

THE PORT WILLIAM

TREBARWITH STRAND, NR TINTAGEL, CORNWALL PL34 OHB
TEL: 01840 770230 FAX: 01840 770936 E-MAIL: phale@william.2ynet.co.uk

OWNER: Peter Hale
CHEF: Brian Corrigan

S: £35–£47
D: £50–£77

Inn: The Port William is a delightful old inn, situated just 50 yards from the sea on the beautiful and unspoilt North Cornwall coast. The small but charming bedrooms have recently been refurbished and offer every modern amenity, including baths with showers, colour TVs, hair dryers and hospitality trays. Each bedroom is positioned so that guests can enjoy spectacular views during the day and dramatic sunsets over the sea in the evening. Well behaved children and dogs are welcome! All the bedrooms are non-smoking. **Restaurant:** The Inn enjoys an excellent local reputation for the quality of its food. An extensive breakfast menu offers a choice including smoked haddock, Cornish kippers or traditional fare. Lunches and dinners are prepared using only the freshest produce, with home-cooked dishes and a range of superb fish courses and seafood among the specialities. A good selection of vegetarian food is always available. Service is friendly and informal. In addition to a wide selection of standard brands of beer, local Cornish ales are also available. In this area, noted for its outstanding natural beauty, there is no shortage of leisure activities. Apart from magnificent walks, there are plenty of opportunities for surfing, sea-fishing and golf. **Nearby:** Tintagel Castle, King Arthur's Great Halls and a host of National Trust properties. **Directions: Follow the B3263 from Camelford to Tintagel, then continue south to Trebarwith via Treknow.**

THE OLD CHURCH HOUSE INN

TORBRYAN, IPPLEPEN, SOUTH DEVON TQ12 5UR
TEL: 01803 812372 FAX: 01803 812180

OWNERS: Eric and Christine Pimm
CHEF: Peter Blythe

 12 rms 12 ens

 S: £45-£55
D: £65-£75

Inn: This is one of England's most famous and beautifully preserved old inns, as welcoming today as it was in Tudor times when the future King Henry VIII and his father, Henry VII, refreshed themselves within its thick stone walls while travelling on the main Exeter to Plymouth road. Family run and with every modern comfort, The Old Church House has immense character and retains its charming, 13th century atmosphere with great inglenook fireplaces, mellowed panelling and massive low beamed ceilings from which hang Elizabethan bowling pins. All ten bedrooms have full en suite facilities and the owners have worked hard to ensure that these and the public rooms are restful and extremely comfortable. **Restaurant:** An impressive à la carte menu and blackboard specialities, with the emphasis on fresh local produce, is offered in the inn's acclaimed old world restaurant and in the intriguing atmosphere of several other dining rooms and bar lounges. **Nearby:** Dartmoor is excellent for walking, fishing and pony-trekking. Local attractions include Buckfast Abbey, Dartington Hall and the Dart Valley Railway. Torquay and Paignton are within easy reach. **Directions: From Exeter take the A380 to Newton Abbot and then the A 381 towards Totnes. After five miles turn right into Ipplepen and follow the sign to Torbryan.**

The Barn Owl Inn

ALLER MILLS, KINGSKERSWELL, TORQUAY, DEVON TQ12 5AN
TEL: 01803 872130 FAX: 01803 875279

OWNERS: Derek and Margaret Warner
CHEF: Denis Le Jette

5 rms | 5 ens

S: £49.50
D: £65–£80

Inn: The Barn Owl Inn has been converted from a farmhouse into a very good value inn. Although the building dates back to the 16th century, it has modern facilities and services, while retaining many original features, including inglenook fireplaces, an ornate plaster ceiling in the largest bar and a sizeable black-leaded range. Hand-crafted furniture can be found in the cottage-style bedrooms, where there are complimentary bottles of spring water and baskets of fruit. **Restaurant:** The restaurant reflects the talents and eagle eye of French chef, Denis Le Jette. Selecting ones meal from the fascinating menu is a challenge, and the excellent but modestly priced wine list complements the superb dishes. Service is immaculate and the ambience is perfect. There is also a very good bar that serves real ale and excellent food. **Nearby:** Torquay is a holiday town par excellence, and the neighbouring seaside towns of Paignton and Brixham are in easy reach. Local places of interest include Compton Castle, once the home of Sir Walter Raleigh, Dartmoor and the underground caves in Kent's Cavern. Tennis and riding can be enjoyed locally. **Directions: Take the M5 to Exeter, then follow the A380 signposted Torquay. Drive one mile past the Penn Inn traffic lights, and the inn is on the right, signposted Aller Mills.**

THE SEA TROUT INN

STAVERTON, NR TOTNES, DEVON TQ9 6PA
TEL: 01803 762274 FAX: 01803 762506

OWNERS: Andrew and Pym Mogford
CHEF: John Hughes

S: £42.50–£4
D: £58–£68

Inn: Runner-up for Johansens Most Excellent Service Award 1996, The Sea Trout Inn dates from the 15th century. It was named by a previous landlord who caught such a fish in the nearby River Dart. Several specimens of the prize fish now adorn the inn in showcases. The two bars retain much of their period charm, with uneven floors, exposed oak beams, brass fittings and log fires. The bedrooms are decorated in an attractive cottage style, while the public rooms are cosy and inviting. Angling permits for trout, sea trout and salmon are available and the inn offers special fishing breaks with tuition. Andrew and Pym Mogford now also own the nearby Malsters Arms, Tuckenhay, formerly Floyds Inn and can offer three further sumptuous bedrooms overlooking Bow Creek on the River Dart. **Restaurant:** The inn's restaurant is highly acclaimed locally and has been mentioned in several guides. Chef John Hughes finely balanced menus are based on the best seasonal produce from local suppliers. Both table d'hôte (£18.50 for three courses including coffee) and à la carte menus are available. **Nearby:** Dartmoor is excellent for walking, fishing and pony-trekking. Local attractions include the Devon coast, the Dart Valley Railway, Buckfast Abbey and Dartington Hall. **Directions: Turn off the A38 on to the A384 at Buckfastleigh (Dartbridge) and follow the signs to Staverton.**

The Mortal Man Hotel

TROUTBECK, NR WINDERMERE, CUMBRIA LA23 1PL
TEL: 015394 33193 FAX: 015394 31261

OWNERS: Christopher and Annette Poulsom
CHEF: Frank Nash

S: £49–£65
D: £98–£125
(including dinner)

Inn: Few country inns can match the spectacular Lakeland position of this 300-year-old hostelry. Lake Windermere is in view from the foot of the Troutbeck Valley, while Grasmere – the home of Wordsworth – and Coniston, where Ruskin lived, are just slightly further away. The inn is an ideal retreat, offering old-fashioned, friendly service in highly traditional surroundings. The interiors have an abundance of beautiful oak beams, panelling, open fires and solid furniture. All of the bedrooms have stunning views of the surrounding countryside and are equipped with every convenience, including hairdryers and trouser presses. **Restaurant:** An excellent value, five course table d'hôte menu is presented in the inn's dining room, with its wonderful views of the valley.

The dishes are all freshly prepared, accompanied by a variety of sauces and garnishes. The menu is supported by a well-chosen wine list. Light lunches can be taken in the bar, which has a warm, inviting atmosphere. The hotel is closed from mid-November to mid-February. **Nearby:** The area is a paradise for country lovers, with fells and mountains to explore. Wastwater, overlooked by Scafell and Great Gable, is a short drive away. Guests have complimentary use of a nearby leisure complex, while sailing and pony-trekking facilities are available close by. **Directions: Take the A592 Windermere–Ullswater road. From the roundabout drive for 2½ miles, then turn left to Troutbeck and right at the T-junction. The hotel is on the right.**

THE ROYAL WELLS INN

MOUNT EPHRAIM, TUNBRIDGE WELLS, KENT TN4 8BE
TEL: 01892 511188 FAX: 01892 511908

OWNERS: David and Robert Sloan
CHEF: Robert Sloan

S: £55–£65
D: £75–£100

20 rms   20 ens

Inn: With a commanding position overlooking Tunbridge Wells Common, just a short walk from the town centre, the Royal Wells is a small, bustling family-run hotel. The inn owes its regal name to Queen Victoria, who visited it frequently as a young princess, and it still carries the royal coat of arms today. There are 20 comfortable en suite bedrooms, all centrally heated and with period furniture and four-poster beds. Guests may enjoy afternoon tea or a pre-dinner drink in the main bar, or a bar meal in the Wells Brasserie surrounded by motoring memorabilia – the hotel owns a 1909 Commer bus once owned by Lord Lonsdale, founder of the Automobile Association. **Restaurant:** A meal in the conservatory restaurant, with its intimate lounge bar, is sure to be one of the highlights of a stay at the Royal Wells. The double attraction of fine food served in delightful surroundings makes it a popular eating place. The three-course dinner menu, based on fresh produce, costs £21.50 and there is also a daily fish speciality. The Restaurant is open Tuesday to Saturday evening. **Nearby:** The inn is an ideal base from which to explore the spa town of Tunbridge Wells, as well as the surrounding countryside of Kent, Surrey and Sussex. Chartwell, Hever Castle and the Bluebell Railway are within easy reach. **Directions: The Royal Wells Inn is situated opposite Tunbridge Wells Common on the section of Mount Ephraim that bypasses the junction of the A26 and the A264.**

For hotel location, see maps on pages 183-189

THE WHITE LION HOTEL

HIGH STREET, UPTON-UPON-SEVERN, NR MALVERN, WORCESTERSHIRE WR8 0HJ
TEL: 01684 592551 FAX: 01684 593333

OWNERS: Jon and Chris Lear

10 rms   10 ens

S: £49.50
D: £67.75

Inn: Henry Fielding wrote part of his novel "The History of Tom Jones" way back in 1749 where he descibed the Hotel as "the fairest Inn on the street" and "a house of exceedingly good repute". The new owners Jon & Chris Lear have committed themselves to upholding this tradition with good old fashioned hospitality along with examples of the finest cuisine in the area cooked for the popular Pepperpot Brasserie. Using only the finest ingredients to produce an interesting menu with flair and imagination, to complement the food Jon and his team make a varied selection of homemade breads that are becoming a source of conversation with the local clientele. A lunch time menu with bar meals can also be enjoyed in the comfortable lounge or bar. All ten bedrooms are for varying periods dating from 1510, the Rose Room and the Wild Goose Room at the White Lion are named in Fielding book. **Nearby:** The White Lion is central for visiting The Malvern Hills, The Three Counties Show Ground, the market town of Ledbury, Tewksburys Norman Abbey, Worcester, Cheltenham and Gloucester. The Cotswolds, Black mountains abnd Shakespears Stratford-Upon-Avon are all within an easy drive from this popular town. **Directions: From M5 junction 8 follow the M50. Exit at junction 1 on to the A38 north. After three miles turn left on to the A4104. Go over the bridge, turn left, then right. The car park is at the rear of the hotel.**

Ye Olde Salutation Inn

MARKET PITCH, WEOBLEY, HEREFORDSHIRE HR4 8SJ
TEL: 01544 318443 FAX: 01544 318216

OWNERS: Chris and Frances Anthony
CHEFS: Graham Leavesley and Frances Anthony

6 rms 6 ens

S: £37–£40
D: £60–£85

Inn: This black and white timbered inn, an inspired conversion of an ale and cider house and a cottage, over 500 years old, is in the centre of Weobley village. The spire of the 900 year old church is a landmark in the green Herefordshire countryside, as yet undiscovered by tourists. The bedrooms are so individual, with delightful chinzes or patchwork quilts, that returning guests demand their favourite, perhaps one with traditional brass bedsteads or a four-poster. Smoking is not allowed in the bedrooms, but is forgiven in the elegant residents' lounge, with its antiques and big, comfortable furniture. Guests will enjoy the well-equipped fitness room. Two self-catering cottages opposite the inn are alternative accommodation.

Restaurant: A non-smoking room, the Oak Room restaurant plays an important role in the inn and has been awarded 2 AA rosettes. Talented chefs prepare sophisticated and aromatic dishes to order, ensuring they arrive fresh at the table. English with a continental accent describes the menu, which refers to puddings as 'the finishing touch'. There is a very well stocked cellar from which to select fine wines. Informal meals are served in the traditonal bar. **Nearby:** Hereford Cathedral, Hay-on-Wye with its antique books, open air Shakespeare at Ludlow Castle, pony-trekking in the Black Mountains and golf. **Directions: Leave Hereford on the A438 Brecon, taking the A480 signed Weobley/Credenhill.**

WEST WITTON (Wensleydale)

THE WENSLEYDALE HEIFER INN

WEST WITTON, WENSLEYDALE, NORTH YORKSHIRE DL8 4LS
TEL: 01969 622322 FAX: 01969 624183

OWNED & MANAGED BY: John and Anne Sharp
CHEF: Adrian Craig

15 rms   15 ens

S: £54
D: £70–£90

Inn: Few inns can claim such a beautiful setting as that of The Wensleydale Heifer. This typical Dales inn, dating from 1631, is situated in the tranquil village of West Witton, in the heart of Wensleydale and set against the backdrop of the Yorkshire Dales National Park. The oak-beamed rooms are furnished in chintz, with antiques and log fires to retain the ancient charm of the building. The quaint bedrooms are located in the inn itself and across the road in The Old Reading Room – they have all been recently refurbished, upgraded to 4 crowns highly commended standard, and three have ground floor access. There are 3 with four-poster beds. A private room can be hired for small meetings of up to 10 people. **Restaurant:** Both the informal bistro and the beamed restaurant offer rustic country cooking. Extensive menus include fresh fish, shellfish and seafood from the North-East Coast and Scotland. Local produce appears frequently including Dales lamb, beef & game. They also use fresh herbs from their own garden. There is a good selection of wines to accompany your meal. Recent awards include AA Red Rosette, RAC Merit and Les Routiers Casserole Award. **Nearby:** The Heifer is situated in the Yorkshire Dales National Park and offers plenty of opportunities for walking, pony-trekking and other country pursuits. Bolton Castle and the racing stables at Middleham are close by. **Directions:** The Wensleydale Heifer is on the A684 trans-Pennine road between Leyburn and Hawes.

THE INN AT WHITEWELL

FOREST OF BOWLAND, CLITHEROE, LANCASHIRE BB7 3AT
TEL: 01200 448222 FAX: 01200 448298

OWNER: Richard Bowman

S: £50–£62
D: £72–£88
Suite: £105

Inn: An art gallery and wine merchant all share the premises of this friendly, welcoming inn, the earliest parts of which date back to the 14th century. It was at one time inhabited by the Keeper of the 'Forêt' – the Royal hunting ground, and nowadays it is not uncommon for distinguished shooting parties to drop in for lunch. Set within grounds of 3 acres, the inn has a spendid outlook across the dramatically undulating Trough of Bowland. Each bedroom has been attractively furnished with antiques and quality fabrics. All rooms have videos and hi-tech stereo systems. **Restaurant:** The cooking is of a consistently high quality. The à la carte menu features predominately English country recipes such as seasonal roast game with traditional accompaniments: grilled red snapper on a savoury confit, home-made puddings and farmhouse cheeses. Good bar meals and garden lunches are also offered. **Nearby:** 8 miles of water is available to residents only from the banks of the River Hodder, where brown trout, sea trout, salmon and grayling can be caught. Other country sports can be arranged locally. Browsholme Hall and Clitheroe Castle are close by and just across the river there are neolithic cave dwellings. **Directions: From the M6 take junction 32; follow A6 towards Garstang for ¼ mile. Turn right at first traffic lights towards Longridge, then left at roundabout, then follow signs to Whitewell and Trough of Bowland.**

THE OLD SCHOOLHOUSE

SEVERN STOKE, WORCESTER, WORCESTERSHIRE WR8 9JA
TEL: 01905 371368 FAX: 01905 371591

OWNERS: The Old Schoolhouse Hotel Ltd
MANAGER: Richard Wells

13 rms | 13 ens

S: £42.50–£57.50
D: £60–£80

Inn: An old-fashioned welcome awaits guests of the Old Schoolhouse, a delightful hotel overlooking the Severn Valley and offering superb views of the Malvern Hills. The building is an interesting combination of 17th century farmhouse and an old Victorian school, with cosy rooms of all shapes and sizes. The bedrooms are decorated in individual styles, most feature beamed ceilings and all offer a range of modern facilities. **Restaurant:** A hearty appetite is the major requirement for guests sampling the very best of British cooking in the award winning but informal Restaurant. Here many regional specialities are incorporated into the menu and dishes are created using fresh local produce wherever possible. Try the Cajun Tuna, a delicious dish dusted with Cajun species, flash grilled with a panaché of roast peppers, sun-dried tomatoes and chicory dressed with tomato salsa. Alternatively sample one of the tasty vegetarian options, asparagus and broccoli risotto or soy glazed linguini – the chef is always happy to cater for special diets. Lighter lunchtime snacks are served in the Headmaster's Study. **Nearby:** A short drive away are the Cotswolds and the lovely towns of Worcester, Tewkesbury and Cheltenham. The villages of Herefordshire, with their oast houses, hops fields and unusual churches, are also within easy reach. **Directions: The Old Schoolhouse is midway between Junction 7 of the M5 and Junction 1 of the M50 on the A38.**

THE TALBOT HOTEL

KNIGHTWICK, WORCESTERSHIRE WR6 5PH
TEL: 01886 821235 FAX: 01886 821060

OWNERS: The Clift Family
CHEF: Annie Clift

S: £26–£35
D: £45–£62

Inn: The Talbot stands sparkling white and proud in one of England's most beautiful river valleys alongside a narrow, winding road reaching up into a rolling, wooded hillside. Opposite stands a tiny church with a small delicate spire. All around are lush riverside meadows, grazing Hereford cattle, Elizabethan and Georgian farmhouses with hop yards, orchards and cornfields, picturesque villages, peace and tranquillity. Built in the late 14th century, The Talbot's charm and hospitality continues today, combining the atmosphere of the past with every modern day amenity. The bedrooms are furnished to a comfortable standard, two bars serve beer brewed with the hotel's own hops and there are squash courts and a sauna. The Talbot has its own fishing stretch on the River Teme and walking, cycling, riding, golf and clay pigeon shooting are available locally. **Restaurant:** Oak panelled, flower filled, warm and cosy. Chefs Annie and Wizzie Clift serves tasteful cuisine using locally grown organic produce to supplement their own game, garden vegetables and herbs. An extensive blackboard menu is available in the beamed lounge bar. **Nearby:** The ancient city of Worcester, with its magnificent cathedral and Dyson Perrins Museum, with one of the world's finest collections of Worcestershire porcelain and bone china, and Elgar's birthplace. **Directions: From the M5, exit at junction 7 and take A4044 Worcester by-pass to A44 Worcester to Bromyard road. The Talbot is on B4197 towards Martley.**

THE OLD TOLLGATE RESTAURANT AND HOTEL

THE STREET, BRAMBER, STEYNING, WEST SUSSEX BN44 3WE
TEL: 01903 879494 FAX: 01903 813399

OWNER: The Old Tollgate Restaurant Ltd
MANAGING DIRECTOR: Peter Sargent
RESTAURANT DIRECTOR: Andrew McNie CHEF DIRECTOR: Peter Arthur

S: £61
D: £61–£83
Suite: £83

Inn: An original Tollhouse centuries ago, travellers now look forward to stopping here and paying their dues for wonderful hospitality. Part of the old building is still in evidence with newer additions attractively blending. There are some splendid suites, even a four-poster, which are excellent value and delightful bedrooms, some of which are reached across the courtyard. The hotel is a popular meeting place for visitors and locals alike, with friendly staff adding to the welcoming ambience. **Restaurant:** The restaurant has built up a fine reputation, extending far beyond Sussex. It has a magnificent award winning carvery and sumptuous cold table. Breakfast, lunch and dinner are all catered for at various price structures according to the number of courses consumed. Soups and broths, fresh and smoked fish, roasts and casseroles, pies and puddings, and vegetarian dishes are in abundance. **Nearby:** Bramber is famous for its Norman Castle and spectacular views over the South Downs. Brighton, with its shops, beach and Pavilion is an easy drive away, as is Worthing. Sporting activities nearby include riding, golf and fishing. **Directions: Bramber is off the A283 between Brighton and Worthing, easily accessed from the A24 or A27.**

THE BARTON ANGLER COUNTRY INN

IRSTEAD ROAD, NEATISHEAD, NR WROXHAM, NORFOLK NR12 8XP
TEL: 01692 630740 FAX: 01692 631122

OWNER: King County Hotels Ltd
MANAGER: John King
CHEF: Jenwyn King MHCIMA

S: £35
D: £58–£80

Inn: While learning to sail on the Norfolk Broads, the young Lord Nelson stayed at this unspoiled hostelry that dates back some 450 years. Set in large gardens, it previously catered exclusively for fishing clubs; but now provides excellent accommodation for anyone wishing to explore North Norfolk. The individually styled bedrooms are pleasantly furnished and some have fine locally crafted four-poster beds. Open fires, exposed beams and antiques feature in the reception rooms all add to the interesting character of this attractive building. Special week or weekend breaks are available during winter months. **Restaurant:** The kitchens are under the supervision of the chef, Jenwyn, and all meals are prepared in the hotel. Bar meals are provided on a first come first served basis. In the Restaurant tables can be reserved – at popular times of the year it is essential to book in advance. Barbecues are a regular summer event on Saturday evenings. **Nearby:** Owned by English Heritage, Barton Broads, which is now within Broadlands National Park, offers plenty of opportunities for birdwatching, fishing, sailing and cruising. Boats can be hired for guests. The coast and many historic churches and houses are nearby. **Directions: A1151 north from Norwich, turn right one mile beyond Wroxham. The inn lies midway between the villages of Neatishead and Irstead.**

THE ROYAL OAK HOTEL

YATTENDON, NEWBURY, BERKSHIRE RG18 0UG
TEL: 01635 201325 FAX: 01635 201926

OWNER: Regal Hotels
MANAGERS: Robbie and Corinne Macrae
CHEF: Robbie Macrae

S: from £75
D: from £90

Inn: The Royal Oak's team of friendly, courteous staff make sure that guests at this lovely old inn are warmly welcomed. Imbued with history, the inn played host to Oliver Cromwell and his generals. There are five elegant bedrooms overlooking the tranquil walled garden or the historic village square. A delightful lounge offers country house comfort, whilst the intimate bar still offers locally brewed real ale. A private room is available for meetings, business lunches and dinner parties and looks onto the walled garden – a picture in itself and ideal for dining on a balmy summer's day. **Restaurants:** (two) Chef Robbie Macrae prepares menus reflecting traditional English, country and mediterranean French cuisine, served in the

AA 3 rosette restaurant or the less formal bar. All dishes cooked to order may include quail paté with foie gras and a sloe gin preserve or pavé of halibut en papillote. Two courses cost from £19.50. **Nearby:** Basildon Park, Reading, racing at Newbury and boat trips on the River Thames. **Directions: From the west, leave the M4 at junction 13 turning up the A34 (north) and take the exit to Hermitage after 300 yds. At the T junction, turn left and then right by the Fox Inn for Yattendon. From the east: leave M4 at junction 12 and head for Theale. Continue towards Pangbourne taking first left, signed Bradfield/Yattendon. Follow road into Yattendon village square where hotel is situated.**

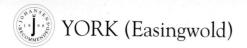

THE GEORGE AT EASINGWOLD

MARKET PLACE, EASINGWOLD, YORK, NORTH YORKSHIRE YO6 3AD
TEL: 01347 821698 FAX: 01347 823448

OWNERS: Steve and Jan Lawrence
CHEFS: Keith Johnson and Bill Murray

15 rms | 15 ens

S: £38–£48
D: £53–£68

Inn: The George at Easingwold is an 18th century coaching inn standing in the old cobbled square of the pretty Georgian market town of Easingwold. Open fires, a wealth of beams and horse brasses all add to its character and cosy atmosphere. The bedrooms vary in style – some are traditionally furnished while others are more modern – but all have a high level of comfort in common. A large inter-connected bar serves a fine selection of real cask ales, including locally brewed beers pulled straight from the cask, and coffee is provided in the relaxing atmosphere of the lounge. **Restaurant:** The inn's original open courtyard is now an attractive candlelit area where a wide selection of freshly prepared bar meals are served. The 'chef's specials' board changes daily. A choice of à la carte or table d'hôte menus is provided in the cosy oak-beamed lamplit restaurant which overlooks the market square, while on Sundays a traditional two or three course Sunday lunch is offered. **Nearby:** The historic city of York is just 10 miles away and Castle Howard and the Howardian hills are also close-by. The George is an ideal base for touring the North York Moors and the National Park. **Directions:** The George is in the centre of the town of Easingwold which is off the A19 midway between York and Thirsk.

THE JEFFERSON ARMS

MAIN STREET, THORGANBY, NR YORK, NORTH YORKSHIRE YO4 6DB
TEL: 01904 448316 FAX: 01904 448837

OWNERS: Tom and Helen Murphy
CHEF: John Blackburn

4 rms | 4 ens

S: £35–£40
D: £55–£60
Suite: £75

Inn: Character, charm and a warm, friendly welcome are guaranteed at this delightful 17th century inn which stands in the pretty little village of Thorganby, just a 15 minutes drive from the medieval delights and splendour of York. Tom and Helen Murphy have totally refurbished the inn since taking over ownership in 1996 without sacrificing any of its traditional virtues and atmosphere. The bedrooms all have en suite shower rooms, have full facilities including colour television and tea and coffee making facilities and enjoy splendid views over the surrounding countryside. Two of the bedrooms are in the inn itself, one is in a former hayloft and a gamekeeper's cottage has been redesigned into a delightful suite. Guests can enjoy drinks and snacks before open fires in an attractive bar and there are two relaxing conservatories hung with grape vines. **Restaurant:** An oak beamed ceiling and superb inglenook fireplace add to the old world atmosphere of the candle-lit dining room where chef John Blackburn presents varied and innovative menus complemented by an extensive wine list and cask-conditioned ales. **Nearby:** York with its Minster, cobbled streets and excellent shopping, Castle Howard, Fountains Abbey and the scenic North Yorkshire Moors. **Directions: From York take A19 south towards Selby. Turn left at Crockley Hill and drive through Wheldrake. Thorganby is the next village.**

SPECIAL SUBSCRIPTION OFFER
TO READERS OF...

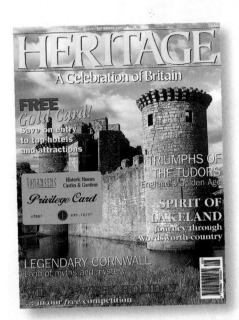

JOHANSENS
GUIDES

SAVE UP TO 15%

Two glorious colour magazines for everyone who enjoys the beauty of Britain

HERITAGE MAGAZINE is a glorious celebration of Britain – her history and traditions, cottages and gardens, castles and cathedrals, crafts and countryside.

Each issue takes you on a fascinating journey of discovery in spectacular colour photographs and captivating text.

Over 60,000 subscribers worldwide.

THE ENGLISH GARDEN is a beautiful new magazine that bursts with pictures of glorious gardens, along with sensible planting tips, plant profiles and imaginative design advice.

Whether you are seeking inspiration for your own garden, or simply wish to share our delight in others, you will be enchanted by THE ENGLISH GARDEN

JOHANSEN'S readers can save up to 15% off the regular 6-issue subscription price of HERITAGE and THE ENGLISH GARDEN

HERITAGE	THE ENGLISH GARDEN
UK £19.70 (usually £23.70)	UK £15.75 (usually £17.50)
Europe £22.70 (usually £26.70)	Europe £17.75 (usually £20.50)
Rest of World £25.70 (usually £29.70)	Rest of World £20.50 (usually £23.50)

TO PAY: Send a cheque payable to Romsey Publishing Co. or your Visa/Mastercard details to: Dept J, Romsey Publishing Co., Tower House, Sovereign Park, Market Harborough, Leicestershire, England LE16 9EF or phone 01858 435308.

US readers may order a 6-issue subscription, price $24.95, direct from The British Connection Inc, PO Box 215, Landisburg, PA 17040-0215 or call 1-800-998-0807 (toll free).

Snowdonia,
Nant Gwynant

Johansens Recommended Inns with Restaurants in
Wales

Magnificent scenery, a rich variety of natural, cultural and modern leisure attractions, and the very best accommodation awaits the Johansens visitor to Wales.

Wales, like Caesar's Gaul, can be divided into three parts – South Wales, Mid Wales and North Wales. These parts are determined by physical geography, mountain groups which break up the country east-west and are fissured by narrow valleys. These lock a large part of the population into small settlements – not dissimilar from those others built around markets and staging posts along the drovers routes – fostering a strong sense of community. The Celtic folk that the Romans encountered were a civilised and artistic people whose sense of design and skills in oratory were greatly admired. These Celtic origins are still apparent today in the language that is spoken by 250,000 – understood by many more – and to be seen everywhere in Wales.

South Wales' industrial past is now enshrined in museums – like Big Pit, the Rhondda Heritage Park and the Industrial and Maritime Museum in Cardiff Bay. For the industrial valleys have been greened again and now house commuter villages for people who work in the new high-tech and service industries along the M4 and the Heads of the Valleys Roads. The old ports that declined with coal and steel are being revived as marinas, with an imaginative mix of commercial and social development.

Nowhere is this more so than in Cardiff Bay,

the former dockland of the capital city. Here a modern maritime city is being catered to compare with any in the world – the centre piece of which is a barrage from Queen Alexandra Dock to Penarth. But the city already has so much to commend it – more parkland per head of population than any other city in the UK and a graceful civic centre modelled on Lutyens' plans for New Delhi.

Swansea is a modern city which over the last 25 years has regenerated a lunar landscape left by 200 years of metal processing in the Lower Swansea Valley into a great green lung in which are set a mixture of commercial and leisure developments. It has also created an attractive marina from its disused dockland. And on its western door-step it has an Area of Outstanding Natural Beauty, the Gower Peninsula.

Carmarthen and Pembrokeshire have lovely beaches, cosy coves, lush pastures and plump hills into which are set golf courses to please the eye and to challenge the handicap. The area boasts fantastic fishing, wonderful walks and watersports galore – and two fantastic parks at Pembrey and Oakwood offering a wide range of attractions and amusements.

Mid Wales is a marvellous land beyond

those blue remembered hills – a rolling, round green country with a silver filigree of rivers and lakes. Buttressed to the north by Cader Idris and to the south by the Brecon Beacons, this lovely hilly region is threaded by rivers and streams and old drovers roads that simply invite exploration – whether on foot, horseback or mountain bike. The land looks and leans towards the west, to the 75 miles long crescent of Cardigan Bay with its magnificent Heritage Coast studded with small ports.

North Wales has mountains offering bracing walks or pre-Everest training, a coast that holds charms for the sailor, the water-sports enthusiast or the sunbather. It has rivers, lakes and forest in which walkers, anglers, mountain-bikers and wild water canoeists can lose themselves and each other. It has castles galore – fine examples built by Welsh lords and by Edward I.

But Wales' greatest asset is its people and the welcome they give the friendly visitor – Croeso I Cymru, Welcome to Wales.

For more information about Wales, please contact:–

Wales Tourist Board
Brunel House
2 Fitzalan Road
Cardiff
Wales CF2 1UY
Tel: 01222 475226

THE CASTLE VIEW HOTEL

16 BRIDGE STREET, CHEPSTOW, GWENT NP6 5EZ
TEL: 01291 620349 FAX: 01291 627397

OWNERS: Martin and Vicky Cardale

12 rms	11 ens

   S: £40–£45
D: £60–£70

Inn: This historic 17th century, ivy-clad hotel is set in a prime location opposite Britain's oldest stone castle, begun in the reign of William the Conqueror. It is a friendly, family-owned hostelry, which offers good value accommodation, with Sky T.V. and all the usual modern comforts, in rooms which still have many original features. There is a hand-turned oak staircase leading to comfortable bedrooms. Some of these have 200-year-old wall paintings and many have views of the castle. There is also a secluded garden which is ablaze with colour during the summer. **Restaurant:** The Kitchen is Egon Ronay and Les Routiers Commended and serves imaginative home-cooked meals. Wye salmon and Welsh lamb often appear on the seasonally changing menu, which always offers fresh vegetables, plus many delicious home-made puddings. There is also an interesting range of bar snacks, real ales, a varied wine list and a few good malts. **Nearby:** Chepstow is on the edge of the Wye Valley and Forest of Dean. It is well situated for international rugby in Cardiff, racing at Chepstow, golf at St Pierre and visits to Tintern Abbey. **Directions: Leave M4 at junction 22, signed to Chepstow, then follow signs to the castle.**

LLANARMON DYFFRYN CEIRIOG

THE WEST ARMS HOTEL

LLANARMON DC, NR LLANGOLLEN, CLWYD LL20 7LD
TEL: 01691 600665 FAX: 01691 600622

OWNERS: Rob and Margaret Evans

S: £40 (inc. dinner £55)
D: £70 (inc. dinner £100)
Suite: £80 (inc. dinner £110)

Inn: Originally a 16th century farmhouse, this charming old inn offers good value for money and unpretentious, warm-hearted hospitality. The old character of the building is evident throughout, with log fires, inglenooks, beams and stone floors. The cosy lounges are furnished with chintz-covered sofas and armchairs. All of the bedrooms are furnished to a high standard to provide the utmost comfort. With formal rose gardens and lawns running down to the river, this really is an idyllic setting for a relaxing break. Dogs can be accommodated by prior arrangement. **Restaurant:** The cooking here is of high quality: all of the Welsh, English and continental dishes are carefully prepared with the emphasis on taste and presentation. Specialities include Ceiriog trout and salmon and the menu presents a choice of delicious puddings. To complement your meal, which is served in the beamed dining room, there is a well chosen list of interesting wines. **Nearby:** The inn can offer its residents free private fishing. The unspoiled hills and valleys of the surrounding countryside give plenty of opportunities for walking and pony-trekking. Among the many local attractions are Chirk Castle, the house of the 'Ladies of Llangollen', Erddig Hall and the Roman city of Chester. **Directions: Tale the A5 to Chirk. From Chirk take the B4500 for 11 miles to Llanarmon DC. Once over the bridge, the inn is situated on the right.**

In association with MasterCard

THE PLOUGH INN

RHOSMAEN, LLANDEILO, CARMARTHENSHIRE SA19 6NP
TEL: 01558 823431 FAX: 01558 823969

OWNERS: Giulio and Diane Rocca

12 rms / 12 ens

S: £45
D: £60

Inn: Originally a farmhouse, The Plough Inn has been elegantly converted and extended to provide good food and accommodation in the rural market town of Llandeilo. In the older part of the building guests will find a public bar, adjoining which is the cosy and intimate Towy Lounge. The 12 en suite bedrooms enjoy glorious views over surrounding countryside and are all well appointed for your comfort. A gym and sauna provide an added dimension to your stay – why not start the day with an invigorating work-out in the gym or unwind in the sauna before a comfortable night's sleep? A conference suite can cater for business meetings: a comprehensive range of audio-visual aids is available for hire. Closed Christmas.

Restaurant: Guests may dine in style and comfort in the à la carte restaurant. Local salmon and sewin, venison, Welsh lamb and beef, cooked simply or in continental recipes, all feature on the menus. An extensive choice of hot and cold bar meals can be enjoyed in the Towy Lounge. One of the inn's specialities is its tradition for Welsh afternoon teas. These are served in the elegant, chandeliered Penlan Lounge. **Nearby:** The Plough Inn is an ideal point of departure for touring the beautiful Towy Valley and surrounding Dinefwr countryside, including the Brecon Beacons National Park. **Directions: A mile from Llandeilo on the A40, towards Llandovery. The inn is 14 miles from exit 49 at the end of the M4.**

YE OLDE ANCHOR INN

RHOS STREET, RUTHIN, DENBIGHSHIRE LL15 1DX
TEL: 01824 702813 FAX: 01824 703050 E-MAIL: hotel@anchorinne.demon.co.uk

OWNER: Rod England and Jean Mills

S: £37.50
D: £65

Inn: Ye Olde Anchor Inn dates back to the 18th century, when it was frequented by travellers journeying from Holyhead to Shropshire. It is just as popular today, with its affable host, Rod England who, without changing its character, has introduced the highest standards of hospitalilty, winning many accolades. The Inn is a welcoming building, the facade very attractive with shutters and colourful window boxes. Inside, the ceilings are low with beams, and intriguing memorabilia decorate the walls. The comfortable bedrooms and the family suite – children and (previously declared) dogs are welcome – have harmonious colour schemes, satellite TV and videos. **Restaurant:** The Restaurant is much in demand and it is advisable to book. A pleasant room, it has a sophisticated menu and excellent wine list. Substantial Welsh breakfasts start the day – which may end in the convivial bars, quaffing cask beer! Ruthin is very interesting; it has a fascinating craft centre and the finest medieval house in Wales. Snowdonia is close by and walkers can go into the Clwydian Hills. **Nearby:** There are museums, castles, a steam railway and gardens to visit, good golf courses, the seaside at Llandudno and fine shops in Chester. **Directions: From Shrewsbury A5, at Llangollen take A542 to A525 finding the inn as you enter the town. Parking is available.**

THE LION HOTEL AND RESTAURANT

BERRIEW, NR WELSHPOOL, MONTGOMERYSHIRE SY21 8PQ
TEL: 01686 640452 FAX: 01686 640604

OWNERS: Brian and Jean Thomas
CHEF: Lance Thomas

6 rms | 6 ens

S: £50–£55
D: £80–£90

Inn: Standing next to the church in one of mid-Wales' prettiest villages, The Lion Hotel is a striking 17th century inn, situated on the Shropshire border. A more genuinely friendly welcome than that extended to guests by the Thomas family would be hard to find. The bedrooms, with dark beams, contrasting white walls and lovely views, are all decorated in an attractive cottage style. Real ales and delicious meals are served in the new style bistro. **Restaurant:** Recommended by Taste of Wales, the restaurant has a graceful and intimate atmosphere and offers a good choice of Welsh dishes as well as a selection of English, continental meals and Far Eastern meals. Choices might include marinated shoulder of Welsh lamb, local game, Thai style chicken and fresh fish dishes. **Nearby:** With the Cambrian Mountains, the River Severn and Shropshire so close, guests can enjoy a variety of beautiful landscapes. The Welshpool Museum contains interesting treasures and historical memorabilia. Powys Castle, just a few miles away, is just one of the many castles to visit in the area. There are three golf courses within 10 miles and pony-trekking nearby too. **Directions: Welshpool is 18 miles west of Shrewsbury on A458. Berriew is signposted off A483 five miles south of Welshpool. Welshpool Airport is 4¹/₂ miles to the north.**

164

THE ROYAL OAK HOTEL AND RESTAURANT

WELSHPOOL, MONTGOMERYSHIRE SY21 7DG
TEL:01938 552217 FAX: 01938 556652

OWNER: Margaret Landgrebe
GENERAL MANAGER: Roger Clutterbuck

S: £50
D: £75

Inn: Overlooked by 500-year-old Powis Castle, The Royal Oak stands in the centre of Welshpool, a Georgian border market town surrounded by rolling green countryside dotted with sheep, castles and timber-framed houses. The hotel, which derives its name from the famous oak tree which marked the cross in the centre of town, is one of the oldest coaching inns in Wales and has been part of the history of Montgomeryshire for some 350 years. It was once owned by the Earls of Powis and for the last three decades has been in the hands of the same family. A more genuine friendly welcome than that extended to guests would be hard to find. The bedrooms are all en suite, spacious, tastefully decorated and have a writing desk, colour television, direct dial telephone, hairdryer and tea/coffee facilities. The Royal Oak also has a purpose built and fully equipped conference suite with meeting and banqueting facilities for up to 200 people. Two attractive lounges also cater for small meetings, buffet receptions, lunches and dinners. **Restaurant:** The Acorn Café Bar and Restaurant serve traditional lighter meals throughout the day and offers a full à la carte menu in the evenings. Good food and cask ales can also be enjoyed in the popular Oak bar. **Nearby:** Powis Castle and gardens, the Montgomery Canal, Welshpool and Llanfair Light Railway, Powysland Museum, Offa's Dyke, golf and fishing. **Directions:** Welshpool is 18 miles west of Shrewsbury on the A458.

AGED CIGARS

SMOKING DAMAGES THE HEALTH
OF THOSE AROUND YOU

Chief Medical Officers' Warning

Johansens Recommended Inns with Restaurants in

Scotland

Isle of Skye

Myths and mountains, lochs and legends – Scotland's stunning scenic splendour acts as a magnet for visitors from all over the globe. Superb as it is, Scotland's charismatic charm is more than just visual.

Rich in history and heritage this ancient nation can trace its origins back over 14 centuries when the 'Scots' tribe from Ireland who had carved out their new Kingdom of Dalriada from land held by the Picts in the 5th Century, eventually gave their name to the united nation of Picts and Scots - Scotland.

Prehistoric sites can be found in almost every corner of Scotland, including the outer islands (Orkney has a particularly rich concentration of bronze age ruins), and ancient standing stones have long been a fascination for curious visitors.

Several new archaeological attractions have opened recently, including Kilmartin House in Argyll. Close to Dunadd, the ancient capital of Dalriada, - the birthplace of Scotland, Kilmartin House brings 6000 years of history to life with imaginative audio visual displays, exhibitions and a range of prehistoric artefacts from Argyll, the original 'coastline of the Gael' (Earraghaidheal in Gaelic).

Across the country in Grampian region, Archeolink at Oyne, around 25 miles north of Aberdeen, is a £4 million interpretative centre which looks set to become a major visitor attraction for the north east. Situated in 40 acres around Berry Hill, an iron age enclosure, the Centre applies state-of-the-art technology to Aberdeenshire's wealth of Stone Circles, Symbol Stones and ancient hill forts.

Far from being stuck in the past, Scotland boasts cosmopolitan cities throbbing with life and vitality. Vibrant arts and culture, magnificent architecture, superb shopping and exciting night-life are all there to be enjoyed.

Getting around is easy with a modern transport infrastructure and communications befitting a nation whose sons invented the telephone, television and tarmacadam! Indeed, air, rail and ferry links are on the increase and competitive economy fares have encouraged many new visitors, but don't worry, beyond the city boundaries space, peace and tranquillity are still the order of the day and you don't have to go far off the beaten track to find solitude and wilderness.

The glorious natural environment remains one of Scotland's most attractive features offering endless options for sports, including walking, cycling, sailing, riding and climbing.

The home of golf and the Highland games, Scotland is an outdoor enthusiast's dreamland. But you don't have to be active to appreciate this wealth of natural brilliance.

Travelling by car is simple and enjoyable; and where but Scotland would you find main roads bordering world-famous beauty spots, such as Loch Lomond and Loch Ness?

You can take your car by ferry to most of Scotland's numerous islands and a new Irish ferry service to Campbeltown has opened up the Kintyre Peninsula - an area of outstanding natural beauty.

Kintyre's coastline, characteristically for Scotland's west coast, is riveted with ruined ramparts and crowned with castellations. The stone walls bear witness to Argyll's bloody past, for this area has seen numerous battles, often between rival clans, with a massacre at Dunaverty Castle on a scale more heinous than Glencoe.

For all their feuding, the clans gave Scotland some of its most recognisable icons. Kilts, bagpipes, Highland Games and dancing - all survived and flourished despite the ban imposed following the Jacobite defeat at Culloden in 1746. Scotland's relationship with England these days is more cordial. The historic 'Stone of Destiny' - the stone which pillowed Jacob's head as he dreamed his dream, later became the property of the migrating Celtic tribe who eventually settled in Scotland in AD498 - was stolen from Scone by Edward I of England in 1296.

Seven hundred years later the Government of Great Britain returned this ceremonial seat for the inauguration of Scots' Kings to Scotland and it can now be seen on display in Edinburgh Castle.

The lavish history and heritage of the oldest Kingdom in Europe is matched by its majestic landscapes and superlative scenery. Friendly and welcoming, the Scots are proud of their country and you'll find them eager to share its many delights and attractions.

For more information on Scotland, please contact:-

The Scottish Tourist Board
23 Ravleston Terrace
Edinburgh
EH4 3EU
Tel: 0131 332 2433

POTARCH HOTEL

BY BANCHORY, ROYAL DEESIDE, KINCARDINESHIRE AB31 4BD
TEL: 013398 84339 FAX: 013398 84493

OWNERS: Michael, Linda and Maureen Boyle
CHEF: Warren Grooby

S: £40
D: £60

Inn: True Scottish hospitality can be enjoyed at this welcoming, friendly inn, which offers attractive accommodation and excellent value for money. A hostelry has stood at Potarch since 1740, when the nearest crossing of the River Dee was half a mile south at Inchbrae. The area is steeped in history, making it popular with sight-seers and sports enthusiasts who come to enjoy the superb fishing and skiing. The bar also draws locals and visitors, as it serves a wide range of whiskies – many of which are quite rare. **Restaurant:** Charmingly furnished, the dining room provides a very pleasant setting in which to enjoy the inn's traditional Scottish cuisine. The Scottish Chef of the Year 1992/93 makes good use of local fare, including the salmon, game and beef for which Deeside is renowned. **Nearby:** The Potarch is surrounded by spectacular scenery, offering plenty of opportunities for all manner of country pursuits. Riding can be arranged at an equestrian centre just 200 yards away. There are also numerous castles in the area, including Balmoral. Aberdeen is 25 miles away, and nearby Aboyne hosts the August Highland Games. **Directions: 25 miles from Aberdeen. The hotel is near Potarch Bridge on the A93 between Banchory and Aboyne.**

THE LOFT RESTAURANT

GOLF COURSE ROAD, BLAIR ATHOLL, PERTHSHIRE PH18 5TE
TEL: 01796 481377 FAX: 01796 481511

OWNER: Stuart Richardson
OWNER/CHEF: Douglas Wright

Restaurant: As its name suggests, The Loft at Blair Atholl was originally a hay loft which formed part of the estate. It has been charmingly converted into an elegant yet informal restaurant, with great care having been taken to retain the original twisted old beams, stone walls and oak flooring. Open daily, the restaurant serves morning coffee, lunches, afternoon tea, pre-theatre supper and dinners. Only the freshest ingredients are used in the compilation of the imaginative menus and all meals are cooked to order. A vegetarian option is available. Menus include whole bream baked and served with its own juices; char grilled rump steak with wild mushroom and onion marmalade; and roast chump of local lamb with crushed garlic potato and shallot confit. Delicious desserts, made in The Loft's own patisserie, feature tempting delights such as hot bread and butter pudding with vanilla anglais; chocolate marquise with passion fruit sauce; and glazed lemon tart with orange confiture sauce. Taste of Scotland and 2 AA rosettes. Accommodation is in 3 adjoining Cottages sleeping from 2 to 6 people. **Nearby:** The surrounding countryside is rich in attractions, including Blair Atholl Castle and the stunning scenery of Glen Tilt and the Forest of Atholl. Pitlochry, a major tourist centre with a large variety of shops and famous Festival Theatre, can be reached within 15 minutes by car. **Directions: From A9, turn off to Blair Atholl, 4 miles north of Pitlochy. The restaurant is well signposted.**

CHEFS' SPECIALITIES
• • • • • • •

caesar salad
with lightly char grilled chicken breast

roast chump of local lamb
with crushed garlic potato & roasted shallot

warm crisp apple tart
with caramel ice cream

THE GLENISLA HOTEL

KIRKTON OF GLENISLA, BY ALYTH, PERTHSHIRE PH11 8PH
TEL: 01575 582223 FAX: 01575 582223 E-MAIL: blake@easynet.co.uk.

OWNERS: Simon and Lyndy Blake

6 rms 6 ens

S: £40–£45
D: £65–£75

Inn: A coaching inn in the 17th century, hospitality has long been a tradition at this attractive hotel in the middle of the tiny village of Kirkton of Glenisla, close to the River Isla. The Drawing Room is filled with flowers, inviting sofas and chairs, and the six bedrooms are charming. Some have a bath, others a shower and there is masses of hot water! Locals and guests frequent the big, friendly bar with its log fire, wooden tables, cask ales and malt whiskies and they enjoy substantial bar lunches and suppers served at wooden tables. The Games Room in the stable block opens on to the Function Hall where Highland Dances are held. **Restaurant:** The elegant dining room serves the best of Scottish fare, winning several accolades including a recommendation from the Taste of Scotland. Orkney herrings, local venison, Aberdeen Angus beef, wild salmon and hill-reared lamb all feature on the menu. There are interesting starters and wicked puddings too! The wine list is impressive. **Nearby:** The Glenisla is an ideal touring centre for Glamis, Scone, Braemar and Royal Deeside, while immediate activities include trout fishing, skiing, stalking, shooting, salmon fishing and golf. Hill walking, bird-watching and pony trekking are also on the doorstep. **Directions: From the M90 take the A93 to Blairgowrie, then A926 by-passing Alyth to next roundabout. Then follow signs to Glenisla for 12 miles, hotel is on the right.**

HOTEL EILEAN IARMAIN OR ISLE ORNSAY HOTEL

SLEAT, ISLE OF SKYE IV43 8QR
TEL: 01471 833332 FAX: 01471 833275

OWNERS: Sir Iain and Lady Noble of Eilean Iarmain
MANAGER: Effie Kennedy
CHEFS: Roger Brown and Morag MacInnes

12 rms   12 ens

 S: £70 D: £95–£110

Inn: Hotel Eilean Iarmain stands on the small bay of Isle Ornsay in the South of Skye with expansive views over the Sound of Sleat and has always meant '*failte is furan*' a warmth of welcomes. The hotel prides itself on its log fires, inventive cooking and friendly Gaelic-speaking staff. 1997 accolades include the RAC Restaurant Award, RAC Merit Award for Hospitality, Comfort and Restaurant, AA Rosette for Restaurant, AA Romantic Hotel of Great Britain and Ireland Award and Les Routiers Corps d'Elite Wine Award. There are 12 bedrooms, all different – six of them in the pretty Garden House – with special views of sea and hills. Original features, period furniture, pretty fabrics and well chosen pictures create a cosy atmosphere.

Restaurant: Every evening the menu features game in season and guests can enjoy seafood landed at the pier that day. There is an extensive wine list, including premier cru clarets. A large selection of malt whiskies includes local Poit Dhubh and Talisker – highly regarded by connoisseurs. The bar offers meals at lunchtime and in the evening is a haunt of yachtsmen, the scene of ceilidhs from time to time. **Nearby:** Clan MacDonald Centre, Armadale Castle and Talisker Distillery. Sea-fishing, stalking, shooting and walking. **Directions: The hotel is in Sleat, between Broadford and Armadale on the A851. 20 minutes from the Skye Bridge and 15 minutes from the Mallaig Armadale Ferry and Lochalsh railway station.**

UIG HOTEL

UIG, ISLE OF SKYE IV51 9YE
TEL: 01470 542205 FAX: 01470 542308

OWNER: Bruce Skelton
CHEF: Steven Moffett

S: £37–£55
D: £74–£140

Inn: Cool, gleaming white-faced walls and a warm Scottish welcome greet visitors to this delightful old coaching hostelry standing in three acres of hillside grounds overlooking beautiful Uig Bay and Loch Snizort. The en suite bedrooms, six in an annexe, have been individually designed and decorated and offer all modern facilities. Pretty fabrics and well chosen watercolours create a cosy atmosphere and a relaxing sun lounge overlooks the bay. Trek into the magnificent surrounding countryside from the hotel's stables of Native Ponies. Excursions in the hotel's vehicles range from off-road Landrover explorations to the cossetted luxury of a Rolls Royce Silver Spirit. The hotel has shooting rights, guided walks arranged. **Restaurant:** Comfortable and welcoming with chef Steven Moffett providing a good choice of menus. Appetites are sure to be tempted by dishes such as a trellis of salmon and sole presented on a pool of ginger scented tomato sauce, or maybe pan seared breast of duck served on stir fried leeks. An interesting wine list includes a number of Scottish vintages. **Nearby:** The fascinating Trotternish Peninsula, Quiraing, Storr, Fairy Glen, Duntulm Castle and Museum of Island Life. One mile from the ferry sailing to the Outer Hebridean Isles of Harris, Lewis and the Uists – day trips available in summer. **Directions: Skye is reached by road bridge via the A87 or by ferry via the A830. Approaching Uig from Portree, the hotel is on the right, beside a white church.**

ANNANDALE ARMS HOTEL

HIGH STREET, MOFFAT, DUMFRIESSHIRE DG10 9HF
TEL: 01683 220013 FAX: 01683 221395

OWNERS: Simon and Margaret Tweedie

15 rms	11 ens

S: £30–£40
D: £40–£64

Inn: True Scottish hospitality can be enjoyed at this welcoming, 200-year-old coaching inn which offers attractive accommodation and excellent value for money. The Annandale Arms stands in the centre of the pretty Southern Upland Hill town of Moffat, where Robert Burns, Sir Walter Scott and John Buchanan found inspiration for many of their works. The area thrives as a sheep farming centre, symbolised by a statue of a ram in the wide High Street. The beautiful surrounding countryside, which looks much like the English Lake District, is steeped in history, making it popular with sight-seers, sports enthusiasts and hill climbers. The panelled bar also draws locals and visitors as it serves a wide selection of malt whiskies. All 15 bedrooms are charming and provide full modern comforts. Some have panoramic views over the magnificent Border countryside. **Restaurant:** In addition to an extensive bar menu there is sophisticated à la carte cuisine with the emphasis on fish, especially salmon, and local produce. **Nearby:** The Annandale Arms is an ideal base for visiting many historic castles and National Trust properties. North of the town is the Devil's Beef Tub, a sheer-sided hollow in the hills, White Coomb (2,696ft) and Grey Mare's Tail, one of Scotland's highest waterfalls. Immediate activities include fishing, golf, shooting, sailing, riding and bird-watching. **Directions: Moffat is two miles off the A74M on the A 701 road from Dumfries.**

 PITLOCHRY

 In association with MasterCard

THE MOULIN HOTEL

MOULIN, BY PITLOCHRY, PERTHSHIRE PH16 5EW
TEL: 01796 472196 FAX: 01796 474098

OWNERS: Chris Tomlinson and Heather Reeves
CHEF: Steven Leslie

15 rms | 15 ens

S: £55
D: £65

Inn: The Moulin Hotel stands pristine white against a towering mountain backdrop of deep blues and greens capped by scudding clouds racing to and from the Highlands. Behind its attractive black framed windows is a welcoming world of peace, tranquillity and Scottish homeliness. Opened as an inn in 1695, The Moulin Hotel stands proudly in the village square just three-quarters of a mile from the bustling town of Pitlochry, gateway to the Highlands. All 17 bedrooms have been recently refurbished to include every modern amenity. The comfortable lounge and lounge bar overlook the hotel's garden and Moulin Burn from where the cooing of doves and water babbling over stones is calming music to the ears of visitors wearied by a day's walking, exploring or sightseeing. **Restaurant:** Spacious and charmingly furnished. Chef Steven Leslie serves a varied choice of imaginatively prepared dishes. Begin with haggis wrapped in filo pastry on an onion cream, followed by salmon wrapped in lemon sole on a prawn sauce and then a desert of highland cranachan with local berries before enjoying an after-dinner coffee and malt. **Nearby:** Many walks and gentle climbs with the 2,759 foot summit of Ben-y-Vrackie three miles away. Golf, fishing, shooting, riding, Pitlochry Theatre, Blair Castle, Scone Palace and numerous historical sites. **Directions: From Perth, take A9 to Pitlochry then turn right onto A924 for Moulin.**

WHINSMUIR COUNTRY INN

POWMILL, BY DOLLAR, CLACKMANNANSHIRE FK14 7NW
TEL: 01577 840595 FAX: 01577 840779

OWNERS: Paul and Diane Brown
CHEF: Paul Brown

13 rms | 13 ens

S: £50
D: £65-£75

Inn: Experience Scottish inn-keeping hospitality at its best at the Whinsmuir Country Inn. Set in a charming location overlooking the Gairney Hills and the countryside all around, this inn combines excellent accommodation with mouth-watering cuisine. The spacious bedrooms are decorated and furnished to the highest standards and include every modern amenity. **Restaurant:** The delightful bistro-style restaurant has open fires and a special private dining area. From the lunch and snack menu why not try a hearty casserole of beef bourgignonne, or penne pasta enriched with a sauce of onion, mushroom, smoked ham and a hint of nutmeg cream sauces. The dinner menu will be equally tempting – roast breast of duck served on buttered leeks with a cassis sauce, or maybe pan fried fillet of trout coated in oatmeal and simply served with citrus fruit and parsley. An interesting wine list and real ales are available to complement this fine food. Fishing, golfing, shooting, falconry and car racing are just a few of the sporting activities than can be arranged for guests. The inn also has access to a number of estates. **Nearby:** The scenic Scottish Perthshire countryside boasts many castles and monuments and Edinburgh and Glasgow are both about 30 miles away. **Directions: From M90 turn off at Kinross service station onto A977 for six miles.**

HIGHLAND.
An almost feminine charm and character all of its own. Light and aromatic, the Gentle Spirit is rich in body with a soft heather honey finish.

ISLE OF SKYE.
Assertive but not heavy. Fully flavoured with a pungent, peaty ruggedness. It explodes on the palate and lingers on. Well balanced. A sweetish seaweedy aroma.

SPEYSIDE.
Finely balanced with a dry, rather delicate aroma, good firm body and a smoky finish. A pleasantly austere malt of great distinction with a character all its own.

WEST HIGHLAND.
Oban is the West Highland malt. A singular, rich and complex malt with the merest suggestion of peat in the aroma, slightly smoky with a long smooth finish.

ISLE OF ISLAY.
Seaweed, peat, smoke and earth are all elements of the assertive Islay character. Pungent, an intensely dry 16 year old malt with a firm robust body and powerful aroma.

LOWLAND.
Typically soft, restrained and with a touch of sweetness. An exceptionally pale smooth malt which, experts agree, reaches perfection at 10 years maturity.

DALWHINNIE	TALISKER	CRAGGANMORE	OBAN	LAGAVULIN	GLENKINCHIE
15 YEARS OLD	10 YEARS OLD	12 YEARS OLD	14 YEARS OLD	16 YEARS OLD	10 YEARS OLD
HIGHLAND	SKYE	SPEYSIDE	WEST HIGHLAND	ISLAY	LOWLAND

Les grands crus de Scotland.

In the great wine-growing regions, there are certain growths from a single estate that are inevitably superior.

For the Scots, there are the single malts. Subtle variations in water, weather, peat and the distilling process itself lend each single malt its singular character.

Each Malt is an authentic, traditional malt with its own identity, inherent in both taste and aroma.

The Classic Malts are the finest examples of the main malt producing regions. To savour them, one by one, is a rare journey of discovery.

SIX OF SCOTLAND'S FINEST MALT WHISKIES

Connemara landscape
Co Galway

Johansens Recommended Inns with Restaurants in
Ireland

Celtic treasures and legends, medieval architecture, racecourses and golf courses, great art collections and a richness of literature are all to be found amongst the green landscapes of Ireland.

While Ireland's number of annual visitors has been breaking its own newly-created record each year in the present decade making it the fastest growing tourism destination in Europe, it is the performance of Irish golf which stands out as the greatest success story of all. Golf has become the Republic's flagship product among a multiplicity of attractions and leisure pursuits which now account for a yearly visitor number which considerably exceeds that of the resident population.

The great historic golf courses of Ireland are well known internationally, Portmarnock, Royal Dublin, Ballybunion and Waterville being formidable among them as links challenges of world standard, while the parkland contrast is confidently provided on the verdant fairways of such as Woodbrook, Mullingar or Headford. In Ireland it is virtually impossible to be more than 20 miles away from a golf course, and every town or village of more than a thousand souls has a course of its very own. The 1990's have seen the development of even more new courses to cater for increasing international demand, and several world status professionals have brought their individual design talents to their construction.

It is the hidden gems, however, when stumbled upon which regularly compel their discoverers to speak of them in whispers, and the scenic, rugged countryside along the Atlantic seaboard provides Ireland's greatest source of such lesser-known treasures. Six of these courses have now come together to form a unique western golfing challenge group known as West Coast Links. Set in the purity of an unspoiled environment and amid the distinct Celtic culture and natural warmth of the rural community, their aim is to ensure that the visitor's golfing holiday will be both invigorating and memorable.

Much of Ireland's history is preserved in the architecture and ancient monuments of many of the towns and villages around the country and an association, Heritage Towns of Ireland, can assist the visitor in achieving the most comprehensive experience during a visit.

In addition to the many beautiful forest parks, Ireland has three internationally recognised national parks. Killarney National Park is perhaps the best known with Muckross House and Gardens as the centrepiece of this magnificent lakeside park. Connemara National Park in Letterfrack is set amid the wild rugged beauty so typical of the West of Ireland, and Glenveagh National Park in County Donegal has a beautiful castle and gardens.

The ancient history of Northern Ireland is comparable to that of the Greeks and Egyptians with the old tales of derring do, bravery and romance of the ancient Celts brought back to life at museums and centres including the Navan Centre of Armagh and the Tower Museum of Derry City.

Visitors to Ireland who make the journey north are inevitably surprised by "how different it is", or "how tidy it is", or "how rural it is". And this is what they enjoy.

Northern Ireland has made a name for itself as a place where welcomes are genuine and the land unspoilt. The last great outdoors playground for western Europe, this part of the island of Ireland remains top favourite among those in the know.

Wild salmon and trout anglers are tempted here by some of the world's best rivers. The Foyle system stands out as one of the best but the Bann, Bush, Erne and Melvin are other rivers and lakes teeming with indigenous sonnghan and dollaghan trout.

Similarly, golfers from the four corners return year after year to the freedom of the great links courses of the north coast. Both Royal Portrush and Royal County Down feature time after time in the world's top ten list of courses which is an indication of the quality available here.

And walkers, ramblers, watersports enthusiasts and other outdoor lovers know Northern Ireland's secret charms and are attracted back again and again.

But it's not all blustery outdoors. With the warmth of the fire in an Ulster bar surrounded by music and friends you will wish never to have to leave. The top class restaurants will seduce you as they have top food connoisseurs from around the world.

The fun of a good night's entertainment with live music, traditional Irish, jazz, rock or classical will help make any stay very memorable and can be enjoyed in most parts of the north.

Ultimately, you'll find an ancient culture here which was already 2,000 years old when St Patrick arrived from Britain 1,500 years ago.

Northern Ireland is special. Once visitors make their way here, they are sure to find what they are looking for – even if they didn't know what they were looking for in the first place!

Heritage Towns of Ireland
City Hall
Main Street
Cashel
Co Tipperary
Tel: 00 353 62 62068

West Coast Links
Teach Sonas
Rinville West
Oranmore
Co Galway
Ireland
Tel: 00 353 91 794500

For more information about Ireland and Northern Ireland please contact:

The Irish Tourist Board
Bord Failte
Baggot Street Bridge
Dublin 2
Tel: 00 353 1 676 5871

Northern Ireland Tourist Board
St Anne's Court
59 North Street
Belfast BT1 1NB
Tel: 01232 246609

In association
with MasterCard

THE OLD INN, CRAWFORDSBURN

CRAWFORDSBURN, CO. DOWN, NORTHERN IRELAND BT19 1JH
TEL: 01247 853255 FAX: 01247 852775

OWNERS: Danny and Don Rice
MANAGER: Brendan McCann
CHEF: Neill Graham

33 rms   33 ens

S: £45–£80
D: £65–£90

Inn: The picturesque Old Inn, a long low building with a partly thatched roof, has been dispensing hospitality since 1614. One of few such hostelries in Northern Ireland, its guest book includes Jonathan Swift, CS Lewis, Dick Turpin and President George Bush. Crawfordsburn is a small village, just 20 minutes from Belfast and 1 mile from the sea. "Good cheer" describes the ambience – warm colours, a big fire, panelled walls and blackened beams, a grandfather clock and millstones by the hearth, fascinating period furniture – and genial hosts. The bedrooms are splendid, antiques vying with exquisite chintz, with several magnificent four-posters, all meeting the demands of today's wayfarer. The romantic Cottage, in the award winning gardens, is wonderfully private, with room service if required! The Inn also has excellent conference facilities. **Restaurant:** Featured in a number of food guides Restaurant 1614 is renowned throughout Ireland; a traditional dining-room where guests feast on fresh seafood from the nearby fishing ports, fine Irish beef and lamb and local vegetables. The cellar is excellent. Informal meals can be enjoyed in the Churn Bistro and the Parlour Bar offers an all-day menu. While draft Guinness is waiting to be sampled in the Bar. **Nearby:** Golf, walking, riding, sailing, museums, gardens, shopping, the theatre in Belfast – the days soon pass. **Directions: From Belfast take the A2 Bangor and City Airport Road, 3 miles past Holywood, Crawfordsburn is signed on the left.**

178

Johansens Recommended Inns with Restaurants in the Channel Islands

St Ouen's Bay Jersey

With a wealth of wonderful scenery, magnificent coastlines, historic buildings, natural and man-made attractions plus mouthwatering local produce, the Channel Islands provide a memorable destination that's distinctly different.

ALL OF THE JOHANSENS RECOMMENDED ESTABLISHMENTS IN THE CHANNEL ISLANDS ARE ABLE TO MAKE FAVOURABLE TRAVEL ARRANGEMENTS FOR YOU.

Jersey and Guernsey offer VAT free shopping, the official language is English, passports are not required and both islands can be reached by sea from Poole or any one of about 30 airports in Britain and Europe.

And don't forget the other islands. Herm has dazzling beaches, Sark lives in a rural timewarp without traffic and Alderney's cobbled streets, pretty cottages and Victorian forts are another world again.

JERSEY

The largest and most southerly of the Channel Islands, Jersey measures only nine miles by five and is just fourteen miles from the French coast. The island slopes from north to south, creating dramatic differences between the high cliffs of the north and broad sandy bays of the south.

Jersey was originally part of Normandy. When William the Conqueror invaded England, it came under English rule until 1204, when King John lost Normandy to France.

The Islanders were given a choice – stay with Normandy or remain loyal to the English Crown. They chose England and gained rights and privileges which to this day are subject not to the British Parliament, but only to the reigning monarch.

The French influence is still strong however, and visitors are often surprised to find the names of streets and villages in French. The granite architecture of the farms and manor houses has a Continental feel too, and in rural areas, you may still hear farmworkers speaking in the local 'patois' or dialect.

Food is also something for which Jersey is renowned. It has an excellent choice of restaurants serving everything from simple family meals to gourmet dishes. Shellfish and fresh fish are the specialities of the Island and

lobster, crab, seafood platter, bass and Jersey plaice feature on many menus. The annual Good Food Festival, held in early summer, is a must for food lovers.

History enthusiasts can trace the Island's development from prehistory to the present day through a variety of different sites. The Channel Islands were the only part of the British Isles to be occupied by the Germans during World War II and there are reminders all over Jersey.

For a small island, Jersey boasts more than its fair share of fascinating museums where the emphasis is very definitely 'hands on' history. Jersey Museum in St Helier; The Hamptonne Country Life Museum; and the new Maritime Museum which opened in July 1997.

You're never far from Jersey's spectacular coastline – all 50 miles of it – but the interior of the Island is worth exploring too. The largely rural landscape is criss-crossed by a network of narrow country roads, some of which have recently been designated as 'Green Lanes', where priority is given to walkers, cyclists and horseriders.

But the cultural attractions of Jersey can never eclipse the Island's natural beauty. Every bend in the lane, every turn in the coast path reveals a new view to be savoured and enjoyed.

GUERNSEY

Guernsey, somewhat smaller than its sister island, supports a successful, self-sufficient economy which mixes finance, horticulture and, of course, tourism – all within a total area of 25 square miles. Its charming little capital, St Peter Port, rises in tiers above the quaysides of the busy harbour where the colourful banners of yachts of all nations flutter in the sunshine. Needless to say, delicious seafood features prominently on the menus, though all tastes are catered for by the chefs of many nationalities who have settled in the island.

Guernsey offers enormous variety within its

relatively small size. The south coast comprises high cliffs, covered, in springtime, with a profusion of colourful flowers, at the foot of which nestle beautiful little sandy coves.

A network of cliff paths provides splendid walking all the way from St Peter Port to Pleinmont Point in the far south west corner of the island. These paths stretch for a total distance of some 25 miles, one spectacular seaview succeeding the other all the way. Inland, high-banked country lanes lead past old granite farmhouses and tiny fields, where the local breed of cows, famed for their superb cream, contentedly graze.

The west and north coasts comprise a series of sweeping sandy beaches where rocky outcrops are dotted with little pools, teaming with sea life, which provide hours of fascination for youngsters.

Guernsey's heritage provides a fascinating choice of subjects to study during a holiday. The island is girded with fortifications dating back to prehistoric times, and of paramount interest is Castle Cornet, dating from the 13th to 17th centuries, which dominates the harbour of St Peter Port and contains imaginatively conceived maritime and other museums. Other fortifications include 18th century coastal defence towers and the many substantial bunkers, tunnels and towers constructed by the occupying German forces during the second World War, a number of which have now been skilfully refurbished.

And it is this feeling of bygone ages which, coupled with the highest modern standards, prove so great an attraction to visitors to the island.

For further information, please contact:

Jersey Tourism
38 Dover Street, London, W1X 3RB
Tel: 0171 493 5278

Guernsey Tourist Board
PO Box 23, St Peter Port, Guernsey, GY1 3AN
Tel: 01481 723557 (24 hrs); 01481 723552

THE MOORINGS HOTEL

GOREY PIER, JERSEY JE3 6EW
TEL: 01534 853633 FAX: 01534 857618 E-MAIL: CASINO@iti.net

OWNER: Renzo Martin
MANAGER: Joe Alvis
CHEF: Daniel Pires

S: £33–£46.50
D: £66–£93

16 rms   16 ens

The Moorings enjoys a unique and idyllic position located between the high and formidable walls of Mont Orgueil (Gorey Castle) and the waterfront of old Gorey Harbour. Once a thriving port and the centre of Jersey's oyster fishing industry, Gorey is now a sleepy haven for sailing boats and pleasure craft with ferry services running to the French ports of Portbail, Granville and Carteret. The hotel offers peace, relaxation and comfort. Awarded three sun register status it has very good standard accommodation for this category. All 16 bedrooms are en suite and many boast superb sea views. There are two bars, one next to the restaurant which is an ideal meeting place for pre-dinner cocktails and after dinner coffees and liqueurs. **Restaurant:** Intimate, stylish, air-conditioned and with a reputation for excellent cuisine recognised by Egon Ronay and Ashley Courtenay recommendations. Specialities are seafood, but the extensive à la carte menu offers a wide range of local and continental gourmet dishes. **Nearby:** Grouville Bay with its safe bathing and water sports, the Royal Jersey Golf Club which runs parallel to the beach, walking, fishing, sailing, riding and all the attractions of Jersey. **Directions: Gorey is on the east side of the island, 30 minutes from the airport and 15 minutes from St Helier.**

SEA CREST HOTEL AND RESTAURANT

PETIT PORT, ST BRELADE, JERSEY JE3 8HH
TEL: 01534 46353 FAX: 01534 47316

OWNERS: Julian and Martha Bernstein
CHEF: Gerard Le Miere

S: £50–£65
D: £75–£105

Inn: The intimate Sea Crest Hotel and Restaurant stands serenely on the sunny south west coast of Jersey in the picturesque bay of Petit Port. It overlooks the beautiful conservation area of La Pulente Headland and is only a short walk from the five-mile stretch of St Ouen's Bay sands. Originally a traditional Jersey granite cottage, Sea Crest has been extended, sympathetically modernised and won a Jersey Tourism Gold Award in 1996 and 1997. All six bedrooms, most of them with their own balcony and sun lounges, have full facilities, hand-made English furniture, pretty French soft furnishings and superb views of the bay. The cosy, beamed cocktail bar leads onto the Sun Lounge and terrace where, overlooking a tempting swimming pool and secluded gardens, guests can enjoy drinks and light meals throughout the day. Excellent value accomodation, service and friendliness are assured. **Restaurant:** Chef Gerard Le Miere has built up an enviable, award-winning reputation for excellent cuisine winning the Chef of the Year Competition 1996 with delicious local seafood dishes and Jersey Fresh Produce. All meals are well presented and complemented by an extensive wine list. The restaurant is air-conditioned with its own distinctive collection of modern art. **Nearby:** Walking beaches and coastal paths, riding, fishing and golf at La Moye. Shopping at the Les Quennevais and Red Houses. **Directions: The hotel is on the south west coast, only seven minutes drive from the airport and 20 minutes from St Helier.**

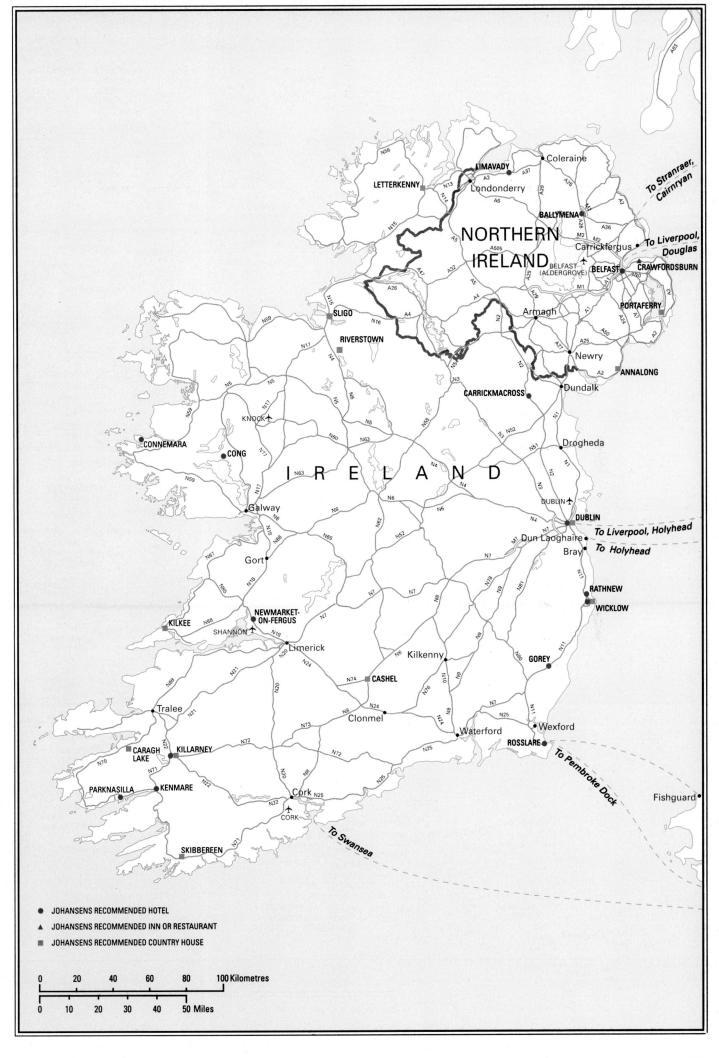

NORTHERN IRELAND

IRELAND

- **LIMAVADY**
- Coleraine
- **LETTERKENNY**
- Londonderry
- **BALLYMENA**
- Carrickfergus
- **CRAWFORDSBURN**
- BELFAST (ALDERGROVE)
- **BELFAST**
- **PORTAFERRY**
- Armagh
- **SLIGO**
- **RIVERSTOWN**
- Newry
- **ANNALONG**
- **CARRICKMACROSS**
- Dundalk
- Drogheda
- KNOCK ✈
- **CONNEMARA**
- **CONG**
- Galway
- DUBLIN ✈
- **DUBLIN**
- Dun Laoghaire
- Bray
- Gort
- **RATHNEW**
- **WICKLOW**
- **KILKEE**
- **NEWMARKET-ON-FERGUS**
- SHANNON ✈
- Limerick
- Kilkenny
- **GOREY**
- **CASHEL**
- Tralee
- Clonmel
- Waterford
- Wexford
- **CARAGH LAKE**
- **KILLARNEY**
- **ROSSLARE**
- **PARKNASILLA**
- **KENMARE**
- Cork
- **SKIBBEREEN**
- CORK ✈
- Fishguard

To Stranraer, Cairnryan
To Liverpool, Douglas
To Liverpool, Holyhead
To Holyhead
To Pembroke Dock
To Swansea

- ● JOHANSENS RECOMMENDED HOTEL
- ▲ JOHANSENS RECOMMENDED INN OR RESTAURANT
- ■ JOHANSENS RECOMMENDED COUNTRY HOUSE

0 20 40 60 80 100 Kilometres

0 10 20 30 40 50 Miles

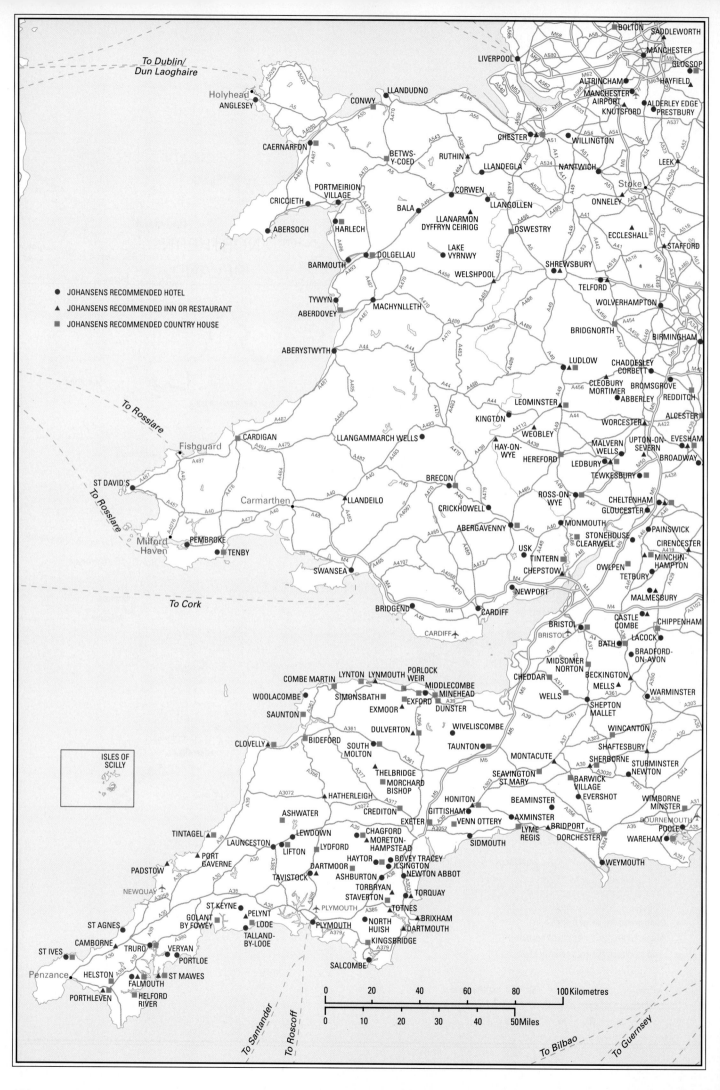

JOHANSENS RECOMMENDED HOTEL

JOHANSENS RECOMMENDED INN OR RESTAURANT

JOHANSENS RECOMMENDED COUNTRY HOUSE

To Dublin/
Dun Laoghaire

Holyhead
ANGLESEY

LLANDUDNO
CONWY
CAERNARFON
BETWS-Y-COED
RUTHIN
LLANDEGLA
NANTWICH
PORTMEIRION VILLAGE
CRICCIETH
CORWEN
LLANGOLLEN
OSWESTRY
ABERSOCH
HARLECH
BALA
LLANARMON DYFFRYN CEIRIOG
BARMOUTH
DOLGELLAU
LAKE VYRNWY
WELSHPOOL
SHREWSBURY
TELFORD
TYWYN
ABERDOVEY
MACHYNLLETH
WOLVERHAMPTON
BRIDGNORTH
BIRMINGHAM
ABERYSTWYTH
LUDLOW
CHADDESLEY CORBETT
CLEOBURY MORTIMER
ABBERLEY
BROMSGROVE
REDDITCH
ALCESTER
LEOMINSTER
WORCESTER
UPTON-ON-SEVERN
EVESHAM
KINGTON
WEOBLEY
MALVERN WELLS
BROADWAY
HAY-ON-WYE
HEREFORD
LEDBURY
TEWKESBURY

To Rosslare

Fishguard

CARDIGAN
LLANGAMMARCH WELLS
BRECON
ROSS-ON-WYE
CHELTENHAM
GLOUCESTER

St DAVID'S
CRICKHOWELL

To Rosslare
Carmarthen
LLANDEILO
ABERGAVENNY
MONMOUTH
PAINSWICK
STONEHOUSE
CLEARWELL
CIRENCESTER
MINCHIN-HAMPTON
Milford Haven
PEMBROKE
TENBY
USK
TINTERN
OWLPEN
TETBURY
SWANSEA
CHEPSTOW
MALMESBURY
To Cork
NEWPORT
BRIDGEND
CARDIFF
BRISTOL
CASTLE COMBE
CHIPPENHAM
CARDIFF
BRISTOL
LACOCK
BATH
BRADFORD-ON-AVON
MIDSOMER NORTON
BECKINGTON
MELLS
WARMINSTER
COMBE MARTIN
LYNTON
LYNMOUTH
PORLOCK WEIR
CHEDDAR
WELLS
WOOLACOMBE
SIMONSBATH
MIDDLECOMBE
MINEHEAD
SHEPTON MALLET
SAUNTON
EXMOOR
EXFORD
DUNSTER
WINCANTON
DULVERTON
WIVELISCOMBE
SHAFTESBURY
CLOVELLY
BIDEFORD
TAUNTON
MONTACUTE
SHERBORNE
STURMINSTER NEWTON
SOUTH MOLTON
SEAVINGTON St MARY
BARWICK VILLAGE
THELBRIDGE
EVERSHOT
WIMBORNE MINSTER
MORCHARD BISHOP
HATHERLEIGH
HONITON
BEAMINSTER
BOURNEMOUTH
ASHWATER
CREDITON
GITTISHAM
VENN OTTERY
AXMINSTER
POOLE
TINTAGEL
LEWDOWN
EXETER
BRIDPORT
DORCHESTER
WAREHAM
PADSTOW
LAUNCESTON
LIFTON
LYDFORD
CHAGFORD
MORETON-HAMPSTEAD
SIDMOUTH
LYME REGIS
PORT GAVERNE
HAYTOR
BOVEY TRACEY
ILSINGTON
WEYMOUTH
NEWQUAY
DARTMOOR
NEWTON ABBOT
TAVISTOCK
ASHBURTON
TORBRYAN
TORQUAY
St KEYNE
PELYNT
STAVERTON
TOTNES
St AGNES
GOLANT BY FOWEY
LOOE
PLYMOUTH
NORTH HUISH
BRIXHAM
CAMBORNE
TALLAND-BY-LOOE
KINGSBRIDGE
DARTMOUTH
St IVES
TRURO
VERYAN
SALCOMBE
Penzance
HELSTON
PORTLOE
St MAWES
PORTHLEVEN
FALMOUTH
HELFORD RIVER

ISLES OF SCILLY

To Santander
To Roscoff
To Bilbao
To Guernsey

0   20   40   60   80   100 Kilometres

0   10   20   30   40   50 Miles

184

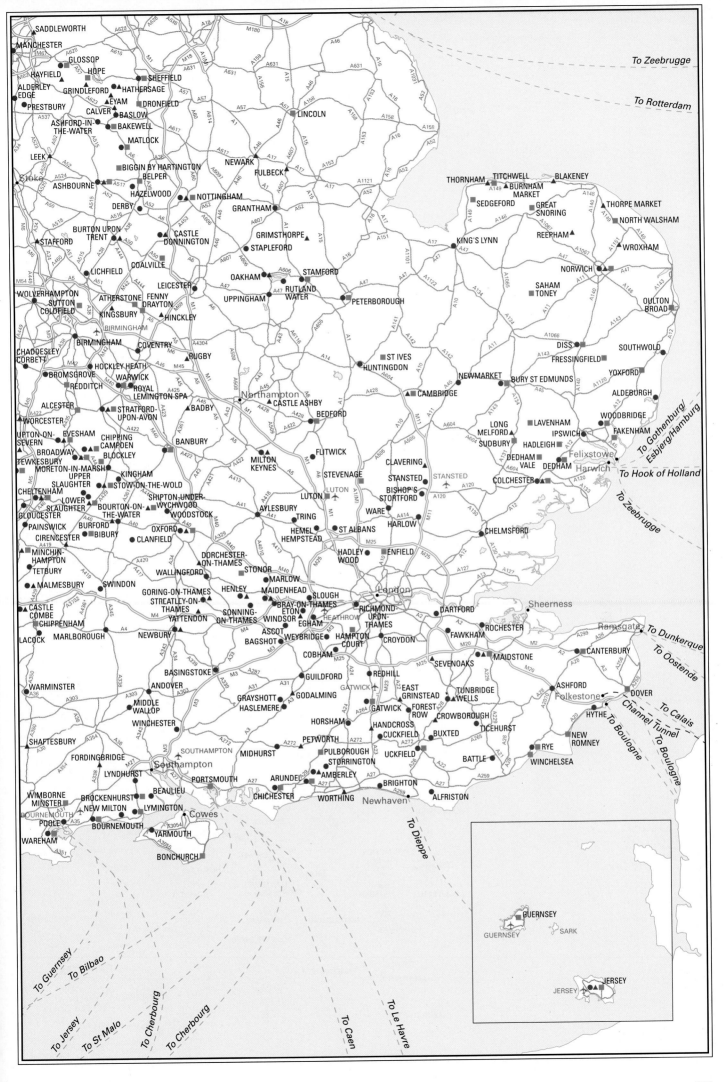

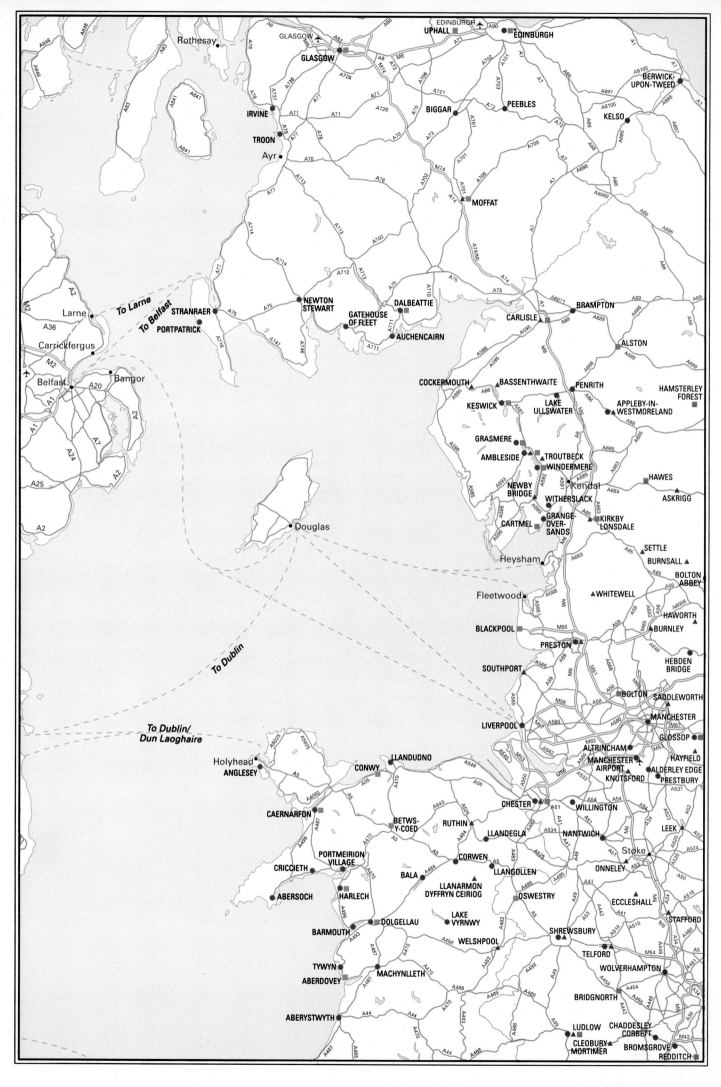

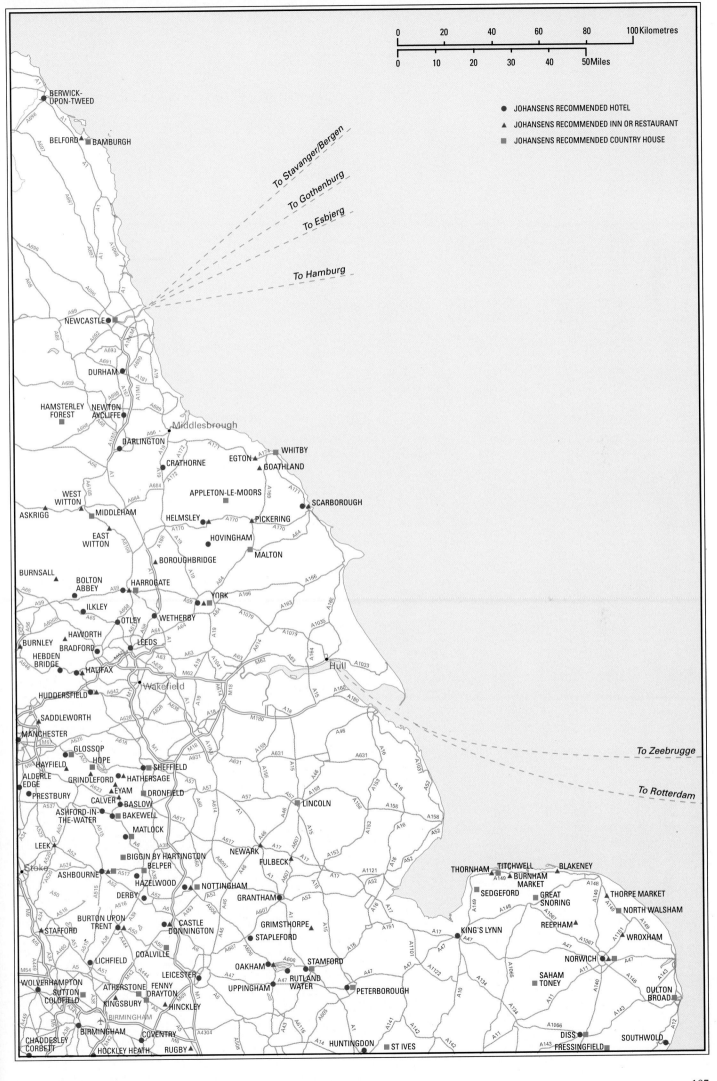

100 Kilometres
0 20 40 60 80

50 Miles
0 10 20 30 40

● JOHANSENS RECOMMENDED HOTEL
▲ JOHANSENS RECOMMENDED INN OR RESTAURANT
■ JOHANSENS RECOMMENDED COUNTRY HOUSE

To Stavanger/Bergen
To Gothenburg
To Esbjerg
To Hamburg
To Zeebrugge
To Rotterdam

BERWICK-UPON-TWEED
BELFORD BAMBURGH
NEWCASTLE
DURHAM
HAMSTERLEY FOREST
NEWTON AYCLIFFE
Middlesbrough
DARLINGTON
CRATHORNE EGTON WHITBY GOATHLAND
WEST WITTON APPLETON-LE-MOORS
ASKRIGG MIDDLEHAM SCARBOROUGH
HELMSLEY PICKERING
EAST WITTON HOVINGHAM
BURNSALL BOROUGHBRIDGE MALTON
BOLTON ABBEY HARROGATE
ILKLEY YORK
OTLEY WETHERBY
HAWORTH LEEDS
BURNLEY BRADFORD
HEBDEN BRIDGE HALIFAX Wakefield Hull
HUDDERSFIELD
SADDLEWORTH
MANCHESTER GLOSSOP
HAYFIELD HOPE SHEFFIELD
ALDERLEY EDGE GRINDLEFORD HATHERSAGE
PRESTBURY EYAM DRONFIELD
CALVER LINCOLN
BASLOW
ASHFORD-IN-THE-WATER BAKEWELL
MATLOCK
LEEK
Stoke BIGGIN BY HARTINGTON NEWARK
BELPER FULBECK
ASHBOURNE HAZELWOOD
DERBY NOTTINGHAM
GRANTHAM
BURTON UPON TRENT GRIMSTHORPE
STAFFORD CASTLE DONNINGTON
STAPLEFORD
COALVILLE
LICHFIELD STAMFORD
LEICESTER OAKHAM
WOLVERHAMPTON UPPINGHAM RUTLAND WATER PETERBOROUGH
SUTTON COLDFIELD ATHERSTONE FENNY DRAYTON
KINGSBURY HINCKLEY
BIRMINGHAM COVENTRY
CHADDESLEY CORBETT HOCKLEY HEATH RUGBY HUNTINGDON ST IVES

THORNHAM TITCHWELL BLAKENEY
BURNHAM MARKET
SEDGEFORD GREAT SNORING THORPE MARKET
NORTH WALSHAM
REEPHAM WROXHAM
KING'S LYNN NORWICH
SAHAM TONEY OULTON BROAD
DISS SOUTHWOLD
FRESSINGFIELD

187

© Lovell Johns Ltd, Oxford

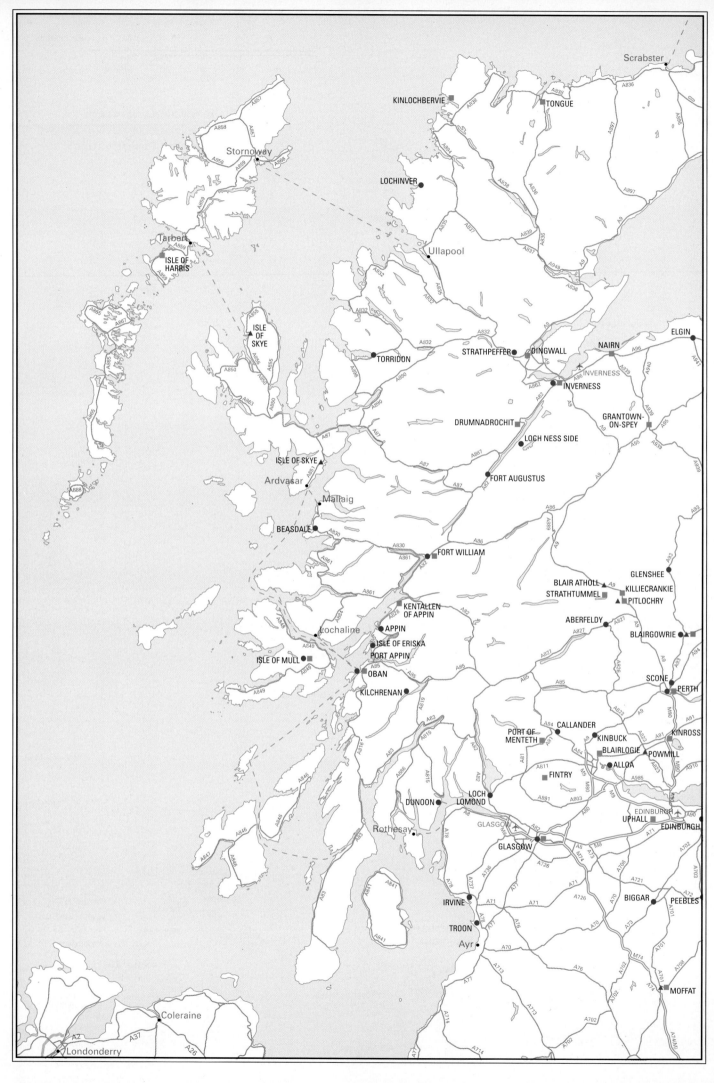

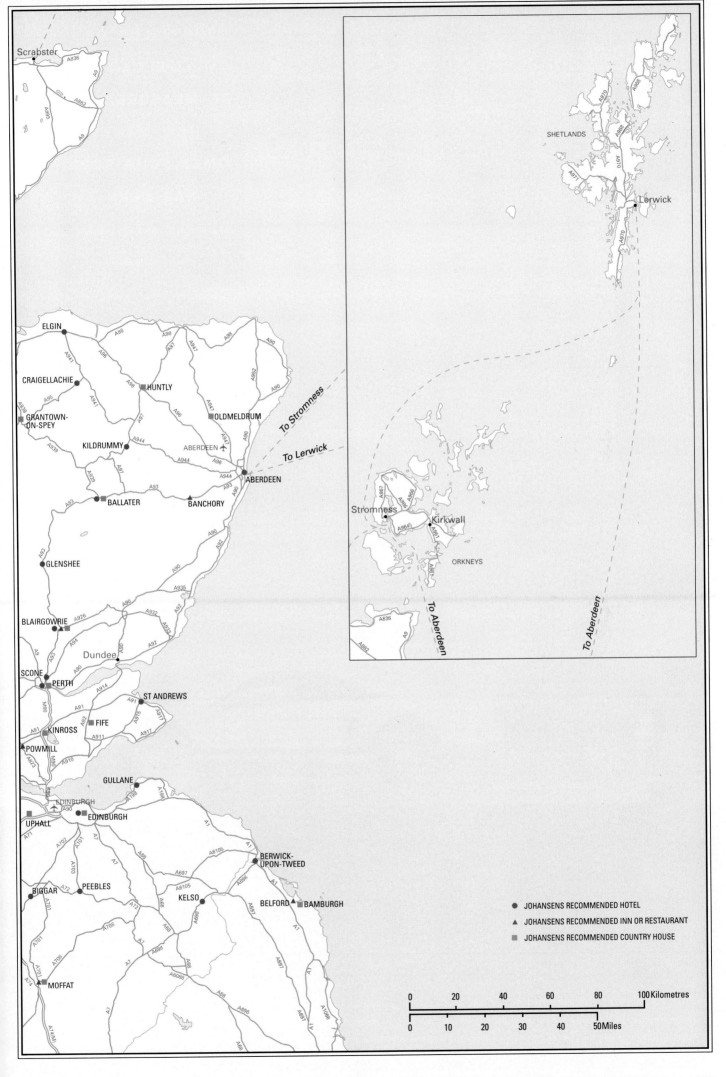

Scrabster

ELGIN
CRAIGELLACHIE
GRANTOWN-
ON-SPEY
KILDRUMMY
BALLATER
GLENSHEE
BLAIRGOWRIE
SCONE
PERTH
KINROSS
POWMILL
GULLANE
EDINBURGH
UPHALL
BIGGAR
PEEBLES
MOFFAT

HUNTLY
OLDMELDRUM
ABERDEEN
BANCHORY

Dundee

ST ANDREWS
FIFE

EDINBURGH

BERWICK-
UPON-TWEED

KELSO
BELFORD BAMBURGH

To Stromness
To Lerwick

SHETLANDS

Lerwick

Stromness
Kirkwall
ORKNEYS

To Aberdeen

To Aberdeen

● JOHANSENS RECOMMENDED HOTEL

▲ JOHANSENS RECOMMENDED INN OR RESTAURANT

■ JOHANSENS RECOMMENDED COUNTRY HOUSE

| 0 | 20 | 40 | 60 | 80 | 100 Kilometres |

| 0 | 10 | 20 | 30 | 40 | 50 Miles |

© Lovell Johns Ltd, Oxford

189

'THE VALUE OF LIFE CAN BE MEASURED BY HOW MANY TIMES YOUR SOUL HAS BEEN DEEPLY STIRRED.'

Soichiro Honda

Soichiro Honda was the inspiration behind what is now the world's largest engine manufacturer. His concern for man and the environment led us to build not only the world's most fuel-efficient car (9426 mpg) but also the winner of the Darwin to Adelaide race for solar-powered vehicles. His search for excellence gave rise to us winning 6 consecutive Formula 1 constructor's championships. It also led to the all-aluminium NSX, a car capable of 168mph and in which, at 70mph with the roof off, you don't need to raise your voice. Soichiro Honda, a softly spoken man, would have approved. For more information on our current range of cars, call **0345 159 159.**

HONDA

First man, then machine

ENGLAND

Alcester (Arrow) – Arrow Mill Hotel And Restaurant, Arrow, B49 5NL. Tel: 01789 762419

Alston – Lovelady Shield Country House Hotel, Nenthead Road, Alston, CA9 3LF. Tel: 01434 381203

Appleton-Le-Moors – Appleton Hall, Appleton-Le-Moors, YO6 6TF. Tel: 01751 417227

Arundel (Burpham) – Burpham Country House Hotel, Old Down, Burpham, BN18 9RV. Tel: 01903 882160

Ashbourne – The Beeches Farmhouse, Waldley, Doveridge, DE6 5LR. Tel: 01889 590288

Ashbourne (Grindon) – Porch Farmhouse, Grindon, ST13 7TP. Tel: 01538 304545

Ashwater – Blagdon Manor Country Hotel, Ashwater, EX21 5DF. Tel: 01409 211224

Atherstone – Chapel House, Friars' Gate, Atherstone, CV9 1EY. Tel: 01827 718949

Bakewell (Rowsley) – East Lodge Country House Hotel, Rowsley, Matlock, DE4 2EF. Tel: 01629 734474

Bakewell (Rowsley) – The Peacock Hotel at Rowsley, Rowsley, DE4 2EB. Tel: 01629 733518

Bamburgh – Waren House Hotel, Waren Mill, Bamburgh, NE70 7EE. Tel: 01668 214581

Barwick Village (Nr Yeovil) – Little Barwick House, Barwick Village, BA22 9TD. Tel: 01935 423902

Bath – Bloomfield House, 146 Bloomfield Road, Bath, BA2 2AS. Tel: 01225 420105

Bath – Apsley House, 141 Newbridge Hill, Bath, BA1 3PT. Tel: 01225 336966

Bath – Eagle House, Church Street, Bathford, BA1 7RS. Tel: 01225 859946

Bath – Paradise House, Holloway, Bath, BA2 4PX. Tel: 01225 317723

Bath – Oldfields, 102 Wells Road, Bath, BA2 3AL. Tel: 01225 317984

Bath (Bradford-On-Avon) – Widbrook Grange, Trowbridge Road, Bradford-On-Avon, BA15 1UH. Tel: 01225 864750 / 863173

Bath (Norton St Philip) – Bath Lodge Hotel, Norton St Philip, Bath, BA3 6NH. Tel: 01225 723040

Bath (Woolverton) – Woolverton House, BA3 6QS. Tel: 01373 830415

Belper (Shottle) – Dannah Farm Country Guest House, Bowman's Lane, Shottle, DE56 2DR. Tel: 01773 550273 / 630

Bibury – Bibury Court, Bibury , GL7 5NT. Tel: 01285 740337

Bideford (Northam) – Yeoldon House Hotel, Durrant Lane, Northam, EX39 2RL. Tel: 01237 474400

Biggin-By-Hartington – Biggin Hall, Biggin-By-Hartington, Buxton, SK17 0DH. Tel: 01298 84451

Blackpool (Singleton) – Mains Hall Hotel & Brasserie, Mains Lane, Little Singleton, FY6 7LE. Tel: 01253 885130

Blockley (Chipping Campden) – Lower Brook House, Blockley, GL56 9DS. Tel: 01386 700286

Bolton (Edgworth) – Quarlton Manor Farm, Plantation Road, Edgeworth,Turton, Bolton, BL7 0DD. Tel: 01204 852277

Bonchurch (Isle of Wight) – Peacock Vane Hotel, Bonchurch, PO38 1RJ. Tel: 01983 852019

Bournemouth – Langtry Manor, Derby Road, East cliff, Bournemouth, BH1 3QB. Tel: 01202 553887

Bourton-On-The-Water – Dial House Hotel, The Chestnuts, High Street, Bourton-On-The-Water, GL54 2AN. Tel: 01451 822244

Bridgnorth – Cross Lane House Hotel, Astley Abbots, Bridgnorth, WV16 4SJ. Tel: 01746 764887

Bristol (Chelwood) – Chelwood House, Achelwood, BS18 4NH. Tel: 01761 490730

Broadway (Willersey) – The Old Rectory, Church Street, Willersey, Broadway, WR12 7PN. Tel: 01386 853729

Brockenhurst – Thatched Cottage Hotel & Restaurant, 16 Brookley Road, Brockenhurst, SO42 7RR. Tel: 01590 623090

Brockenhurst – Whitley Ridge & Country House Hotel, Beaulieu Road, Brockenhurst, SO42 7QL. Tel: 01590 622354

Cambridge (Melbourn) – Melbourn Bury, Melbourn, Cambridgeshire, SG8 6DE. Tel: 01763 261151

Canterbury (Boughton under Blean) – The Garden Hotel, 167-169 The Street, Boughton under Blean, Faversham, ME13 9BH. Tel: 01227 751411

Carlisle – Number Thirty One, 31 Howard Place, Carlisle, CA1 1HR. Tel: 01228 597080

Carlisle (Crosby-On-Eden) – Crosby Lodge Country House Hotel, High Crosby, Crosby-On-Eden, Carlisle, CA6 4QZ. Tel: 01228 573618

Cartmel – Aynsome Manor Hotel, Cartmel, Grange-Over-Sands, LA11 6HH. Tel: 015395 36653

Chagford – Easton Court Hotel, Easton Cross, Chagford, TQ13 8JL. Tel: 01647 433469

Cheddar (Axbridge) – The Oak House Hotel, The Square, Axbridge, BS26 2AP. Tel: 01934 732444

Cheltenham (Charlton Kings) – Charlton Kings Hotel, Charlton Kings, Cheltenham, GL52 6UU. Tel: 01242 231061

Cheltenham (Withington) – Halewell, Halewell Close, Withington, GL54 4BN. Tel: 01242 890238

Chichester (Apuldram) – Crouchers Bottoms, Birdham Road, Apuldram, PO20 7EH. Tel: 01243 784995

Chichester (Charlton) – Woodstock House Hotel, Charlton, PO18 0HU. Tel: 01243 811666

Chippenham – Stanton Manor, Stanton Saint Quinton, SN14 6DQ. Tel: 01666 837552

Chipping Campden (Broad Campden) – The Malt House, Broad Campden, GL55 6UU. Tel: 01386 840295

Clearwell – Tudor Farmhouse Hotel & Restaurant, High Street, Clearwell, GL16 8JS. Tel: 01594 833046

Coalville (Greenhill) – Abbots Oak, Greenhill, Coalville, LE67 4UY. Tel: 01530 832 328

Colchester (Frating) – Hockley Place, Rectory Road, Frating, Colchester, CO7 7HG. Tel: 01206 251703

Combe Martin (East Down) – Ashelford, Ashelford, East Down, EX31 4LU. Tel: 01271 850469

Crediton (Coleford) – Coombe House Country Hotel, Coleford, Crediton, EX17 5BY. Tel: 01363 84487

Dartmoor (Nr Two Bridges) – Prince Hall Hotel, Two Bridges, Dartmoor, PL20 6SA. Tel: 01822 890403

Dedham Vale (Nayland) – Gladwins Farm, Harpers Hill, Nayland, CO6 4NU. Tel: 01206 262261

Diss – Salisbury House, Victoria Road, Diss, IP22 3JG. Tel: 01379 644738

Dorchester (Lower Bockhampton) – Yalbury Cottage Hotel, Lower Bockhampton, Dorchester, DT2 8PZ. Tel: 01305 262382

Dover (Temple Ewell) – The Woodville Hall, Temple Ewell, Dover, CT16 1DJ. Tel: 01304 825256

Dover (West Cliffe) – Wallett's Court, West Cliffe, St. Margaret's-at-Cliffe, CT15 6EW. Tel: 01304 852424

Dronfield – Manor House Hotel & Restaurant, High Street, Old Dronfield, SY18 6PY. Tel: 01246 413971

Dulverton – Ashwick Country House Hotel, Dulverton, TA22 9QD. Tel: 01398 323868

Dunster – The Exmoor House Hotel, West Street, Dunster, TA24 6SN. Tel: 01643 821268

Enfield (London) – Oak Lodge Hotel, 80 Village Road, Bush Hill Park, Enfield, EN1 2EU. Tel: 0181 360 7082

Evesham (Harvington) – The Mill At Harvington, Anchor Lane, Harvington, Evesham, WR11 5NR. Tel: 01386 870688

Exeter (Dunchideock) – The Lord Haldon Hotel, Dunchideock, EX6 7YF. Tel: 01392 832483

Exford (Exmoor) – The Crown Hotel, Exford, Exmoor National Park, TA24 7PP. Tel: 01643 831554/5

Fakenham (Weekly Let) – Vere Lodge, South Raynham, Fakenham, NR21 7HE. Tel: 01328 838261

Falmouth (Mawnan Smith) – Trelawne Hotel-The Hutches Restaurant, Mawnan Smith, TR11 5HS. Tel: 01326 250226

Fenny Drayton (Leicestershire) – White Wings, Quaker Close, Fenny Drayton, CV13 6BS. Tel: 01827 716100

Fressingfield (Diss) – Chippenhall Hall, Fressingfield, Eye, IP21 5TD. Tel: 01379 588180 / 586733

Gatwick (Charlwood) – Stanhill Court Hotel, Stanhill, Charlwood, RH6 0EP. Tel: 01293 862166

Glossop – The Wind In The Willows, Derbyshire Level, Glossop, SK13 9PT. Tel: 01457 868001

Golant by Fowey – The Cormorant Hotel, Golant, Fowey, PL23 1LL. Tel: 01726 833426

Grasmere (Rydal Water) – White Moss House, Rydal Water, Grasmere, LA22 9SE. Tel: 015394 35295

Great Snoring – The Old Rectory, Great Snoring, Fakenham, NR12 0HP. Tel: 01328 820597

Hadleigh (Nedging) – The Old Rectory, Nedging. Tel: 01449 740745

Hampton Court (Hampton Wick) – Chase Lodge, 10 Park Road, Hampton Wick, Kingston Upon Thames, KT1 4AS. Tel: 0181 943 1862

Hamsterley Forest (Near Durham) – Grove House, Hamsterley Forest, DL13 3NL. Tel: 01388 488203

Harrogate – The White House, 10 Park Parade, Harrogate, HG1 5AH. Tel: 01423 501388

Hawes (Upper Wensleydale) – Simonstone Hall, Hawes, DL8 3LY. Tel: 01969 667255

Hawes (Wensleydale) – Rookhurst Georgian Country House Hotel, West End, Gayle, Hawes, DL8 3RT. Tel: 01969 667454

Haytor (Dartmoor) – Bel Alp House, Haytor, TQ13 9XX. Tel: 01364 661217

Helford River (Gillan) – Tregildry Hotel, Gillan Manaccan, Helston, TR12 6HG. Tel: 01326 231378

Helston – Nansloe Manor, Meneage Road, Helston, TR13 0SB. Tel: 01326 574691

Hereford (Fownhope) – The Bowens Country House, Fownhope, HR1 4PS. Tel: 01432 860430

Hereford (Ullingswick) – The Steppes, Ullingswick, HR1 3JG. Tel: 01432 820424

Honiton (Yarcombe) – The Belfry Country Hotel, Yarcombe, EX14 9BD. Tel: 01404 861234

Hope (Castleton) – Underleigh House, Off Edale Road, Hope, Hope Valley, S33 6RF. Tel: 01433 621372

Keswick (LakeThirlmere) – Dale Head Hall Lakeside Hotel, Thirlmere, Keswick, CA12 4TN. Tel: 017687 72478

Keswick (Newlands) – Swinside Lodge Hotel, Grange Road, Newlands, Keswick, CA12 5UE. Tel: 017687 72948

Keswick-On-Derwentwater – Grange Country House Hotel, Manor Brow, Keswick-On-Derwentwater, CA12 4BA. Tel: 017687 72500

Kingsbridge (Chillington) – The White House, Chillington, Kingsbridge, TQ7 2JX. Tel: 01548 580580

Kirkby Lonsdale – Hipping Hall, Cowan Bridge, Kirkby Lonsdale, LA6 2JJ. Tel: 015242 71187

Lavenham – Lavenham Priory, Water Street, Lavenham, Sudbury, CO10 9RW. Tel: 01787 247404

Leominster – Lower Bache, Kimbolton, HR6 0ER. Tel: 01568 750304

Lifton (Sprytown) – The Thatched Cottage Country Hotel And Restaurant, Sprytown, Lifton, PL16 0AY. Tel: 01566 784224

Lincoln – D'Isney Place Hotel, Eastgate, Lincoln, LN2 4AA. Tel: 01522 538881

Lincoln (Washingborough) – Washingborough Hall, Church Hill, Washingborough, Lincoln, LN4 1BE. Tel: 01522 790340

Looe (Talland Bay) – Allhays Country House. Tel:

– Talland Bay, Looe, PL13 2JB, COUNTRY HOUSE. Tel:

Looe (Widegates) – Coombe Farm, Widegates, PL13 1QN. Tel: 01503 240223

Ludlow (Diddlebury) – Delbury Hall, Diddlebury, Craven Arms, SY7 9DH. Tel: 01584 841267

Ludlow (Overton) – Overton Grange Hotel, Overton, Ludlow, SY8 4AD. Tel: 01584 873500

Luton (Little Offley) – Little Offley, Hitchin, SG5 3BU. Tel: 01462 768243

Lydford (Vale Down) – Moor View House, Vale Down, Lydford, EX20 4BB. Tel: 01822 820220

Lyme Regis (Charmouth) – Thatch Lodge Hotel, The Street, Charmouth, DT6 6PQ. Tel: 01297 560407

Lymington (Hordle) – The Gordleton Mill Hotel, Silver Street, Hordle, SO41 6DJ. Tel: 01590 682219

Lynton – Hewitt's Hotel, North Walk, Lynton, EX35 6HJ. Tel: 01598 752293

Maidstone (Boughton Monchelsea) – Tanyard, Wierton Hill, Boughton Monchelsea, ME17 4JT. Tel: 01622 744705

Malton – Newstead Grange, Norton-On-Derwent, Malton, YO17 9PJ. Tel: 01653 692502

Matlock (Dethick) – The Manor Farmhouse, Dethick, Matlock, DE4 5GG. Tel: 01609 534246

Middlecombe (Minehead) – Periton Park Hotel, Middlecombe, TA24 8SW. Tel: 01643 706885

Middleham (Wensleydale) – Millers House Hotel, Middleham, Wensleydale, DL8 4NR. Tel: 01969 622630

Midsomer Norton (Bath) – The Old Priory, Church Square, Midsomer Norton, Bath, BA3 2HX. Tel: 01761 416784

Minchinhampton – Burleigh Court, Minchinhampton, GL5 2PF. Tel: 01453 883804

Minehead – Channel House Hotel, Church Path, Minehead, TA24 5QG. Tel: 01643 703229

Minehead (Exmoor) – The Beacon Country House Hotel, Beacon Road, Minehead, TA24 5SD. Tel: 01643 703476

Morchard Bishop – Wigham, Morchard Bishop, EX17 6RJ. Tel: 01363 877350

New Romney (Littlestone) – Romney Bay House, Coast Road, Littlestone, New Romney, TN28 8QY. Tel: 01797 364747

North Walsham – Beechwood Hotel, Cromer Road, North Walsham, NR28 0HD. Tel: 01692 403231

North Walsham – Elderton Lodge Hotel & Restaurant, Gunton Park, Thorpe Market, NR11 8TZ. Tel: 01263 833547

Norwich – The Beeches Hotel & Victorian Gardens, 4-6 Earlham Road, Norwich, NR2 3DB. Tel: 01603 621167

Norwich (Coltishall) – Norfolk Mead Hotel, Coltishall, Norwich, NR12 7DN. Tel: 01603 737531

Norwich (Drayton) – The Stower Grange, School Road, Drayton, NR8 6EF. Tel: 01603 860210

Norwich (Hethel) – The Moat House, Rectory Lane, Hethel, Norwich, NR14 8HD. Tel: 01508 570149

Norwich (Old Catton) – Catton Old Hall, Lodge Lane, Catton, Norwich, NR6 7HG. Tel: 01603 419379

Norwich (Thorpe St Andrew) – The Old Rectory, 103 Yarmouth Road, Thorpe St Andrew, Norwich, NR7 0HF. Tel: 01603 700772

Nottingham (Ruddington) – The Cottage Country House Hotel, Ruddington, Nottingham, NG11 6LA. Tel: 01159 846882

Oswestry – Pen-y-Dyffryn Country Hotel, Rhydycroesau, SY10 7JD. Tel: 01691 653700

Oulton Broad – Ivy House Farm, Ivy Lane, Oulton Broad, Lowestoft, NR33 8HY. Tel: 01502 501353

Owlpen – Owlpen Manor, GL11 5BZ. Tel: 01453 860261

Oxford (Kingston Bagpuize) – Fallowfields, Kingston Bagpuize With Southmoor, OX13 5BH. Tel: 01865 820416

Peterborough (Southorpe) – Midstone House, Southorpe, Stamford, PE9 3BX. Tel: 01780 740136

Porlock Weir – The Cottage Hotel, Porlock Weir, Porlock, TA24 8PB. Tel: 01643 863300

Porthleven (Nr Helston) – Tye Rock Hotel, Loe Bar Road, Porthleven, TR13 9EW. Tel: 01326 572695

Portsmouth – The Beaufort Hotel, 71 Festing Road, Portsmouth, PO4 0NQ. Tel: 01705 823707

Pulborough – Chequers Hotel, Church Place, Pulborough, RH20 1AD. Tel: 01798 872486

Redditch (Ipsley) – The Old Rectory, Ipsley Lane, Redditch, B98 0AP. Tel: 01527 523000

Ross-On-Wye (Glewstone) – Glewstone Court, HR6 6AW. Tel: 01989 770367

Rye – White Vine House, High Street, Rye, TN31 7JF. Tel: 01797 224748

Saham Toney (Thetford) – Broom Hall, Richmond Road, Saham Toney, Thetford, IP25 7EX. Tel: 01953 882125

Saunton – Preston House Hotel, Saunton, Braunton, EX33 1LG. Tel: 01271 890472

Seavington St Mary, Nr Ilminster – The Pheasant Hotel, Seavington St Mary, TA19 0QH. Tel: 01460 240502

Sedgeford (Weekly Let) – The Sedgeford Estate, Bordering Royal Estate, Sedgeford, PE36 5LT. Tel: 01485 572855

Sheffield (Chapeltown) – Staindrop Lodge, Lane End, Chapeltown, Sheffield, S30 4HH. Tel: 0114 284 6727

Sherborne – The Eastbury Hotel, Long Street, Sherborne, DT9 3BY. Tel: 01935 813131

Shipton Under Wychwood – The Shaven Crown Hotel, High Street, Shipton Under Wychwood, OX7 6BA. Tel: 01993 830330

Simonsbath (Exmoor) – Simonsbath House Hotel, Simonsbath, Exmoor, TA24 7SH. Tel: 01643 831259

South Molton – Marsh Hall Country House Hotel, South Molton, EX36 3HQ. Tel: 01769 572666

St. Ives (Cambridge) – Olivers Lodge Hotel & Restaurant, Needingworth Road, St. Ives, PE17 4JP. Tel: 01480 463252

St Ives (Trink) – The Countryman At Trink Hotel & Restaurant, Old Coach Road, St Ives, TR26 3JQ. Tel: 01736 797571

St Mawes (Ruan Highlanes) – The Hundred House Hotel, Ruan Highlanes, TR2 5JR. Tel: 01872 501336

Stamford (Ketton) – The Priory, Church Road, Ketton, Stamford, PE9 3RD. Tel: 01780 720215

Stamford (Tallington) – The Old Mill, Mill Lane, Tallington, Stamford, PE9 4RR. Tel: 01780 740815

Staverton (Nr Totnes) – Kingston House, Staverton, Totnes, TQ9 6AR. Tel: 01803 762 235

Stevenage (Hitchin) – Redcoats Farmhouse Hotel & Restaurant, Redcoats Green, SG4 7JR. Tel: 01438 729500

Stonor (Henley-on-Thames) – The Stonor Arms, Stonor, RG9 6HE. Tel: 01491 638345

Stow-On-The-Wold (Kingham) – Conygree Gate Hotel, Kingham, OX7 6YA . Tel: 01608 658389

Stratford-upon-Avon (Loxley) – Glebe Farm House, Loxley, CV35 9JW. Tel: 01789 842501

Sudbury – Tarantella Hotel & Restaurant, Sudbury Hall, Melford Road, Sudbury, CO10 6XT. Tel: 01787 378879

Sutton Coldfield – Marston Farm Country Hotel, Bodymoor Heath, Sutton Coldfield, B76 9JD. Tel: 01827 872133

Taunton (Fivehead) – Langford Manor, Fivehead, Taunton, TA3 6PH. Tel: 01460 281674

Taunton (Lydeard St.Lawrence) – Higher Vexford House, Higher Vexford, Lydeard St.Lawrence, TA4 3QF. Tel: 01984 656267

Tewkesbury (Kemerton) – Upper Court, Kemerton, GL20 7HY. Tel: 01386 725351

Tintagel (Trenale) – Trebrea Lodge, Trenale, Tintagel, PL34 0HR. Tel: 01840 770410

Titchwell – Titchwell Manor Hotel, Titchwell, Brancaster, King's Lynn, PE31 8BB. Tel: 01485 210221

Truro – The Royal Hotel, Lemon Street, Truro, TR1 2QB. Tel: 01872 270345

Uckfield – Hooke Hall, High Street, Uckfield, TN22 1EN. Tel: 01825 761578

Venn Ottery (Near Ottery St. Mary) – Venn Ottery Barton, Venn Ottery, Ottery St. Mary, EX11 1RZ. Tel: 01404 812733

Wareham (East Stoke) – Kemps Country House Hotel & Restaurant, East Stoke, Wareham, BH20 6AL. Tel: 01929 462563

Warwick (Claverdon) – The Ardencote Manor Hotel & Country Club, Lye Green Road, Claverdon, CU35 8LS. Tel: 01926 843111

Wells – Glencot House, Glencot Lane, Wookey Hole, BA5 1BH. Tel: 01749 677160

Wells – Beryl, Wells, BA5 3JP. Tel: 01749 678738

Whitby – Dunsley Hall, Dunsley, Whitby, YO21 3TL. Tel: 01947 893437

Wimborne Minster – Beechleas, 17 Poole Road, Wimborne Minster, BH21 1QA. Tel: 01202 841684

Wincanton (Holbrook) – Holbrook House Hotel, Wincanton, BA9 8BS. Tel: 01963 32377

Winchelsea – The Country House At Winchelsea, Hastings Road, Winchelsea, TN36 4AD. Tel: 01797 226669

Windermere – Braemount House Hotel, Sunny Bank Road, Windermere, LA23 2EN. Tel: 015394 45967

Windermere – Quarry Garth Country House Hotel, Windermere, LA23 1LF. Tel: 015394 88282

Windermere (Bowness) – Fayrer Garden House Hotel, Lyth Valley Road, Bowness-On - Windermere, LA23 3JP. Tel: 015394 88195

Woodbridge – Wood Hall Hotel & Country Club, Shottisham, Woodbridge, IP12 3EG. Tel: 01394 411283

York (Escrick) – The Parsonage Country House Hotel, Escrick, York, YO4 6LF. Tel: 01904 728111

Yoxford – Hope House, High Street, Yoxford, Saxmundham, IP17 3HP. Tel: 01728 668281

WALES

Aberdovey – Plas Penhelig Country House Hotel, Aberdovey. Tel: 01654 767676

Abergavenny (Glangrwyney) – Glangrwyney Court, Glangrwyney, NP8 1ES. Tel: 01873 811288

Abergavenny (Govilon) – Llanwenarth House, Govilon, Abergavenny, NP7 9SF. Tel: 01873 830289

Abergavenny (Llanfihangel Crucorney) – Penyclawdd Court, Llanfihangel Crucorney, Abergavenny, NP7 7LB. Tel: 01873 890719

Betws-y-Coed – Tan-y-Foel, Capel Garmon, LL26 0RE. Tel: 01690 710507

Brecon (Three Cocks) – Old Gwernyfed Country Manor, Felindre, Three Cocks, Brecon, LD3 0SU. Tel: 01497 847376

Caernarfon – Ty'n Rhos Country House, Llanddeiniolen, Caernarfon, LL55 3AE. Tel: 01248 670489

Cardigan (Cilgerran) – The Pembrokeshire Retreat, Rhosygilwen Mansion, Cilgerran, SA43 2TW. Tel: 01239 841387

Conwy – Berthlwyd Hall Hotel, Llechwedd, LL32 8DQ. Tel: 01492 592409

Conwy – The Old Rectory, Llansanffried Glan Conwy, Nr Conwy, Colwyn Bay, LL28 5LF. Tel: 01492 580611

Dolgellau (Ganllwyd) – Dolmelynllyn Hall, Ganllwyd, Dolgellau, LL40 2HP. Tel: 01341 440273

Harlech (Llanbedr) – Aber Artro Hall, Llanbedr, LL45 2PA. Tel: 01341 241374

Tenby (Waterwynch Bay) – Waterwynch House Hotel, Waterwynch Bay, Tenby, SA70 8TJ. Tel: 01834 842464

Tintern – Parva Farmhouse and Restaurant, Tintern, Chepstow, NP6 6SQ. Tel: 01291 689411

SCOTLAND

Ballater,Royal Deeside – Balgonie Country House, Braemar Place, Royal Deeside, Ballater, AB35 5NQ. Tel: 013397 55482

Blairlogie (Nr Stirling) – Blairlogie House, Blairlogie by Stirling, FK9 5QE. Tel: 01259 761441

Dalbeattie – Auchenskeoch Lodge, By Dalbeattie, DG5 4PG. Tel: 01387 780277

Dalbeattie – Broomlands House, Haugh Road, Dalbeattie, DG5 4AR. Tel: 01556 611463

Dingwall (Highlands) – Kinkell House, Easter Kinkell, By Dingwall, IV7 8HY. Tel: 01349 861270

Drumnadrochit (Loch Ness) – Polmaily House Hotel, Drumnadrochit, Loch Ness, IV3 6XT. Tel: 01456 450343

Edinburgh – No 22, Murrayfield Gardens, Edingburgh, EH12 6DF. Tel: 0131 337 3569

Fife (Kettlebridge) – Chapel House, Kettlebridge, KY15 7TU. Tel: 01337 831790

Fintry (Stirlingshire) – Culcreuch Castle Hotel, Fintry, Loch Lomond, G63 0LW. Tel: 01360 860555

Fort William – Ashburn House, 5 Achintore Road, Fort William, PH33 6RQ. Tel: 01397 706000

Glasgow (Stewarton) – Chapletoun House, Stewarton, KA3 3ED. Tel: 015604 82696

Grantown-on-Spey – Ardconnel House, Woodlands Terrace, Grantown-on-Spey, PH26 3JU. Tel: 01479 872104

Huntley (Bridge of Marnoch) – The Old Manse of Marnoch, Bridge of Marnoch, By Huntley, AB54 5RS. Tel: 01466 780873

Inverness – Culduthel Lodge, 14 Culduthel Road, Inverness, IV2 4AG. Tel: 01463 240089

Isle Of Harris – Ardvourlie Castle, Aird amhulaidh, Isle Of Harris, HS3 3AB. Tel: 01859 502307

Isle Of Mull – Killiechronan, Killiechronan, PA72 6JU. Tel: 01680 300403

Kentallen Of Appin – Ardsheal House, Kentallen Of Appin, PA38 4BX. Tel: 01631 740227

Killiecrankie,By Pitlochry – The Killiecrankie Hotel, Killiecrankie, By Pitlochry, PH16 5LG. Tel: 01796 473220

Kinlochbervie – The Kinlochbervie Hotel, Kinlochbervie, By Lairg, IV27 4RP. Tel: 01971 521275

Kinross (Cleish) – Nivingston House, Cleish, By Kinross, KY13 7LS. Tel: 01577 850216

Moffat – Well View Hotel, Ballplay Road, Moffat, DG10 9JU. Tel: 01683 220184

Nairn (Auldearn) – Boath House, Auldearn, Nairn, IV12 5TE. Tel: 01667 454896

Oban – The Manor House Hotel, Gallanch Road, Oban, PA34 4LS. Tel: 01631 562087

Oban – Dungallen House Hotel, Gallanach Road, Oban, PA34 4PD. Tel: 01631 563799

Old Meldrum (By Aberdeen) – Meldrum House, Old Meldrum, AB57 0AE. Tel: 01651 872294

Perth – Dupplin Castle, Dupplin Estate, By Perth, PH2 0PY. Tel: 01738 623224

Perth (Guildtown) – Newmiln Country House, Newmiln Estate, Guildtown, Perth, PH2 6AE. Tel: 01738 552364

Pitlochry – Dunfallandy House, Logierait Road, Pitlochry, PH16 5NA. Tel: 01796 472648

Port Appin – Druimneil, Port Appin, PA38 4DQ. Tel: 01631 730228

Port Of Menteith – The Lake Hotel, Port Of Menteith, FK8 3RA. Tel: 01877 385258

Strathtummel (By Pitlochry) – Queen's View Hotel, Strathtummel, By Pitlochry, PH16 5NR. Tel: 01796 473291

Tongue (Sutherland) – Borgie Lodge Hotel, Skerray, By Tongue, Sutherland, KW14 7TH. Tel: 01641 521332

IRELAND

Annalong (Co Down N.Ireland) – Glassdrumman Lodge Country House & Restaurant, 85 Mill Road, Annalong, BT34 4RH. Tel: 013967 68451

Caragh Lake Co Kerry – Caragh Lodge, Caragh Lake. Tel: 00 353 66 69115

Carragh Lake Co Kerry – Ard-Na-Sihde. Tel: 00 353 66 69105

Cashel Co Tipperary – Cashel Palace Hotel, Cashel. Tel: 00 353 62 62707

Dublin – Aberdeen Lodge, 53-55 Park Avenue, Ailesbury Road. Tel: 00 353 1 2838155

Kilkee Co Clare – Halpins Hotel & Vittles Restaurant, Erin Street, Kilkee. Tel: 00 353 65 56032

Killarney Co Kerry – Earls Court House, Woodlawn Junction, Muckross Road. Tel: 00 353 64 34009

Letterkenny (Co Donegal) – Castle Grove Country House, Ramelton Road, Letterkenny. Tel: 010 353 745 1118

Portaferry (Co Down N Ireland) – Portaferry Hotel, The Strand, Portaferry, BT22 1PE. Tel: 012477 28231

Riverstown,Co Sligo – Coopershill House, Riverstown. Tel: 00 353 71 65108

Skibbereen Co.Cork – Liss Ard Lake Lodge, Skibbereen . Tel: 00 353 28 22365

Sligo,Co Sligo – Markree Castle, Colooney. Tel: 00 353 71 67800

Wicklow,Co Wicklow – The Old Rectory, Wicklow Town. Tel: 00 353 404 67048

CHANNEL ISLANDS

Guernsey (Castel) – Hotel Hougue Du Pommier, Hougue Du Pommier Road, Castel, GY5 7FQ. Tel: 01481 56531

Guernsey (Fermain Bay) – La Favorita Hotel, Fermain Bay, GY4 6SD. Tel: 01481 35666

Guernsey (St Martin) – Bella Luce Hotel & Restaurant, La Fosse, St Martin, Guernsey. Tel: 01481 38764

Jersey (St Aubin) – Hotel La Tour, Rue de Croquet, St Aubin, Jersey, JE3 8BR. Tel: 01534 43770

PARTNERS IN INSURANCE

*Lakesure is the Exclusive Partner to
Johansens Recommended Inns with Restaurants and offers
SAVINGS ON YOUR PREMIUMS*

*We understand the market and have developed a
number of schemes giving extremely wide cover at a
competitive price and with first class security.*

*We also offer a special basis of quoting each risk using
'OUR UNIQUE NO CLAIMS
BONUS AT INCEPTION'.*

*Call 01702 471135 or 471185 (Phone and fax)
Talk to Bruce Thompson for further details*

WE KNOW OUR BUSINESS

To enable you to use your 1998 Johansens Recommended Inns with Restaurants Guide more effectively, the following four pages of indexes contain a wealth of useful information about the establishments featured in the Guide. As well as listing them alphabetically, by region and by county, the indexes also show at a glance which Inns with Restaurants offer certain specialised facilities.

The indexes are listed as follows:

- Alphabetically by region
- By county
- With a swimming pool
- With fishing nearby
- With shooting locally
- With conference facilities for 100 delegates or more

- Double rooms for £50 or under
- Johansens Preferred Partners
- Inns accepting Johansens Privilege Card

1998 Johansens Recommended Inns with Restaurants listed alphabetically by region

1998 Johansens Recommended Inns and Restaurants by county

Inns with a swimming pool

ENGLAND

The Feversham Arms Hotel	Helmsley	80
The George Hotel	Hatherleigh	74
The Old Brewery House Hotel	Reepham	120
The Old Schoolhouse	Worcester	151
Tree Tops Country House Restaurant & Motel	Southport	131
Wheelbarrow Castle	Leominster	88
Winston Manor	Crowborough	50

CHANNEL ISLES

Sea Crest Hotel And Restaurant	Jersey	181

Inns with fishing nearby

ENGLAND

The Anchor Country Inn	Dulverton	53
Badgers	Petworth	114
Barnacles Restaurant	Hinkley	82
The Barton Angler Country Inn	Wroxham	154
The Black Horse Inn	Grimsthorpe	68
The Blue Bell Hotel	Belford	18
The Blue Lion	East Witton	55
The Boar's Head Hotel	Harrogate	72
Boulters Lock Hotel	Maidenhead	92
The Bulls Head Inn	Eyam	61
The Castle Inn	Castle Combe	37
The Christopher Hotel	Eton/Windsor	58
The Coppleridge Inn	Shaftesbury	126
The Countrymen	Long Melford	89
The Cricketers	Clavering	45
The Crown Hotel	Boroughbridge	20
The Falcon Hotel	Castle Ashby	36
The Feathers Hotel	Helmsley	79
The Feversham Arms Hotel	Helmsley	80
The Garden House Hotel	Norwich	104
The George at Easingwold	York	156
The George Hotel	Hatherleigh	74
The George Hotel	Dorchester-On-Thames	52
The George Hotel	Eccleshall	56
The Golden Lion Inn of Easenhall	Rugby	121
Green Farm Restaurant And Hotel	Thorpe Market	140
The Harbour Inn	Porthleven	118
Hare & Hounds	Fulbeck	64
Home Farm Hotel	Honiton	83
The Horse and Groom	Stow-on-the-Wold	133
The Horse And Groom Inn	Malmesbury	95
The Hoste Arms Hotel	Burnham Market	27
Hotel Des Clos	Nottingham	105
The Hundred House Hotel	Telford	137
The Inn At Whitewell	Whitewell	150
The Jefferson Arms	York	157
The Jersey Arms	Oxford	109
Jubilee Inn	Pelynt,Nr Looe	113
The Kings Arms Hotel	Askrigg	14
The Kings Head Inn	Stow-On-The-Wold	134
The Lamb Inn	Burford	26
The Low Hall Hotel	Harrogate	73
Mallyan Spout Hotel	Goathland	65
The Manor Hotel	Bridport	22
The Masons Arms	Cirencester	43
The Maynard Arms	Grindleford	69
The Mill & Old Swan	Oxford	110
The Mortal Man Hotel	Troutbeck	145
The Nesscliffe	Shrewsbury	130
The New Dungeon Ghyll Hotel	Ambleside	11
The New Inn	Cirencester	44
New Inn Hotel	Clovelly	48
The New Inn Hotel	Settle	124
The Noel Arms	Chipping Campden	42
The Old Bell Inn Hotel	Saddleworth	123
The Old Brewery House Hotel	Reepham	120
The Old Church House Inn	Torbryan Nr Totnes	142
The Old Custom House Hotel	Padstow	112
The Old Manse	Bourton-On-The-Water	21
The Old Schoolhouse	Worcester	151
Old White Lion Hotel	Haworth	76
The Pheasant Inn	Bassenthwaite Lake	16
The Port Gaverne Hotel	Port Gaverne	117
The Port William	Tintagel	141
The Ragged Cot	Minchinhampton	98
The Red Lion	Burnsall	29
Red Lion Inn	Ashbourne	13
The Redfern Hotel	Cleobury Mortimer	47
Rhydspence Inn	Hay-On-Wye	77
The Rising Sun	Lynmouth	91
The Rising Sun	St Mawes	122
Riverside Restaurant And Hotel	Evesham	59
The Rock Inn Hotel	Halifax/Huddersfield	70
The Roebuck	Ludlow	90
The Royal Oak Inn	Appleby-In-Westmorland	12
The Royal Oak Inn	Exmoor	60
The Sea Trout Inn	Totnes	144
The Shaven Crown Hotel	Shipton-Under-Wychwood	129
The Swan Hotel	Newby Bridge	103
The Swan Hotel	Newbury	102
The Swan Hotel	Chester	40
The Talbot	Worcester	152
The Talbot Inn at Mells	Mells Nr Bath	96
The Talkhouse	Oxford	111
The Tarn End House Hotel	Carlisle	35
Thelbridge Cross Inn	Thelbridge	138
Trengilly Wartha Country Inn & Restaurant	Falmouth	62
The Victoria Hotel	Dartmouth	51
The Waltzing Weasel	Hayfield	78
The Wensleydale Heifer Inn	West Witton	149
The Wheatsheaf Inn	Egton	57
The Whipper-In Hotel	Oakham	106
The White Hart Hotel	Moretonhampstead	100
White Horse Hotel	Blakeney	19
White Horse Inn	Petworth	115
The White Lion Hotel	Upton-Upon-Severn	147
The White Swan	Pickering	116
Whoop Hall Inn	Kirkby Lonsdale	84
Wild Boar Hotel	Chester	41
The Willow Tree	Newark	101
Winston Manor	Crowborough	50
The Woodcock Inn	East Grinstead	54
The Woolpack Inn	Beckington Nr Bath	17
Ye Horn's Inn	Preston	119
Ye Olde Churston Court Inn	Brixham	23
Ye Olde Salutation Inn	Weobley	148

WALES

The Castle View Hotel	Chepstow	160
The Lion Hotel	Welshpool	164
The Plough Inn	Llandeilo	162
The Royal Oak Hotel	Welshpool	165
The West Arms Hotel	Llanarmon Dyffryn Ceiriog	161
Ye Olde Anchor Inn	Ruthin	163

SCOTLAND

Annandale Arms Hotel	Moffatt	173
The Glenisla Hotel	Blairgowrie	170
Hotel Eilean Iarmain or Isle Ornsay Hotel	Isle Of Skye	171
The Moulin Hotel	Pitlochry	174
Potarch Hotel	Banchory	168
Uig Hotel	Isle Of Skye	172
Whinsmuir Country Inn	Powmill	175

CHANNEL ISLANDS

The Moorings Hotel	Jersey	180
Sea Crest Hotel	Jersey	181

Inns with shooting nearby

ENGLAND

The Anchor Country Inn	Dulverton	53
Badgers	Petworth	114
The Black Horse Inn	Grimsthorpe	68
The Blue Bell Hotel	Belford	18
The Blue Lion	East Witton	55
Boar's Head Hotel	Burton Upon Trent	30
The Boar's Head Hotel	Harrogate	72
Boulters Lock Hotel	Maidenhead	92
The Castle Inn	Castle Combe	37
The Chequers At Slaugham	Handcross	71
The Christopher Hotel	Eton/Windsor	58
The Coppleridge Inn	Shaftesbury	126
The Countrymen	Long Melford	89
Crown At Hopton	Cleobury Mortimer	46
The Crown Hotel	Boroughbridge	20
The Falcon Hotel	Castle Ashby	36
Feathers Hotel	Ledbury	86
The Feathers Hotel	Helmsley	79
The Feversham Arms Hotel	Helmsley	80
The Fox Country Hotel	Henley	81
The George Hotel	Hatherleigh	74
The George Hotel	Dorchester-On-Thames	52
The George Hotel	Eccleshall	56
Green Farm Restaurant And Hotel	Thorpe Market	140
Hare & Hounds	Fulbeck	64
Holcombe Hotel	Oxford	108
The Horse and Groom	Stow-on-the-Wold	133
The Horse And Groom Inn	Malmesbury	95
The Inn At Whitewell	Whitewell	150
The Jefferson Arms	York	157
The Jersey Arms	Oxford	109
The Kings Arms Hotel	Askrigg	14
The Kings Head Inn	Stow-On-The-Wold	134
The Lamb Inn	Burford	26
The Lamb Inn	Shipton-Under-Wychwood	128
The Leatherne Bottel Riverside Inn & Restaurant	Goring-On-Thames	67
The Manor Hotel	Bridport	22
The Maynard Arms	Grindleford	69
The Mill & Old Swan	Oxford	110
The Mortal Man Hotel	Troutbeck	145
The Nesscliffe	Shrewsbury	130
The New Dungeon Ghyll Hotel	Ambleside	11
New Inn Hotel	Clovelly	48
The Noel Arms	Chipping Campden	42
The Old Brewery House Hotel	Reepham	120
The Old Church House Inn	Torbryan Nr Totnes	142
The Old Schoolhouse	Worcester	151
Old White Lion Hotel	Haworth	76
The Port William	Tintagel	141
The Ragged Cot	Minchinhampton	98
The Red Lion	Burnsall	29
Rhydspence Inn	Hay-On-Wye	77
The Rising Sun	Lynmouth	91
The Rock Inn Hotel	Halifax/Huddersfield	70
The Roebuck	Ludlow	90
The Royal Oak Inn	Appleby-In-Westmorland	12
The Royal Oak Inn	Exmoor	60
The Sea Trout Inn	Totnes	144
The Shaven Crown Hotel	Shipton-Under-Wychwood	129
The Swan Hotel	Newby Bridge	103
The Swan Hotel	Newbury	102
The Swan Hotel	Chester	40
The Talbot	Worcester	152
The Talbot Inn at Mells	Mells Nr Bath	96
The Talkhouse	Oxford	111
The Tarn End House Hotel	Carlisle	35
The Victoria Hotel	Dartmouth	51
The Waltzing Weasel	Hayfield	78
The Wheatsheaf Inn	Egton	57
The Whipper-In Hotel	Oakham	106
The White Hart Hotel	Moretonhampstead	100
White Horse Hotel	Blakeney	19
White Horse Inn	Petworth	115
The White Swan	Pickering	116
Whoop Hall Inn	Kirkby Lonsdale	84
Wild Boar Hotel	Chester	41
The Willow Tree	Newark	101
Winston Manor	Crowborough	50
The Woodcock Inn	East Grinstead	54
The Woodfalls Inn	Fordingbridge	63
The Woolpack Inn	Beckington Nr Bath	17
Ye Horn's Inn	Preston	119
Ye Olde Salutation Inn	Weobley	148

Play the role of Hotel Inspector

At the back of this book you will notice a quantity of Guest Survey Forms. If you have had an enjoyable stay at one of our recommended hotels, or alternatively you have been in some way disappointed, please complete one of these forms and send it to us FREEPOST.

These reports essentially complement the assessments made by our team of professional inspectors, continually monitoring the standards of hospitality in every establishment in our guides. Guest Survey reports also have an important influence on the selection of nominations for our annual awards for excellence.

'Diversity and excellence for the independent traveller'.

Hallid

ARCHITECTS • INTERIOR DESIGNERS

JOHANSENS PREFERRED ARCHITECTURAL ADVISOR PARTNER

A complete architectural and interior design service for hoteliers and restauranteurs supported by a truly personal and professional practice founded in 1908.

We take great care in the design and management of contracts for the repair, refurbishment, extension and interior design of contemporary, period and listed buildings, and in the design of new uses for old buildings.

Our experience extends to hotels, restaurants and bars, swimming and leisure facilities, conference and seminar venues.

We work nationally and are interested in projects of all sizes. The hallmark of our work is an attractive project finished on time, within cost and without disruption.

Why not have an exploratory discussion to see how we can help you achieve your objectives?

RECIPIENTS OF OVER TWENTY AWARDS IN THE LAST TEN YEARS

0161 661 5566

Peter House, St. Peter's Square

Oxford Street

Manchester M1 5AN

Guest Survey Report

Name/location of hotel: _____   Page No: _____

Date of visit: _____

Name & address of guest: _____

_____   Postcode: _____

Please tick one box in each category below:	Excellent	Good	Disappointing	Poor
Bedrooms				
Public Rooms				
Restaurant/Cuisine				
Service				
Welcome/Friendliness				
Value For Money				

PLEASE return your Guest Survey Report form!

Occasionally we may allow other reputable organisations to write with offers which may be of interest.
If you prefer not to here from them, tick this box ☐

To: Johansens, FREEPOST (CB264), 175-179 St John Street, London EC1B 1JQ

✂ ....

Guest Survey Report

Name/location of hotel: _____   Page No: _____

Date of visit: _____

Name & address of guest: _____

_____   Postcode: _____

Please tick one box in each category below:	Excellent	Good	Disappointing	Poor
Bedrooms				
Public Rooms				
Restaurant/Cuisine				
Service				
Welcome/Friendliness				
Value For Money				

PLEASE return your Guest Survey Report form!

Occasionally we may allow other reputable organisations to write with offers which may be of interest.
If you prefer not to here from them, tick this box ☐

To: Johansens, FREEPOST (CB264), 175-179 St John Street, London EC1B 1JQ

Order Coupon

To order Johansens guides, simply indicate which publications you require by putting the quantity(ies) in the boxes provided. Choose you preferred method of payment and return this coupon. You may also place your order free on
1 800 448 4337 or by fax on **(212) 683 2672**.

❑ I enclose a cheque for US$_____ payable to Johansens.

❑ Please debit my credit/charge card account the amount of US$_____

❑ MASTERCARD ❑ VISA ❑ DINERS ❑ AMEX ❑ DISCOVER

Card No [____|____|____|____]

Signature _____ Expiry Date _____

Name (Mr/Mrs/Miss) _____

Address_____

_____ Zip _____

(We aim to despatch your order within 10 days, but please allow 28 days for delivery)

Post to: Johansens, 244 Madison Avenue, Box 368, New York, NY 10016

Occasionally we may allow reputable organisations to write to you with offers which may interest you. If you prefer not to hear from them, tick this box ❑

save $7.80

	PRICE	QTY	TOTAL
The Collection of 4 Johansens Guides + *Recommended Hotels & Inns –* North America **FREE** ~~$76.80~~	**ONLY** $69.00		
The 2 CD ROMS ~~$59.90~~	$54.00		
Recommended Hotels – Great Britain & Ireland 1998	$24.95		
Recommended Country Houses and Small Hotels – GB & Ireland 1998	$16.95		
Recommended Inns with Restaurants – GB & Ireland 1998	$14.95		
Recommended Hotels – Europe 1998	$19.95		
Recommended Hotels – North America 1998	$14.95		
Historic Houses Castles & Gardens, Published and mailed to you in March 1998	$17.95		
CD ROM – Hotels, Country Houses & Inns Great Britain & Ireland 1998 with Historic Houses Castles & Gardens	$34.95		
CD ROM – Recommended Hotels & Inns N. America and Recommended Hotels Europe 1998	$24.95		
1998 Privilege Card – *10% discount, room upgrade when available. VIP Service at participating establishments*			FREE
The Independent Traveller – *Johansens newsletter including many special offers*			FREE
Shipping & Handling *Please add $10 – or $6 for single orders and CD-Roms All items shipped UPS Ground Service*			
TOTAL	**$**		

CALL THE JOHANSENS CREDIT CARD ORDER SERVICE FREE ☎ **1 800 448 4337**

PRICES VALID UNTIL 31/08/98 **J14**

✂ ┈┈

Order Coupon

To order Johansens guides, simply indicate which publications you require by putting the quantity(ies) in the boxes provided. Choose you preferred method of payment and return this coupon. You may also place your order free on
1 800 448 4337 or by fax on **(212) 683 2672**.

❑ I enclose a cheque for US$_____ payable to Johansens.

❑ Please debit my credit/charge card account the amount of US$_____

❑ MASTERCARD ❑ VISA ❑ DINERS ❑ AMEX ❑ DISCOVER

Card No [____|____|____|____]

Signature _____ Expiry Date _____

Name (Mr/Mrs/Miss) _____

Address_____

_____ Zip _____

(We aim to despatch your order within 10 days, but please allow 28 days for delivery)

Post to: Johansens, 244 Madison Avenue, Box 368, New York, NY 10016

Occasionally we may allow reputable organisations to write to you with offers which may interest you. If you prefer not to hear from them, tick this box ❑

save $7.80

	PRICE	QTY	TOTAL
The Collection of 4 Johansens Guides + *Recommended Hotels & Inns –* North America **FREE** ~~$76.80~~	**ONLY** $69.00		
The 2 CD ROMS ~~$59.90~~	$54.00		
Recommended Hotels – Great Britain & Ireland 1998	$24.95		
Recommended Country Houses and Small Hotels – GB & Ireland 1998	$16.95		
Recommended Inns with Restaurants – GB & Ireland 1998	$14.95		
Recommended Hotels – Europe 1998	$19.95		
Recommended Hotels – North America 1998	$14.95		
Historic Houses Castles & Gardens, Published and mailed to you in March 1998	$17.95		
CD ROM – Hotels, Country Houses & Inns Great Britain & Ireland 1998 with Historic Houses Castles & Gardens	$34.95		
CD ROM – Recommended Hotels & Inns N. America and Recommended Hotels Europe 1998	$24.95		
1998 Privilege Card – *10% discount, room upgrade when available. VIP Service at participating establishments*			FREE
The Independent Traveller – *Johansens newsletter including many special offers*			FREE
Shipping & Handling *Please add $10 – or $6 for single orders and CD-Roms All items shipped UPS Ground Service*			
TOTAL	**$**		

CALL THE JOHANSENS CREDIT CARD ORDER SERVICE FREE ☎ **1 800 448 4337**

PRICES VALID UNTIL 31/08/98 **J14**